'Susan Schwartz, drawing creatively on Jung and French psychoanalytical traditions, has produced a beautiful and insightful book on the "as-if" personality. The study uniquely combines theoretical and clinical dimensions so that one gets a full feel for the richness of actual therapy with these most challenging of patients. The text is replete with exquisite quotes that set the emotional tone. This volume, *The Imposter Syndrome and the "As-If" Personality in Analytical Psychology: The Fragility of Self*, is at the cutting edge of Jungian and psychoanalytic thinking'.

Henry Abramovitch, *Founding President,*
Israel Institute of Jungian Psychology, in honour of Erich Neumann,
and Professor Emeritus, Tel Aviv University

'Susan Schwartz's compelling and timely study of the "as-if" personality explores the phenomenology of a person who exists unseen, as if living behind a wall. Dr Schwartz captures with great empathy the struggles of both individuals and collectives to cope with feelings of acute estrangement, isolation and loneliness by uncovering the underlying emptiness that negates depth and substance. Drawing on the works of C.G. Jung, André Green, Donald Winnicott, Julia Kristeva, Judith Butler and others, Dr Schwartz describes the "as-if" person as stuck between the mirror and the mask and trapped in personal, cultural and historical wounds that include unfinished mourning. She suggests that integration can occur by differentiating untouched, unacceptable "shadow" aspects that open creative dialogues in order to venture beyond the "as-if" façade. This book is essential reading for making sense of the effects of our turbulent psycho-social environment of post-COVID, climate change, environmental disasters and war-torn zones that all exacerbate global trauma'.

Dr Elizabeth Brodersen, *Accredited Training Analyst*
and Supervisor, C.G. Jung Institute, Zürich,
and co-editor of Jungian Perspectives on Indeterminate States:
Betwixt and Between Borders, *2021*

'Susan Schwartz addresses the popular topic of impostor syndrome. In an expanded, careful and exhaustively researched way, she presents reflections on the topic from not only classic Jungian, post-Jungian and psychoanalytic authors, but also from scholars of philosophy and sociology. The clear and precise description of such a personality, named by the author as "as if", helps us to identify the massive existence of these symptoms in our practices and in the narcissistic and fragmented Western culture in which we currently live. This gives the reader, although facing difficulties in the diagnosis, treatment and transference involved with the syndrome, the possibility of envisioning a kind of "cure" for the subjects who seek in Jungian symbolic analysis a way to experience and better relate with their psychic multiplicity'.

Luciana Ximenez, *Jungian analyst in Sao Paulo, Brazil, and*
Co-Director of the online program, Thiasos – Shared Imagination
Workshop

Imposter Syndrome and the 'As-If' Personality in Analytical Psychology

This insightful book explores the 'as-if' personality through the lens of Jungian analytical psychology, illuminating how the same forces that can disturb personal development relationally, socially and culturally are equally an impetus towards expressing and relating with one's more complete self.

The book describes persons expressing an 'as if' personality as facing a conundrum around whether to hide or expose the truth of who they are. It describes the analytic container as a place of growth from that place, affecting person and culture, self and other. Using a myriad of clinical examples (across a range of cultures, contexts and personal experiences), the author describes people who are moving through feelings of not belonging, sexual addiction, ageing, the cultural influence of social media, the role of the father, and body image challenges. All these issues reveal the valuable recognition of the unconscious – a hallmark of Jungian analytical psychology – incorporates the dissociated others into selfhood. The theories of French psychoanalysts Andre Green on absence and the negative, Julia Kristeva on abjection, French philosopher Jacques Derrida on Narcissus and Echo and American philosopher Judith Butler on precarity expand the Jungian analytical thought to reflect the multiplicity of the psyche.

Using understandable language to interweave various psychoanalytical and philosophical frameworks, *Imposter Syndrome and the 'As-If' Personality in Analytical Psychology: The Fragility of Self* is both accessible to general readers and highly relevant to professional analysts, therapists, clinicians and social workers.

Susan E. Schwartz, PhD, trained in Zurich, Switzerland as a Jungian analyst. A member of IAAP, she presents at numerous conferences and has many journal articles and book chapters. Her previous book *The Absent Father Effect on Daughters: Father Desire, Father Wounds* is translated into several languages. She practises in Paradise Valley, Arizona, www.susanschwartzphd.com

Imposter Syndrome and the 'As-If' Personality in Analytical Psychology

The Fragility of Self

Susan E. Schwartz

Routledge
Taylor & Francis Group

LONDON AND NEW YORK

Designed cover image: ©Barbara Aliza

First published 2024
by Routledge
4 Park Square, Milton Park, Abingdon, Oxon OX14 4RN

and by Routledge
605 Third Avenue, New York, NY 10158

Routledge is an imprint of the Taylor & Francis Group, an informa business

British Library Cataloguing-in-Publication Data
A catalogue record for this book is available from the British Library

Library of Congress Cataloging-in-Publication Data
Names: Schwartz, Susan E., 1946- author.
Title: Imposter syndrome and the 'as-if' personality in analytical psychology : the fragility of self / Susan E. Schwartz.
Description: Abingdon Oxon; New York, NY : Routledge, 2024. | Includes bibliographical references and index. |
Identifiers: LCCN 2023015140 (print) | LCCN 2023015141 (ebook) | ISBN 9781032324814 (hardback) | ISBN 9781032324807 (paperback) | ISBN 9781003315254 (ebook)
Subjects: LCSH: Identity (Psychology) | Self. | Self-perception. | Jungian psychology.
Classification: LCC BF697 .S383 2024 (print) | LCC BF697 (ebook) | DDC 155.2—dc23/eng/20230623
LC record available at https://lccn.loc.gov/2023015140
LC ebook record available at https://lccn.loc.gov/2023015141

ISBN: 978-1-032-32481-4 (hbk)
ISBN: 978-1-032-32480-7 (pbk)
ISBN: 978-1-003-31525-4 (ebk)

DOI: 10.4324/9781003315254

Typeset in Times New Roman
by Deanta Global Publishing Services, Chennai, India

This writing is dedicated to Frederic whose loving and steadfast support of my endeavours helps take them into reality. There are no words ...

Contents

Acknowledgements

My appreciation goes to Daniela Roher, PhD, who patiently read many chapters of this manuscript. Her commentary was invaluable, offering an acute and tender perspective for understanding the psyche. Barbara Aliza spent hours creating another wonderful cover and generously gave of her time, also in reading and commenting on some of the chapters. This book would not have emerged without the careful editing of LeeAnn Pickrell whose collaborative guidance wisely drew the book into coherence. And the book would not exist without the analytic relationships with those who shared their inner worlds as together we found a way through the mire to their real selves.

Credits

Introduction

I have been intrigued with the 'as-if' personality type since I first read an article by British analyst Hester Solomon (2004). It has long roots in analytical thought but has usually been dismissed as being only applicable to women and originally to those assumed to be unanalysable. I decided to explore it further as I was seeing so many of the 'as-if' personality types in my analytical practice and it seemed relatively unexplored in Jungian thought. Each person I saw verbalised in various ways how they were a fraud. Each one knew no one saw who they really were. They weren't present and often felt unreal. There was a touching and tender vulnerability, a raw and unexplored potential evident to me but not yet evident to them. Their unformulated question, as expressed so succinctly by André Aciman, was, in essence, who am I really?

> Nothing was as it seemed. I was not as I seemed... I was confronted by the possibility that perhaps the truest thing about me was a coiled identity, my irrealis self, a might-have-been self that never really was but wasn't unreal for not being and might still be real, though I feared it never would.
>
> (Aciman, 2021, p. 111)

This book is an attempt to engage with the work and thought of Jungian analytical psychology and its modern value. This is not disembodied esoterica but delves into the issues that many wrestle with around being real. In the modern era of technological advances, real has become more difficult to actualise. More people feel the need to pose, be an imposter, create an image, or rely on the façade 'as-if'.

In his *Red Book* (2009), C.G. Jung addressed the spirit of the depths and spirit of the times. The spirit and the depth of our times are defined personally, culturally and collectively. Many of us live with estrangement, isolation, loneliness and emptiness, much like what the 'as-if' person experiences. This reflects our increasingly fragmented and precarious world with its underlying feeling of fragility. Discontinuities are a part of life and one of the issues raised in this book is how we cope.

The 'as-if' personality type manifests in a different form in each culture, but the psychological structure remains similar. By exploring this personality with its

DOI: 10.4324/9781003315254-1

fractured bits and pretend façades, I am delving into some of the most diverse and complex issues of our times. This book is an exploration into this complex personality, a journey to discover new ways of resolving conflicts, broadening the circle of comprehension of and connection with the real self.

Our era is one of personal and cultural fluidity combined with confusion and disintegration. The world is fraught with social unrest and challenges to our quality of life. This parallels the significant rise in the 'as-if' personality or, in popular psychology terms, *imposter syndrome*. The current global and societal crises and movements seem contradictory to this personality type, which is often associated with superficiality and self-centredness. However, both indicate the need for a serious psychological approach to the deeper issues with their effects on the personal and collective psyche and body.

> Comprehension does not mean denying the outrageous, deducting the unprecedented from precedents, or explaining phenomena by such analogies and generalizations that the impact of reality and the shock of experience are no longer felt... Comprehension, in short, means the unpremeditated, attentive facing up to, and resisting of, reality – whatever that may be.
>
> (Arendt, 1976, p. viii)

This book is an in-depth exploration of the 'as-if' personality through the lens of Jungian analytical psychology. The writing throughout recognises the analytical or psychological container as a place of growth for the individual and culture, personally and relationally. Using understandable language and a many-sided approach, the book's concepts are accessible to general readers as well as professionals. The 'as-if' personality, with its underlying insecurity, highlights the mystery of being alive. We each pursue this aliveness in various ways that lead us to open more gates and surmount higher walls in the search for greater knowledge of self and others.

The 'as-if' person faces a conundrum – whether to hide or expose the truth of who they are. Filled with case studies, this work recognises those who otherwise feel alone and bereft and who question their identity. This is one of the hardest places to be, when the 'as-if' person knows they are unreal, especially when this 'reality' is unseen by most others.

Known for a slickly contrived persona or ego image, the 'as-if' person withdraws into fantasy and illusion. These issues affect intimacy with themselves and others due to the difficulty of being present. The 'as-if' person is faced with the sense of not belonging; they sometimes deal with issues around sexual addiction, ageing, the cultural influence of social media, the role of the father and mother, body image, and split selves. The recognition of the unconscious, a hallmark of Jungian analytical psychology, aims to incorporate the inner dissociated others into a more unified selfhood.

Through my work in Jungian analytical psychology, I've discovered the 'as-if' personality has many exhibited components, among them envy and low self-worth, denial of the shadow, an appealing but elusive persona, and lack of self-connection. All these aspects are promoted by the culture of social media where reality and illusion are often blurred. This replicates the 'as-if' person who is both the mirror and the mask and presents with artifice.

Clinical psychology tends to address merely the ego, the conscious world, and leaves out the unconscious. This is apparent in much of the commentary describing imposter syndrome; the terminology parallels some of the 'as-if' personality. This book, however, through the depth perspective of Jungian analytical psychology, deepens into the underlying issues. The various psychoanalytical and philosophical approaches noted here give a broad platform to the fragile ego existing 'as-if'. I draw on the theories of French psychoanalysts André Green on absence and the negative and Julia Kristeva on abjection, the French philosopher Jacques Derrida on Narcissus and Echo, and the American philosopher Judith Butler on precarity, all of whom extend Jungian analytical thought and reflect the multiplicity of the psyche. Throughout I include quotes from literature, fairy tales and myths, weaving together the interdisciplinary patterns that course through our lives.

Expansion is towards the more complete self. This personality type challenges our cultural tendencies for coverups, superficiality and the search for easy fixes, especially as found on the internet. The psychological isolation of this personality type also contains the yearning for body, self and other connections, stymied in the unreal and illusionary. Being real rather than 'as-if' is a process of release and personal emergence from inner emptiness and loss to a place of desire and aliveness.

Each chapter includes clinical composite examples, dreams and the narratives illustrative of the process of personality integration for more conscious relationship to self and others. The chapters begin with a portion of a fairy tale or story, each from a different culture. The symbols within them illustrate the stripping of old attitudes, facing the real, and eventually transforming the personality. The examples clarify the theoretical points and assist readers in finding their own psychological resonance. All unite under the umbrella of the Jungian analytical model for becoming the author of one's real self.

Integration occurs through addressing the throes of despair and depression and bringing together the personality with those formerly untouched, unacceptable and unknown aspects. The imposter surface is no longer needed when one can be real. Attention to this personality type brings out the deeper individuation urge within as one opens to creative and authentic expression beyond the 'as-if' façade. We live in a particularly challenging time, given the magnitude of uncertainties and transitions humanity is now facing. The purpose of exploring the 'as-if' personality is to nurture awareness of what can be replenishing and regenerative for each person and culture.

References

Aciman, A. (2021). *Homo irrealis*. Farrar, Straus and Giroux.

Arendt, H. (1976). *The origins of totalitarianism*. Mariner Books.

Jung, C.G. (2009). *The red book* (S. Shamdasani, Ed.). (S. Shamdasani, M. Kyburz & J. Peck, Trans.). W.W. Norton & Co.

McFarland Solomon, H.M. (2004). Self creation and the limitless void of dissociation: The 'as-if' personality. *Journal of Analytical Psychology*, *49*(5), 635–656. doi: 10.1111/j.0021-8774.2004.00493.x.

Chapter 1

As-if defined

This parable from *The Trial* by Franz Kafka relates the very problem of the 'as-if' person who does not realise how to manifest what is theirs and how to inhabit their existence:

> To the doorkeeper there comes a countryman who prays for admittance. But he is told he cannot be allowed in at the moment. Maybe later. On this the man stays until the end of his life. At that time the doorkeeper says no one else was allowed in except the man and now it will be shut. The point is that the man did not realize that the intangibility of what we confront stems not from its concealed essence but from its very accessibility.
>
> (Franz Kafka, 2022)

They do not go through the door as in the story because they do not know it is theirs. To further highlight the importance of this issue, in 2018, *Time Magazine* published an article with an accompanying short video entitled, 'Yes, imposter syndrome is real. Here's how to deal with it'. The imposter, and what is here called the 'as-if' personality, is defined by the central question – who am I, really?

Who is this person? The answer will reflect a deep sense of identity, speaking to something more like 'What are you really about?' This means goals, purposes, meanings in life rather than the superficial answer to the superficial question, 'What is your name and where are you from?' Identity in this more encompassing sense isn't fixed, handed down or unconscious. Rather, it is something shaped and determined over time. A person's identity is what they are about as reflected in the passions that give direction to life.

A woman heard a voice. Was she dreaming? It seemed so real and present in her room. *The woman's voice said, 'Now is the time of healing, beginning from the past'.* There was no one in the room as Loggan awoke. Whose voice was speaking? What about the past? What was the healing? All these are questions covered in this exploration of the 'as-if' personality, describing a mixture of talent and conundrum, affecting life in the social, personal and cultural spheres, combining both the conscious and unconscious realms.

DOI: 10.4324/9781003315254-2

The call in the dream is to become who she really is. This points to a process for growth and development, and as the dream says, it means going from the past to the present for healing to occur. The dream, although short, is directive and the voice seems to arise from the larger self, or the part of the personality that gives clarity and direction. It signals the need to access a higher order of being as healing requires knitting together the past personal, collective, cultural, familial and relational. Once the past is understood, the present can expand.

A man commented,

> The mirror was in a space I had to walk past every day. Though I did not have to look in it, I did anyway and didn't feel good in the mirror regardless of how I looked. Every day I walked past that mirror I looked at a man who was hurt and confused.

This short comment is typical of the 'as-if' personality. There is a low level of discomfort, an uneasy separateness adhering to even the smallest moments. Gradually, the feeling becomes a part of each day, a level of despair that swells until its thunderous noise drowns out any presence for oneself. Many attempts are made to escape the inner disappointment and heaviness. This is part of the complexity behind the adopted masks and illusions put forth by this personality type. The attempted dissimulation actively works to mystify and deceive both themselves and others.

This person has an impoverished or emotionally and physically uncomfortable relationship to the world belied by their presentation of glitz and shine. They cannot bear, even momentarily, to be seen up close, beneath the skin. Others might perceive them as winners, as having made it, but often they are internally empty, disillusioned, anxious, confused, alienated and, most of all, estranged from themselves. Looking successful to others does not fill the empty spaces within.

A woman described, 'Today I had a moment of feeling real. Usually, I am somewhere else. But now I caught it and could tell the difference for the first time'. The 'as-if' person narrates a story of personal and collective history composed of the secret vicissitudes with which they engage. This personality has a penchant for illusions and poses, an imposter based on inner distress and psychological confusion. Their soul feels wrecked from within, swarmed by instability and the pain of existence.

The 'as-if' person has yet to travel the road inward, even when faced with the truths they know unconsciously, including discontent and discontinuity. The courage it takes is there but has yet to be recognised and accessed. The 'as-if' person cannot stop long enough to do so. They need to cover the real and just go on because it hurts too much. At some point, however, life catches up and they must address issues formerly denied. The process will evolve out of the fog of denial into the experience of presence. This is a journey inwards to evolve outwards.

The dream: *I am giving a presentation on the 'as-if' personality and someone asks me how I do it. I say I think I've always felt a kind of floating feeling – I don't know how else to put it. But I've always also, even more, had this feeling that nothing is quite real – what are we doing – and it is sort of strange. All this has always been present in my feelings and in my thoughts. It made me feel displaced and ungrounded while moving through life.*

This dream positioned at the beginning of a person's analytical process pointed towards fostering the process of individuation and finding meaning in life. The dream describes my reason for writing this book. There are so many people who feel similarly, skimming by on the surface but not really living. These people are internally isolated, although they look competent, creative, unusual, with quirky perspectives, but insecure. What does their inner mirror show that they both believe and negate?

This 'as-if' person exhibits an elusive, flighty and often dramatic approach to life, but this belies the internal abyss. No one is to see their emotional, interpersonal and behavioural fragility. They have an underlying sense of distrust and lack of confidence in their place in the world. Filling the emptiness with people, places and things is an attempt to compensate for the feeling of being unreal. This emptiness often arises from early emotional wounding and a lack of correct or close-enough attachment with consistent caregivers. As adults these people become performers, needing attention and seeming superficial. The question is… how to bridge the gap to access who they really are.

They relate to the world through mimicry, although the adaptation of 'as-if' comes at the expense of authenticity. They feel as flat as the social media screen, yet they often hide this from themselves and others. The signals of internal division are trapped in unconscious personal, cultural and historical wounds. These include unfinished mourning processes, intergenerational issues and archetypal anxieties. The unconscious calls to be more deeply known, relationships with self and others open rather than closed, life no longer avoided with emotional distancing, compulsions or perfectionism.

This personality type, although clever at disguise, feels emotional and psychological distress, haunted by aims and aspirations not yet achieved along with the pressure of nothing ever being enough. 'What to the rational mind seems a flaw is often a profoundly mysterious key to the secret of individual life… When we pathologize human foibles in our relentless way, trying to subdue and "purify" life, we kill the soul' (Hinton, 1993, p. 58). An enigma to themselves and others, people with this personality type are impenetrable, avoiding themselves and intimate relationships and apprehensive at being present. These people 'defend against aspects of reality concerned with absence and loss that are felt to be intolerable' (Colman, 2006, p. 22). They need the illusions and idealisations of others focused on them so life can seem other than it is. They construct a solid and tight package as a defence. In dreams they might appear inappropriately dressed or insufficiently rehearsed because they do not feel ready for life.

Loggan dreamt *I notice a small door at the bottom of my closet and realise it's been unlocked. I am worried that all this time I've been painstakingly locking the front and back doors of my apartment and didn't even know this door existed. It's a thin door that separates the wall of my unit to the hallway. I feel vulnerable and lock the door. The lock is only a small hook latch and doesn't feel like it's strong enough to keep me safe.*

She said, 'When I woke up the next day, I was faced with the mysterious door I did not know or see previously'. The dream deeply stirred Loggan emotionally, awakening her to something forgotten or ignored. She was not only intrigued but also scared as she thought she had been careful and prepared but had missed the door. How did that happen and what could it represent? A single dream, like this one, remarkable for its surprise, power and simplicity can completely change the mood and intentions for the day, week and foreseeable future.

'In analysis the reflector is the dream, which can mirror psyche to reality and reality to psyche' (Shorter, 1986, p. 182). Loggan could not shake the dream or its feeling and referenced it on and off during analysis. Looking into the dream for clues, the small door expresses there is material hidden away and now there is only a small lock on it. What is inside the door? Where does it go? Why has it gone unnoticed in the recesses of her closet? She reacts as if the door represents something unknown or threatening to her emotional stability. As we spoke, Loggan realised she has been defending against some aspects she considered shameful. This attitude has blocked the capacity for imagination; however, the dream and its memory activate the now necessary material.

What was excluded from consciousness was unconsciously holding her a prisoner. This is indicated by the insecurely latched door, more upsetting as she did not even know about it. If locked, she felt safe but now what? What might be lurking in her personality she has tried to ignore? The timing of the dream is important as it opened a space of exploration on the bumpy path of self-discovery. A small dream, a small latch and a small door but opening into a vast and until now unknown space.

The dream draws Loggan to access personality pieces needed for the psyche to assist in achieving individuation and a deeper connection with life. The dream positioned at the beginning of her analytical process is leading her into herself. This will be more complex than she thought and more involved than just locking the door, however.

When it comes down to it, this personality type will put in much time to prepare and wishes to perform but often does not and backs off. Loggan seems dream-like, living 'as-if', ethereal; she feels she doesn't count for much. Hurt, she tells no one the totality of what she wants and needs. Yet, she is bored by the daily grind and the average because it is neither exciting nor glamorous. The fantasy world has brighter appeal, but she is never satisfied and always needs more.

In fact, she has not adequately formed a secure identity, which has made relationships to self and others a series of confusing mishaps and poor choices. Her behaviour and ways of relating might include aggressive and self-destructive elements, often hidden from the purview of others. Worried she is behind and cannot catch up, she feels defeated and lost. Needing to be perfect and marvellous, she detests mediocrity, especially her own. Yet she becomes caught in negative thought cycles, self-denigrating to the point of paralysing. In these cycles she cannot find where she fits or what to develop. Due to her internal confusion, mimicry and falsity take over. She becomes an imposter to herself.

Her inner discourse is composed of the selves she is not able to face as they lead to addressing the question, 'Who am I'? She was supposed to be someone, but not who she is. There are also various dissociations between mind and body as the personality is crumpled. This is the struggle, with the inner negative scrutiny making reality disappointing and fraught with anticipated rejection. She is a spectator; she keeps a distance from others, yet she needs them, although she simultaneously assumes them to be smarter and more attractive. In this eternal conflict, she feels separated by a thick curtain she cannot open.

False self

The *false self* is a concept named by British psychoanalyst Donald Winnicott in the mid-20th century. 'A word like self knows more than we do, it uses us and it can command us' (1987, p. 158). The false self is a popular term, although few realise how much the personality is compromised. The construction of the false self is not a substitute for the true self, but rather serves as a protective covering for it. The 'as-if' personality, however, is 'constructed from very early experiences attempting to establish the self in the face of a blank or inappropriate environment that is so misattuned to the subjective reality of the self that it feels unseen and/or noxiously related to' (Solomon, 2004, p. 641).

'The False Self has one positive and very important function: to hide the True Self, which it does by compliance with environmental demands' (Winnicott, 1987, pp. 146–7). By *true self*, Winnicott refers to the authentic identity with which the child is born. The idea is that infants depend on their primary caregivers not only to meet their basic needs for survival, but also for reliable, accurate and empathic emotional responsiveness. When this is not the case, the false self protects, defends and keeps the true self from harm. It develops as the infant is subjected to what intrudes upon, rejects or abandons the child's experience. When this is the case, the child increasingly loses the sense of initiative and spontaneity. 'There is a growing sense in the individual of futility and despair' (p. 133). The false self develops through early environmental failure, and the true self potential is unrealised and hidden. Christopher Bollas, American psychoanalyst, has termed this a sense of 'fatedness' (1989, p. 33).

The parents are not attuned to the child's natural desire to be enlivened and assertive. They might want a compliant child who exerts little independent will with modulated and contained affect and behaviour. The child becomes responsive to the desires of these parents who are almost totally unaware of the imaginative and creative aspects of the child. The parents exhibit recurring and/or intermittent non-responsiveness and emotional abandonment. 'Where the mother [and father] cannot adapt well enough, the child is seduced into a compliance, and a compliant False Self reacts to environmental demands and the infant seems to accept them' (Winnicott, 1987, p. 146). The child's outer compliance, conformism and submission are central to the constellation of the false self.

As basic emotional needs are either unmet, or met unreliably, the infant gradually learns not only to distrust the environment, but also to distrust the self. A
basic mistrust develops because infants rely on primary caregivers to mirror their
emotional experiences accurately. Through this accurate mirroring, infants learn
to label their emotions and trust the validity of their internal experiences. When
the parents do not sufficiently acknowledge or respond to the child's basic needs,
the child feels invisible and alone. This child is left wondering what is wrong with
them. Winnicott essentially viewed the false self as a 'defence against the unthinkable, the exploitation of the True Self which would result in its annihilation' (1987,
p. 141).

The ego or sense of 'I' in the 'as-if' personality is fragile and frequently
threatened with falling apart. The sense of self or concreteness of being is often
fragmented. Experiences, both internal and external, are fraught with emotional
turmoil. There is a feeling of grandiosity and unease when criticised, and a dependency on recognition and praise from others. It sounds extreme but there is a terrifying vulnerability. This is compounded by the 'as-if' person being insufficiently
rooted in the body, so that psyche and soma do not feel solidly held together.

To protect and avoid, the child and then adult learns to conform through adopting a polite and compliant social attitude. The process is designed to maintain the
true self, but in a hidden state. The emotional deadness of the parent and inability
to make the parent happy leaves a hole in the personality. A black hole of depression originates not only from the dual fear and want of connection but also with the
realisation it is not forthcoming. This involves some form of retreating away and
into the mind, into a pretend world and the illusions needed to avoid impositions
from the outside world. What can take over is self-condemnation for being imperfect. This can lead to a loss of vitality without access to the true self. The 'as-if'
person acts like they can be this or that, able to perform but never really occupying
a place of depth or substance.

The therapeutic transference and any relationship can become complicated and
characterised by subtly hidden nests of mistrust – disguised, denied and difficult
to address. When self-understanding ceases and feelings overwhelm, all is hidden
from the eyes of others. Persevering through this and with the despair accessed
in therapy, the 'as-if' person's adapted attitudes and learned responses can begin
to shift.

The imposter

There has been a dearth of descriptors and serious attention to the 'as-if' or imposter
personality in the psychological literature. Most approaches centre on 'how to'
ideas for fixing behaviour but without attention to or inclusion of the unconscious.
This reflects a lack of psychological depth or curiosity towards the intricacy of this
personality type. The popularised term and descriptions of imposter syndrome do
not adequately get at the depth of the distress extending beyond the borders of culture, social class, status or economics. Without the symbolic and the unconscious

and delving into deeper meanings, the totality of a person is inadequately addressed, leaving them stuck in a quandary of pain and distress.

The 'as-if' person's life is based on a façade, on posing, unable to access a solid and confident self. 'For there is nothing to lay hold of. I am made and remade continually. Different people draw different words from me' (Woolf, 1931, p. 58). This is a personality trapped in the image, attempting the ideal, without the ability to be their individual self. For the imposter making a life based on self-deception, the reality of self is painfully shame filled.

Rooted in the need for protection and self-reliance, the imposter shapeshifts to fit the occasion. An imposter does not feel a definitive identity and operates in the absence of a fully knowable self. Therefore, any slight can spur defeat. These often high-achieving individuals are apprehensive that they will be found out or unmasked as incompetent or unable. Success cannot be solidly achieved or maintained because the personality is weakened from within, the personality parts disparate and identity disjointed. They can look lively but feel lifeless as a mannequin.

Each day the question arises about which costume to put on. The costume represents an ego/persona or outer image approach to life. The persona will appear intact, but underneath, the personality is in shreds. 'As-if' people seek to avoid anxiety, loneliness and emotional losses. They retreat from reality, as they feel impotent to cope with it. The creation of these alternative worlds prevents access to the interior for the means of self-preservation (Modell, 1996, p. 77). Identity shifts to please, stand out or fit in, but basically to avoid depth and visibility. So busy complying with outer constraints imposed personally, culturally and socially, the real self has become unavailable. Whether noticed or not, this person is hidden while in plain sight.

The search after image manufactures a false existence. The personality has become one-sided, adorned with an exterior consciously and carefully arranged for inner concealment. The 'as-if' personality lives out only one side in favour of the approved external role, repressing anything considered unacceptable to the group. This might seem like inflation and grandiosity, but it is in place, so the personality does not disintegrate.

The regime of images imposed on the body from the outside creates violence and anger turned inward, leading to an accompanying disappearance of the body. Estranged from their affective core (Modell, 1996, p. 150), this person loses contact with an authentic self, closing off from others. An independent self or omnipotent self is convinced it needs no others due to the perceived absence of safety. The self is felt as fragile and vulnerable, empty and dead, as if nothing were there (p. 151). The inner darkness, the shadow, potential and energy lies secreted beneath the surface making this person seem brittle, hollow and false. T.S. Eliot (1998), in his famous poem 'The Waste Land', written in 1922, refers to life's images as damaged or without meaning at all.

As an example, in this next narrative, the gradual process of self-alienation and the imposter development began from childhood. Tahira said she did not know how to be other than to please and appear happy, that she never had an idea who she really was. She relayed many fond memories of being young and spending hours with her father who made up stories about people. Each was more fanciful and enchanting than the last. He was clever, a marvel, and did much to fabricate reasons for his many bankruptcies and just as many affairs. Her father was an imposter, and he made everything seem more glamorous than it was. Real was irrelevant, as was honesty, to this father always in debt, making up reality. She looked up to him. She also learned not to reveal her real self to others and made up stories as well.

Soon she held almost everything in secret and altered the truth to make it look better and more palatable to herself and the world. She was worried her opinion would hurt others and felt she should not burden anyone with her unhappiness. As she considers it now, she has always been ashamed, lying about her childhood, the family poverty, a home without emotional satisfaction or pleasure, wanting to be like others. But there was a chasm, and she did not know how to cross it, so she pretended, like her father taught. Always there was the nagging worry she would be judged for doing something wrong. As a result of this fear of being judged, she put herself last. She made 'as-if' that was alright, but she had been miserable, working hard to create an image and hide the real, also mostly from herself. Now in her late fifties she wonders how long she can keep up the façade.

She has been busy making life a play, staged, offered to the applause of others. This drama plays out at the expense of real living. Even with the fanciful father making up stories of seeming delight, she quite early met with disillusionment in their economic poverty, their unstable home, their frequent moves. Saddened and struggling to be otherwise, without sufficient clothes, sometimes without food or basic attention, she learned to put off her desires. The story presented to the world was all is well, but behind it lay other truths, hence the need for the ruse of the imposter.

The imposter is often filled with shame and fear, dealt with by their outstanding performance. When life is based on being a performer, gaining approval, concerned with being acceptable to some elusive standard, they have no way to acknowledge inner distress. It must be buried each day. There is no comfort, only a nervous watching and hypervigilance. Peace and contentment are unknown in the face of the need to exert control and eliminate suffering.

Tahira was basically deeply unhappy. Because so much had to be denied and hidden, the 'as-if' person pretends, and this attitude fosters discontinuity. These people are not what they seem. The world quite early did not give support for authenticity, and this results in bewilderment about how to live. As children they are lonely, depressed and sensitive to the environmental atmosphere. As adults the pattern is repeated.

Tahira was in an unhappy long-term partnership. She never spoke of her misery to family and pretended to friends. Inside she was looking for an escape route. Yet, she feared the anger, wrath even, of her partner. She was trapped by her fears and worries. She was insecure about how to survive; she had always felt uneasy, ashamed, worried and then compliant.

Dreams

Tahira dreamt *she was on a beach and three men in black capes with a flock of black birds behind them walked past her. One of the men laid down a book with the cover decorated in jewels and the pages in an old manuscript style.* When she looked up the image online, she found it was an alchemical codex from the Middle Ages. These are powerful images to play with and unravel, and they took her into the mystery of herself. What was she to do with this? She did not yet appreciate the wealth of her psyche or the depth of understanding she could acquire. She did not realise the value of the codex or the knowledge it contained appearing in her dream.

In the Jungian analytical process, she is uncovering her background, but it is not the one she was told. The repression that results from trying not to become conscious of desires or uncover secrets contributes to psychological confusion. The descent into the unconscious leads to a revelation about the truths of her heritage. This and other secrets of the family and herself emerge. This dream image with its symbolism and historical roots is beyond the personal and reaches into the collective unconscious, the storehouse of images and meanings. These were guiding her ever deeper to answer the question, Who am I really?

Jung described dreams as the psyche's attempt to communicate things to the dreamer about what is really going on. They are symbolic representations of the elements within the dreamer's psyche. The personal associations to the dream as well as the amplifications of the images with archetypal, collective and cultural themes fill in the conscious attitude. This compensates for what is incomplete in the personality.

Dreams are understood through uncovering their meaning, timing and wisdom. They are a rich storehouse of personal and collective information, guiding and assisting the narrative for self-discovery. They are vehicles for the embodiment of the invisible world rendered visible through their metaphors and images. 'The elimination of the symbolic, polysemy, is one of the fundamental exterminations perpetrated by this order, since the symbolic is the true subversion of ideology' (Bollas, 1998, p. 161). Dreams reflect personal, cultural and collective issues specific to and yet beyond each era. Jung wrote, 'The dream is a spontaneous self-portrayal, in symbolic form, of the actual situation in the unconscious' (Jung, 1970b, para. 505). Like Tahira's dream, dreams pursue insight and increase awareness by also being ahead of the dreamer's consciousness.

Characters in dreams can appear one-dimensional, like actors in a play, whereas others demonstrate psychological depth. We encounter these characters whose actions elicit a range of physical and emotional responses. Through their words, faces, expressions, voices and mannerisms, they pull us into numerous interactions, some known and some unknown. Dreams encourage emotional engagement in their narratives.

Dreams reveal what has been lost and reflect the rhythm of how we live inside. They are a study of the psychological processes and complexes affecting development. The disconnections and dissociations from self are also a seeking of self, ultimately taking the person inward. As Jung said, 'This struggle has something to do with creation, with the unending battle between affirmation and negation' (1956/1967, p. 48).

One of the gifts of depth psychology is the capacity to understand the invisible forces at work in the unconscious. We grasp their context and understanding as we pay attention to dreams. Tahira had neglected her inner life with its wealth of images and symbols for years. Now it is coming back through the messenger man in the black cape. She is left to explore this text referring to alchemy, the mystical, the masculine presenting this gift to her, the meaning of his black cape from another earlier era and what all this signifies for her life. At this point she knew nothing about alchemy or the value of the codex until she checked on Google and then she was quite surprised.

The dream is a psychic fact and a spontaneous self-portrayal, in symbolic form, mirroring the situation in the unconscious. The psyche is self-regulating, seeking to compensate the conscious attitude. The dream is neither isolated nor separate from daily life; it is presented to restore balance and wholeness. Dreams reveal personal problems, the current situation of the psyche, the past and future through the images presented. In the process of becoming known to herself and unpeeling the layers built up from family secrets, the symbolic meaning of the dream reveals truths.

Dreams help liberate, clarifying the psyche as it reflects personal and collective issues, offering complexes, strengths and values in a quest for information and guidance. In dreams we discover the many parts of ourselves, unleashing the psychological attitude for self-reflection. If the dreamer can understand and apply what the dream is saying, the imbalances existent even through the generations can be corrected. All these opportunities were implied in Tahira's dream.

Defining self

The self, as defined in Jungian analytical psychology, transcends the ego as the centre of consciousness. It is beyond the ego and contains more than can be known only by the ego sphere of consciousness. The self is considered the central organising principle of the entire psyche. This is a complex concept, as Jung himself used many descriptors of the self, encompassing a wide range of definitions and symbols as he continued to refine and clarify it. Jung described 'the self as an inclusive term that embraces our whole living organism' (1970a, CW 7, para. 303). The self is a core concept referring to the expansiveness of the personality, uniting conscious and unconscious and bringing meaning to existence. The self enlivens, guides and stretches the personality in the continual path of individuation. 'The self is an inner, guiding center whose energies manifest symbolically' (Schwartz-Salant, 1982, p. 18). The images of the self coalesce towards integration of the personality. Warren Colman, British Jungian analyst, describes the self as 'the centre of the personality and the goal of individuation but also as action allowing for the totality of being' (2008, p. 364).

The self is numinous, genuine and more than the narrow, grandiose or exhibitionistic ego. 'The experience of the self is the ground of our own being' (Colman, 2008, p. 355). This is where the symbolism of dreams illustrates the unconscious river of life opening into the knowledge and accessing the guidance from the 'invisible centre that is the self' (Jung, 1956/1967, para. 77). The self is vast, the greater part of a person attempting to be realised and pushing the ego beyond its known reality. The self as the inner other is also what facilitates transformation (Schwartz-Salant, 1982, p. 20). The guidance of the self gives a sense of direction, personal identity and meaning. 'The self stands for wholeness… toward formation of the ego and consciousness, but it goes further toward individuation… [there is] progressive character of the self' (Neumann, 1971, p. 131). Life-enhancing psychological development leads ever further to awareness of the self. This is not a concept that can be held or kept static. It is ever moving and elusive; it is there without being seen.

When development is obstructed, self experiences may remain suppressed, somatised, acted-out in ways unusable for its unfolding. When the true self must split off, the 'as-if' person is depleted of energy (Schwartz-Salant, 1982, p. 135), split from reality, their inner world in shambles. The 'as-if' person often feels divided within and cut off from the deeper aspects of the self, especially from bodily experience (Colman, 2008, p. 362). Their behaviour turns destructive, indicating they are at odds with themselves. Without registering basic bodily needs or when treating the body as a distant object, the feelings of self and body-self are disjointed.

Life is hanging by a thread; frantic they will not get whatever they are after, they are hounded by insecurities.

> This collision between one's image of oneself and what one actually is, is always very painful and there are two things you can do about it, you can meet the collision head-on and try and become what you really are or you can retreat and try to remain what you thought you were, which is a fantasy, in which you will certainly perish.
>
> (Baldwin, 1985, p. 244)

These people keep themselves together through routines and schedules to follow rather than relying on natural instincts. The physical becomes overwhelming, and they are easily decentred, ungrounded in the world. When something goes awry, it feels like their very survival has become precarious and threatened.

Perfectionism

One of the hallmarks of the 'as-if' personality is perfectionism. Anything is excluded that might displease, and the 'as-if' person aims to avoid whatever could be interpreted as discordant or misshapen.

> If it were only resistance that he felt, it would not be so bad. In fact, however, the psychic substratum, that dark realm of the unknown, exercises a fascinating

attraction that threatens to become the more overpowering the further he penetrates into it.

(Jung, 1968, para. 439)

This person is lured by the relief of fantasy, creating images, ideas and events to cover assumed personality flaws. There is much shame and panic to be hidden and denied. Striving to be perfect, adopting a persona of confidence and surety, they become false. Perfection is never satisfied and inevitably turns destructive. Nothing and no one are good enough or last long enough. The good easily dissipates in each next endeavour needed to prop up the personality. This way of thinking and perceiving the world occurs when a person grows up without a sense of support, safety or sufficient nurturing. It can be a reaction to childhood trauma, cultural expectations or unconscious reactions to transgenerational issues. Appearing perfect becomes a strategy for emotionally surviving and coping with distrust of the environment, self and others.

Adaptation substitutes for authenticity. Gnawing emptiness signals the lack of a secure identity. The 'as-if' person is always uneasy and needs validation and positive evaluation by others. They must be stellar and without any issues, or there is the crush of despair and defeat. The sense of solid identity is easily jeopardised in the anticipated abandonment for any infraction. Anguished by the smallest detail and assessed as doing poorly, the 'as-if' person's reaction is based on low self-esteem and feeling battered but without reserves or defences to make it through.

Self-negating thoughts and actions are set against imagined standards of perfection. In the progressive deadening of the self, the person enters a sort of wandering, repeating the original losses while escaping introspection. Relationships are based on hiding and learned inauthenticity. Although social with the expected presentation, seemingly capable of warmth, their emotional depth is stunted, and they feel unable to emerge or be safely seen.

Creating a falsity of image and acting for approval protects them against any of this and against the world. Focus is on inadequacy and internal disregard. This is compensated by the search for perfection as if it could rectify lack while emptiness remains unresolved. In addition, there is a relationship between perfectionism and depression. Invaded by saturnine moods, the melancholy psyche is faced with fear of collapse, crushed by the assumed expectations of not measuring up. Self-reproach weighs heavily on this personality. Anxiety, not belonging, loneliness and genuine pain mix with feeling misunderstood, different from others, insignificant, flawed, ridden with internal conflict. There is isolation, broken identity, shattered and divided personality. The emotional distress has been so expertly and often unconsciously obscured, the cloak perfection cannot slip, or it could reveal the underlying loneliness.

There is also the issue of self-hatred, which indicates 'a basic division between the ego and self when the spontaneous being of the person is always hated, feared and attacked' (Colman, 2008, p. 363). There is a frantic need to avoid the impact of shame and self-hatred. Hatred turns a person against their own self with wishes to destroy and is not easily eradicated.

> Hatred is paradoxical. It emerges from traumatic origins and involves primitive defence mechanisms of the self ... but it manifests itself at a sophisticated level of consciousness where ego fragments have coalesced, albeit in a distorted way, to form a fixed complex.
>
> (Weiner, 1998, p. 499)

In other words, hatred of self, driven by perfectionism, leads them to become frozen, separated from within.

The childhood problem of lack

When the parental figure is too distant, a person can become inhibited, frightened and unable to access healthy assertion. This derives from a lifelong script of inferiority and aggression turned inward. As Jung commented, 'Children are so deeply involved in the psychological attitude of their parents that it is no wonder that most of the nervous disturbances in childhood can be traced back to a disturbed psychic atmosphere in the home' (Jung, 1956/1967, para. 80).

The match between the parents and the child's temperaments is inadequate if parents are self-absorbed, depressed and preoccupied, or otherwise emotionally unreliable. In these cases, the parents' image of the child was of someone who needed nothing from them. These become the proverbial perfect children expected to behave with maturity beyond their years, 'as-if' they were competent but they were too young. However, the child complied and moulded their behaviour to fit the family and culture. The child fills the parents' expectations but over time loses who they really are. When the good is not available, they respond with protest, despair and detachment.

This limited form of identification is problematic. The traumatic interactions become replicated within as an internalised withholding – an angry, depressed relationship to oneself (Modell, 1996, p. 86). This person retreats as the sense of personal authenticity slowly diminishes. Life is measured by what is appropriate rather than what is genuine and depends on staging performances with the socially constructed correct persona.

Failure in the parental holding environment gives the child no sense of safety in the external world and so a grandiose self substitutes for the real to provide magical protection (Modell, 1996, p. 88). There might have been verbal and/or physical violence and abuse at home, denigration by siblings or parents, neglect and needs ignored. One or both parents may have been dictatorial and harsh. The inner world is not bearable for the 'as-if' person who cannot manage the range of feelings as there was little modelling for this (Zoppi, 2017, p. 703). These experiences affect and change them, they leave their mark, and this person has little sense of self. 'As children they were lonely, depressed, and with innate sensitivity' (Solomon, 2004, p. 640). This went unnoticed. There was little opportunity to express feelings or have their subjective reality recognised. The child experiences the world as negating or trying to destroy their reality, leading to feelings of despair and emptiness.

The depression that results from repressing what is real is a complex process composed of many aspects. This wound can become a central organising factor in the personality, and they continue to react, expecting to be re-wounded. The self is shrouded in make believe. There is internal alienation, self-destruction in thoughts and behaviours, not necessarily apparent to others but taking up much space in the 'as-if' personality. The mind is populated with lack.

Relating to the world is based on the imaginary and pretend. The imagined now replaces the real. This helps defend against aspects of reality having to do with absence and loss as these were experienced as unbearable quite early. 'The [psychic] retreat then serves as an area of the mind where reality does not have to be faced, where phantasy and omnipotence can exist unchecked and where anything is permitted' (Steiner, 1983, p. 3). They learn to put on a sparkling appeal, a cover usually fostering positive projections, but these are neither seen nor believed. The consistency of self is porous and the sense of self-value not within their purview. The emotional insulation wants to be filled with adulation. Although this person is very alone, they cannot easily be alone, and it is difficult to bear absence. The façade makes it seem the person is there when she is not. But where is she?

Imagery of the body

Attention to inner work includes the presence rather than pretence of the physical self. The body and its expressive connection to the psyche is an important part of the personality but, until recently, has received comparatively little attention in analytical psychology. Recognising the body aspects of the psyche addresses this lacuna. Healing occurs through physical and psychological reciprocal interaction and exchange. Jungian psychology seeks to understand communications from the unconscious, and the body is a place where the psyche speaks, consciously and unconsciously. In thinking about our body, we recognise it represents both our specificity and multiplicity – it means to examine and be conscious of the automatic set of assumptions we have and project around our physical abilities, shape, gender, sexuality, social justice, cultural and class status.

Everything we know, do and are, is mediated through the body. 'One's body is a container/communicator of personal complexes that have not been integrated by the person's consciousness, while, in the collective sense, it constitutes the somatic expression of the instinctual impulse of the Self towards the transformation of the individual' (Martini, 2016, p. 20).

Adorning oneself and enhancing the body's appearance is integral to most, if not all, cultures. We derive pleasure from contemplating those who are beautiful and from beautifying ourselves. Not only that, but beauty work is relative, as what is beautiful in one instance can be viewed from another perspective as unappealing.

Beauty work can also be a source of resistance to oppression by celebrating bodies outside rigid norms.

Many scenarios contribute to a body image becoming damaged through emotional wounds. Narrow ideas of beauty create anguish, self-alienation, eating problems, body distortion, body hatred and invisibility. Diverse representations of beauty can help release from body shame. If, however, traditional standards of beauty are the only currency for valuing our bodies, we remain stuck in a paradigm preserving stereotypes and perpetuating an unattainable beauty myth.

Mental states are expressed through fantasies about body image. The body is fundamental to our conscious awareness, as it is a storehouse of memories ranging from trauma to joy. Physicality is a kind of stage on which psychic pain can be dramatised and eventually relieved (Sidoli, 1993, p. 187). The preoccupation of the 'as-if' person too often represents physical unease and discomfort in their skin. Something always needs to be altered, is wrong or must be improved. Although the body of the 'as-if' person seems attended to, they usually dislike it and observe their body 'as-if' from a distance. They might feel ugly, unattractive, and this disease relates to an insecure identity, not liking to be seen yet putting themselves on display, continually wondering how others view and think about them. All this counts to the 'as-if' person and can send them into emotional depression and decline if their body is not to their standards.

Appearance and beauty are of import to the 'as-if' personality, expressing the need for applause and appeal, to be alluring but remain unattainable. There are struggles with weight, body shame and discomfort; clothes are changed often as a means of seeking ease or peace. But this rarely happens. Exemplifying defensive mind/body splitting, they devalue their body, reflecting a lack of corporeal engagement with the world. The 'as-if' person cannot easily find internal coherence or compassion. Estranged from their internal and external worlds, they are often unable to locate their body in space.

For one woman, glimpsing herself in mirrors outside her home brings a slight shock and the image is not as good as when safely at home. The mismatch from private to public is a disparity followed by judgement and self-reproach and accompanied by symptoms of depersonalisation and derealisation. It is based on shame and self-loathing, difficulty self-soothing, internal conflicts and struggles. Of course, this body unease complicates relationships.

Traumatising events, attachment failures and oppression, both historical and current, define our experiences of how we learn to appreciate our bodies. These powerfully influence expectations of self, others and the world. Established early on, these patterns of thinking, feeling and acting influence how we navigate unsafe and oppressive environments. They solidify with repetitive use and can become resistant to modification with time, held in place by automatic, unconscious physical and physiological habits. The body then becomes a negative complex and, as such, is a drain on the psyche. The point of analysis is to uncover these unconscious areas and provide freedom from the rigidity of habitual defence against the body.

It is hard to look inward. Continuously hiding their negative emotions and cognitions generated by anxiety and depression, 'as-if' people wear a social mask they do not take off. The fear of being discovered as a fraud does not allow them to reveal themselves. Internally they define as intellectual phonies (Clance & Imes, 1978, p. 1). Many of these people, although smart, engage in intellectual inauthenticity in one way or another. They often do not reveal their real ideas or opinions. Instead, they have accurately psyched out others and given them what they want to hear, using charm and perceptiveness to win approval.

Healing wounds

Heeding the call of our character means acknowledging the marginalised, chaotic aspects of our being.

> If a man embraces his wholeness, he can avoid 'the unhappy consequences of repressed individuation' … If he voluntarily takes the burden of completeness on himself, he need not find it "happening" to him against his will in a negative form.
>
> (Jung, 1951, para. 125)

It is precisely these qualities that make us inimitable and irreplaceable. Our subjectivity carries answers to the questions, Who am I? What kind of person am I? Subjectivity is not about any particular belief, but rather is the investigation into one's actual and individual personality.

Attempts to understand the 'as-if' person are frustrated by the impression of a disingenuous nature although the outer presentation appears complete, even spectacular. Yet, something intangible and indefinable obtrudes. Defences and projections, splits and dissociations, avoiding vulnerability or being seen, all inhibit access to the unconscious and disrupt the dialogical relationship with self and others. Self and world are disjointed for the 'as-if' person. This becomes problematic for development as it holds the basic material for accessing the imaginative and intuitive and for personality cohesion.

The process of recovery means giving up illusions about parents, partners, relationships and themselves. It takes an honest look in the mirror, questioning how they are on the surface, skimming and not seeing. These people are internally alone, ungrounded, looking competent but not feeling so. Bewildered, where do they turn? Interweaving theory with examples of people and their dreams gives professional and personal substance to the conundrum of the 'as-if' personality. This person is often misread, not understood and in need of gaining access to their inner world. Given the magnitude of uncertainties and transitions we are now undergoing, it is a particularly challenging time. The purpose of exploring the 'as-if' personality is to nurture a more expanded awareness and find what can be replenishing and regenerative.

There is pain, tremendous loss and grief, along with the relief of feeling alive and real. To recover existence and one's realness through the process of Jungian psychotherapy opens a pathway through the complex and challenging wounds of the 'as-if' personality. The point of Jungian work and the challenge of the 'as-if' personality is to find security and the uniqueness of self, including establishing genuine relationships with others. 'As-if' fragmentation and disunion then function as opportunities for unique re-patterning.

Jungian analytical psychology, with its use of symbols, dreams and exploring meaning in the psychological complexes, invites the quest through the personal and collective stories connecting us to ourselves and others. There is a gap for the 'as-if' personality between who one is and who one wants to be. This creates an endless series of painful re-creations of past troubles and rigid limiting behaviours and attitudes. And it is the opening to the personality.

Analytical and psychological treatment is a place where the chaos and the anxieties absorbed from childhood can begin to become thinkable. The search is for the underlying order, the connection to the self.

> We discover, indeed that we do not know our part, we look for a mirror, we want to rub off the make-up and remove the counterfeit and be real. But somewhere a bit of mummery still sticks to us that we forget.
>
> (Rilke, 2016, p. 194)

The hope under all the defences and layers is to accept the vulnerability and fragility, but at the same time enable belief in and support for the future. Finally accessing this, a person expressed,

> I feel for years I built up this protection around me. I was always on the fence, and life was like walking or running on a minefield. And you never knew when the mine would explode. But now I feel like I'm walking without looking down. I feel like I'm open. I was raised to never show weakness but no longer must accept living like that.

References

Baldwin, J. (1985). *The price of the ticket*. St. Martin's Press.

Bollas, C. (1989). *Forces of destiny*. London: Free Association Books.

Bollas, C. (1998). State of the fascist mind. In *Being a character*. Routledge.

Clance, P.R. & Imes, S.A. (1978). The imposter phenomenon in high achieving women: Dynamic and therapeutic intervention. *Psychotherapy: Theory, Research and Practice*, *15*(3), 241–7.

Colman, W. (2006). Imagination and the Imaginary. *Journal of Analytical Psychology*. *51*(1), pp. 21–41.

Colman, W. (2008). On being, knowing and having a self. *Journal of Analytical Psychology*, *53*(3), 351–66. doi: 10.1111/j.1468-5922.2008.00731.x.

Eliot, T.S. (1998, May 1). The waste land. Project Gutenberg. Ebook #1321. https://gutenberg.org/cache/epub/1321/pg1321-images.html.

Hinton, L. & Zokowsky, P. (1993). A return to the animal soul. *Psychological Perspectives*, *28*(1), 47–60.

Jung, C.G. (1951). *The collected works of C.G. Jung: Vol. 9ii. Aion*. Princeton University Press.

Jung, C.G. (1956/1967). *The collected works of C.G. Jung: Vol. 5. Symbols of transformation*. Princeton University Press.

Jung, C.G. (1968). *The collected works of C.G. Jung: Vol. 12: Psychology and alchemy*. Princeton University Press.

Jung, C.G. (1970a). *The collected works of C.G. Jung: Vol. 7. Two essays on analytical psychology*. Princeton University Press.

Jung, C.G. (1970b). *The collected works of C.G. Jung: Vol. 8. Structure and dynamics of the psyche*. Princeton University Press.

Kafka, F. (2022, April 8). The trial. (D. Wylie trans.). *Project Gutenberg. Ebook #7849*. www.gutenberg.org/files/7849/7849-h/7849-h.htm.

Martini, S. (2016). Embodying analysis: The body and the therapeutic process. *Journal of Analytical Psychology, 61*(1), 5–23. doi: 10.1111/1468-5922.12192.

Modell, A. (1996). *The private self*. Harvard University Press.

Neumann, E. (1971). *Amor and psyche*. Princeton University Press.

Rilke, R. (2016). *The notebooks of Malte Laurids brigge*. Penguin.

Schwartz-Salant, N. (1982). *On narcissism*. Inner City Books.

Shorter, B. (1987). *An Image Darkly Forming: Women and Initiation*. London: Routledge.

Sidoli, M. (1993). When the meaning gets lost in the body: Psychosomatic disturbances as a failure of the transcendent function. *Journal of Analytical Psychology, 38*(2), 175–89. doi: 10.1111/j.1465-5922.1993.00175.x.

McFarland Solomon, H.M. (2004). Self creation and the limitless void of dissociation: The 'as-if' personality. *Journal of Analytical Psychology, 49*(5), 635–56. doi: 10.1111/j.0021-8774.2004.00493.x.

Steiner, J. (1983). *Psychic retreats: Pathological organizations in psychotic, neurotic and borderline patients*. Routledge.

Wiener, J. (1998). Under the volcano: Varieties of anger and their transformation. *Journal of Analytical Psychology, 43*(4), 493–508. doi: 10.1111/1465-5922.00049.

Winnicott, D.W. (1987). Ego distortion in terms of true and false self. In *The maturational processes and the facilitating environment*. International Universities Press.

Woolf, V. (1931). *The waves*. Hogarth Press.

Zoppi, L. (2017). Chilled to the bone: Embodied countertransference and unspoken traumatic memories. *Journal of Analytical Psychology, 62*(5), 701–9. doi: 10.1111/1468-5922.12357.

Chapter 2

Through the looking glass of persona

In *The Picture of Dorian Gray* (1890), by Oscar Wilde, Lord Henry, a friend of the artist who is painting the portrait of Dorian Gray, upsets Dorian when he muses on the transient nature of beauty and youth.

> Yes, Mr. Gray, the gods have been good to you. But what the gods give they quickly take away. You have only a few years in which to live really, perfectly, and fully. When your youth goes, your beauty will go with it, and then you will suddenly discover that there are no triumphs left for you ... Every month as it wanes brings you nearer to something dreadful. Time is jealous of you, and wars against your lilies and your roses. You will become sallow, and hollow-cheeked, and dull-eyed. You will suffer horribly ...

Dorian, horrified that he will age while the portrait remains fixed, pledges his soul that it be the other way around.

> But this picture will remain always young. It will never be older than this particular day of June ... If it were only the other way! If it were I who was to be always young, and the picture that was to grow old! For that – for that – I would give everything! Yes, there is nothing in the whole world I would not give! I would give my soul for that!
>
> (Wilde, 1890)

Lord Henry's influence over Dorian grows and he devotes himself to the 'new Hedonism', pledging to dedicate his life to pleasure. Dorian falls in love with Sibyl Vane, an actress, and then cruelly breaks their engagement because he doesn't love her, only her ability to act. Returning home, he sees the face in his portrait is now sneering. Fearing the portrait will reflect his sins, he hides it away.

Dorian spends the next 18 years living a life of sensation and pleasure, and although his reputation suffers in society, his friends love him because he remains young and beautiful, while the portrait, hidden away, transforms.

DOI: 10.4324/9781003315254-3

Often, on returning home … he himself would creep upstairs to the locked room, open the door with the key that never left him now, and stand, with a mirror, in front of the portrait … looking now at the evil and ageing face on the canvas … He would examine with minute care, and sometimes with a monstrous and terrible delight, the hideous lines that seared the wrinkling forehead or crawled around the heavy sensual mouth, wondering sometimes which were the more horrible, the signs of sin or the signs of age.

(Wilde, 1890)

This story is one of personal deception and betrayal. Dorian thinks he can get away with the crimes committed against others and himself. He is seductively and compulsively drawn to the deception. He is lawless and lives against social and personal mores. Of course, in the end, he must perish as he cannot continue to carry the secret or his crimes without them turning against the personality. This is also true psychologically when we come to a point where the façade will no longer suffice, and the total personality must come forth.

In the last analysis every life is the realization of a whole, that is, of a self, for which reason this realization can also be called individuation. All life is bound to individual carriers who realize it, and it is simply inconceivable without them. But every carrier is charged with an individual destiny and destination, and the realization of these alone makes sense of life.

(Jung, 1944/1968, CW 12, para. 330)

Many people are readily and unquestionably conditioned by society to adopt what Jung regarded as the persona. Through this image and for the sake of acceptance and approval people pretend but feel like imposters, acting 'as-if'. This chapter focuses on the persona when used as a coverup. In this case it prevents access to the total person, although simultaneously it can be a pathway to the real self. Double-sided, the persona can be the connecting link to self, the possibility the outer can represent the inner as part of real personal and deep self-expression. We often assume personas are at the surface level, literally shallow, to be pierced through to get to what's deep and important. But the persona can be the real rhythm and beat of a person when connected to the self. Persona can be how we present ourselves to the world with conscious individuality. However, examining the persona means looking at the ways the 'as-if' person uses it to cover the fragility of ego while obstructing the possibility of connection to self and others.

One man said with little affect, 'I cannot tell when the mask is not me as it feels stuck to my skin. I do not think I can take it off'. We all develop masks, shields, personas, protections and defences in form and substance. We think we need them, and, at times, we do. But do we truly control these layers of identities and personalities? Or, like Dorian Gray, do our persona creations, in fact, control us by presenting only part and not the whole? The various personas, whether true to the total self or not, are ways to find ourselves. The 'as-if' person plays a game of mirrors and fragments, however, in which the persona is multiplied infinitely, thus postponing and avoiding the possibility of the personality being totally perceived.

The forces making for both deception and unmasking are various and powerful. They are composed of unsurpassed danger, whether real or not, the urgent need for protection and self-sufficiency, the opposite and equal need for joy, communication and connection. Any of these can serve either truth or falsity, as the occasion demands. Within a plurality of inner and discordant voices, the 'as-if' personality is bombarded by the cacophony of themselves.

There is breakdown in the perception of a 'me' and a split between the perceived and the real. 'As-if' people are definitively divided due to issues of trust, identity, security and missed connection to self. They are trying to figure out why they feel a certain way, can't find satisfaction and always feel behind or rudderless. They are perplexed, feel alone, bereft. Their identity is in question. Therefore, the 'as-if' person is a master at the art of mask making, adopting various personas to conceal haunting inner monsters or to prevent being judged as lacking by others. Personal meaning becomes increasingly transient, precarious, dizzying, unmoored in a panoply of apprehensions. This person engages in many manoeuvres to hedge against being found out, unmasked as incompetent or unable to replicate past successes. They put on masks of beauty, confidence, bravado or various forms of illusion to avoid being transparent and revealed. In this regard they are not attached to the self.

According to Jung the persona mediates between individual consciousness and the surrounding social community. The personal can be absorbed by the collective. In relation to this he stated, 'When we analyse the persona we strip off the mask, and discover that what seemed to be individual is at bottom collective' (1956/1972, CW 7, para. 246). The outer appearance or image can become the entirety of focus for the 'as-if' person.

Yet, some people become aware this guise does not fit; based on falsity, lack of fulfilment, they realise something crucial is missing. This morphs into the search for the individual self along with genuine connection to others. Self-creation emerges from acts of reaching back to move forward into promise and challenge as they assume a shape and definition unique to themselves.

After a long analytical relationship, a man recounted he felt on stage at home, like an actor performing. He was not real. He realised he had never shared this and knew it was important. In any family situation and up close, he froze. This affected all his relationships and was seriously eroding the one with his partner. He withdrew from his partner at any hint of disapproval. The memory of early repressions and feeling squashed in his family as a child were insidious. He was always on guard with family, feigning and acting 'as-if'. He did it so well, no one could tell, but he could, and he was exhausted. It was the up close that brought about the 'as-if' performance; it didn't occur at work or professionally. People liked him so much, yet at home he was stilted and a false version of his natural self.

The continuation of an artificial personality will trigger unconscious turbulence, bringing people into the journey for individuation. This call to self-realisation compels the search for truth. This is a natural impetus, although one can be unconscious about it until necessity pushes them to pay attention. If the inner self is suppressed, the unconscious comes forward to rebalance the imbalance. The 'as-if' person is dealing with, not just an outer mask, but the path to the self. The persona will alter as they become more aware of the unconscious forces impacting the scope of the personality.

When not used consciously the personality suffers and the persona can become rigid and fragmented from the self. The problem arises when people conform to a contrived image rather than their real self. To be inordinately identified with the persona signals susceptibility to the shadow or what are considered the shameful, repressed, denigrated and unused qualities. In addition, the shadow contains important energy, traits or qualities thus far unused yet a part of the self. If the persona is too defended and the shadow too hidden this suggests a significant part of the personality lies below the surface. Surface and shadow together round out the personality. The persona can reflect the true personality, not just a pasting on of stereotypes or following the herd, current style or cultural and traditional customs. The persona is not to be disregarded in the search for one's true self, but rather can be an essential part of the rich and complex configuration of the whole person. No one is a single image but a tapestry of colour and variety.

The 'as-if' person relies on the persona to buffer the yearning, hunger and desperate need to be recognised as something. Jung described the persona as a 'complicated system of relations between individual consciousness and society, fittingly enough a kind of mask, designed on the one hand to make a definite impression upon others, and, on the other, to conceal the true nature of the individual' (1956/1972, CW 7, para. 305).

The 'as-if' type presents a face to the world laced with complexities, paradoxes and ambiguities. This person lives with incongruity between self and image due to an absence or loss of a stable sense of being. Used unconsciously, the persona becomes a husk, the person appearing like an automaton, everything organised but without liveliness. Their presentation is constructed or manicured, with defences erected to present the cohesion and consistency the person does not feel inside.

The persona illustrates to us and others our experiences – painful, disorienting, joyful, rewarding. It can illuminate with a brief flash or thoughtful reflection to bring the landscape of our existence into bold relief so we can be all we are. Being the truth of ourselves, we manifest real around us. Out of this we create and come alive by unwrapping the façade and no longer trivialising ourselves.

The persona reveals the rationales, justifications and myths we tell ourselves, whether false or accurate. How does the 'as-if' personality use the persona to open to the world? This is a simple and complex question and, in a sense, the crux of the conundrum these people face. The trouble is the insistent and often frantic emphasis on the persona and ego as if these often-assumed superficial aspects suffice for the entire personality. Presence means coming from behind the mask.

The word *persona* derives from the ancient Greek plays and refers to the huge masks through which the actors spoke to project their voice and to be seen. Psychologically, the mask of this person hides the real with layers of actions and images to garner approval and success, but according to others. In marketing, a prime place for image and surface, the word *persona* denotes the imaginary customer who is appealed to through outer design.

The pose of clothes

When the potentiality of the psyche is not used it becomes perverted (Leonard, 2000, p. 89). This applies to the necessity of persona development beyond the superficial, so it is not a mask but a form of authentic self-expression. This chapter tracks through a dream series and case examples the ways in which the persona becomes the true self-reflection, aligned with creativity and one's distinctive style for affirming the self. These are expressive of the clarion call challenging people to express their emotional, psychological and physical life through persona adornment. People might be most themselves in what and how they appear, and a person can use the persona to be human, thoughtful and responsive (Bari, 2020, p. 2), showing care and consciousness. Clothes are one example of how people connect persona to self, making them susceptible to being seen, declaring who they really are. 'Clothes change our view of the world and the world's view of us' (Woolf, 1928).

At the beginning of her Jungian analysis a woman began to dream about a series of clothes. She was surprised as this was completely unexpected. They were all the clothes she would wear and in her style. The dream images included the material, colour and the details and the intricacy of design. As she wondered about this dream series its many meanings began to unfold. Her family had been tailors or seamstresses for generations. Her mother, who had died the previous year, sewed her clothes that were much loved, representing care, colour and the unusual. It was a ritual between them to find the right pattern, the right fabric – it had to be unique. Clothes represented the mother's love and creativity, a way to confidently present herself as distinct from others. Through the clothes dreams, she was both mourning the death of her mother while also creating herself. The drawings she made of clothes at the start of a long analytic process were cherished by her as special and valuable pieces of her identity. She felt validated by these images, and although they did not repeat later in the analysis, the images remained within her and helped support her ego/self-development. Her mother, the feminine and maternal symbolically unfolded through the clothes to reveal deeper aspects of the self she could never have previously imagined.

Dress is considered trivial, significant, defining; it makes life statements and ignites unending discussions, debate and even collective disputes. Clothes reflect ideas and dilemmas about what is proper or not and according to whom. They show where we come from, how we regard ourselves, how close we live to our essence. How we dress can be both inhibiting and emancipatory. Clothing choice and appearance reveal us, and through those choices we make a statement about person, body, psyche, culture and individuality. For some this is an art form and how they assert distinctiveness, composing a true picture of who they are. For others it is a means to hide and blend into the average or the crowd or perhaps disappear behind the stage.

Dress is about memory, meaning and intimacy, connecting us to ourselves and others in complicated ways (Bari, 2020, p. 3). In clothes and appearance are enacted the social mores of an era, culture and generation. They not only reflect the body and its real representation, but also provide protection and are illustrative statements of bodily form, representing both desire and denial. Clothes mean different things to different people. They invite another to reach out and/or ask to be noticed or ignored; they can be off-putting and rebellious; they make statements, sometimes angry and defiant, sometimes aesthetic and delicate.

Obviously, the persona has many layers of meaning in daily life. Persona is a way of apprehending the world, making statements about us and our relationships to others. The persona presents overtly our ideas of selfhood and soul, stating our experiences, social class, ethnicity, place in the world, how and where we live. All these reflect in various ways our interior life. They are a language opening to the soul or a means of being shielded against this opening. For example, the people in this chapter use their personas for disguise; they are uncomfortable standing out as real. Yet, they also desire to be noticed, even perceived as spectacular. Whatever the case, the persona of the 'as-if' person is calculated to be a weighty guise with layers of protection against anyone getting close. The 'as-if' person might have an outstanding persona putting one off with defensive posturing while hiding behind is insecurity. They believe the mask is needed to preserve themselves.

We are always in relationship to our outer presentation whether we try to deny it or not. Persona brings with it responsibility to the deepest self, to the honesty of the inner world. How we wear ourselves defines and brings focus to the body. Some might take a position of non-care, or that it does not matter. They might wear pain outwardly while thinking they are camouflaging it. Yet, the desperation remains, the vulnerability present, no matter what attempts are manufactured to cover or override what they feel and who they are.

Our outer appearance and personality are in constant flux and transformation. We are not who we were yesterday as the body and psyche shift. Dressing for ourselves confirms our existence. Yet this can be difficult for the 'as-if' person who is both seeking acclaim yet feeling ashamed and inadequate. Moments of being seen can cause them to crumple from the inside. The world feels like it will fall apart unless they present the right appearance. Although it seems otherwise, the discomfort of self-consciousness and self-preservation may need the dissimulation and disguise. In this instance, the persona provides refuge from others. It can be like a shield of protection and extra skin for the vulnerable feelings underneath, a disguise in which one dissolves (Bari, 2020, p. 7).

The persona is a physical and psychological layer responsive to life, demonstrating a range of feelings. It can express glamour, excitement, pleasure, despair, depression, loss, all aspects springing from within. Considered by some as trivial, the persona can be interwoven with the deepest layers of being and our individual particularities.

The outer objects and images put forth illustrate the life and variety of the person within them. However, they can also elicit falsity, even idolatry as though they possess some power or spirit. Appearances can be deceptive and consciously set up to be so. 'Sometimes who we are is judged by how we appear. Maybe there is no opposition between a style one assumes and one's true being ... our manner of appearing is our manner of being' (Sontag, 1966, p. 26). People see themselves in those things that are dear to them. Style and image can be a way to blend in and/or to create the real and unusual self as it exists within. The outer tells a story of how we express our chosen life path.

An imposter guise formed for self-protection can deny the self and hide the issues calling to be addressed. As one woman said, 'I do not wear shorts'. Behind this sentence was an entire history with a father who all her life was a scary figure, brutal, who made crude sexualised comments about women. She remained cautious about being seen, backed away from intimacy and ignored her body. Her clothing was based on how much she could cover up and not be seen. She focused on others to deflect energy and attention away from herself. There was little security at home, and from childhood she had felt unprotected in the presence of an intrusive father and a mother who also feared him. Confidence in her body and healthy attentiveness was nowhere to be found. She refused a relationship to her body. The goal was to be nondescript, distant. She presented this persona of invisibility to the world. She emphatically did not wear shorts.

The outer image and how we clothe it without words speaks volumes, indicating identity, diversity and the delicacy of lived experience. The persona shows how we wear our body – what we show, reveal, conform, emphasise, in essence what we value and devalue. The guise or costume can display the reality of destruction, health or illness. It imparts moods, feelings, status and psychological and physical situations. The outer impression gives signals and seeks notice, communicating actively with others through evasion or a desire for connection. There is life in the unspoken language of persona. Even when we think otherwise, we state ourselves by how we appear, hide, expose, declare, flaunt, invite or dissuade. The body has a clear language as nonverbal as it is verbal.

But what does it mean when the persona denies individuality in favour of blending in or conforming to an unconscious agreement to be 'as-if'? The outer can conceal the distress, the self-sabotage or personality out of alignment, the ambivalent desire for attention. The assessment of a person's appearance and anatomy can signal a crumbling personality. It can show the dramatic statements of a body disowned and emotional disconnection from others. How we appear reveals the gaze we elicit and why. Persona is manipulative, inviting, enticing, off-putting. What are we saying each day and in each costume about ourselves? Or do we put on some image to fit someone else's fantasy? Each day it is possible to be real. However, the 'as-if' person struggles to balance the fantasy with reality as these rarely fit.

The outer image also reminds people of their age, body shape, self-denigration or appreciation and the inevitability of change. The outer places one in relationship to self and others in the comfort or discomfort of the image put forward. Self-care has been often associated with narcissism and self-absorption, yet self-care is self-value with its connection to body and soul.

If there is ease or not, persona conveys whether someone is living 'as-if' – whether this person has lost the self-connection. In a rather tortured consciousness, blank spaces, the vulnerability and complexity of the self, can be in stark relief when there is an overemphasis on the persona. And herein lies the issue. What seems superficial and adaptive also holds promise for development and creativity. These people are also sparkling stars. They are not failures, but often are unusual and have much energy. They are attractive, and others desire to be with them. Their persona glitters, with exceptional talent, unique qualities. How real does this feel to the person and to others in intimate relationship with them?

The 'as-if' personality, the imposter, is often associated with high-achievers, performers geared to elicit the admiration they need. The imposter uses their persona to get attention but worries about being found as phoney. Inner alienation and insecurity are aspects of the imposter syndrome but are disguised behind the agility of a smoke and mirror persona image. These people report feeling superficial and unreal. Feelings of estrangement and not really belonging detract from living a meaningful life. Insecurity, envy and resentful qualities are sometimes hidden under the appealing persona. Underneath is a personality quaking, insecure, frantic to cover the assumed holes. The 'as-if' person can put on masks with a multiplicity of disguises, retaining singular and isolative positions for emotional safety. This assumed need to rely on the persona as façade can impede recognition of depth and uniqueness.

We all develop personas, exposing certain aspects and hiding others. Dreams remind us of these aspects to integrate, rather than negate. The 'as-if' person is often unaware how much they rely on and are led by the persona. When persona deflects from the real, the spontaneity to be oneself has usually been long forgotten. The 'as-if' person lives with a façade, not knowing otherwise.

In the film *Persona* by Ingmar Bergman, the intertwining of the personalities between two women occurs as each takes on the other's persona, revealing the inner life of the other, otherwise unseen by either of them. The exchange and interchange of personality is enacted with the loss and gain of the persona in a confusing mix. The audience is left with the question of who is who, wondering if the actresses are also left with the question, Who am I?

The persona man

Fritz, a man in his fifties, says his life is a mess. He began Jungian analytical therapy after reading Jung, intrigued by the concept of the collective unconscious. He comes to the first analytical session dressed in a suit, matching socks, tie, immaculate. He has put obvious attention into his appearance. He is mindful in speech, enunciating with clarity, and is obviously intelligent. He has a prestigious scientific job he enjoys. His gestures are modulated and careful as if he does not want to disturb.

He begins saying it is his third divorce, but he is not sad and feeling little if anything. In fact, his face shows no emotion, and although he retains eye contact, it is unclear what is happening within. He also casually and somewhat rapidly said he knows he is a fraud, but no one else does. He adds he is used to being this way, and he recognises something is wrong and there is more to life but does not know what that is. He almost proudly says no one can guess anything about him. He no longer wants to be a fraud and wants to be honest in therapy; however, he does not know how to express anything else, much less find his real self, or even know what that is. He has not cared about this before. Several sessions later he dreams *of being in a card game in which he was looking for pairs. Two boys try to steal the cards. His wallet split in half, and he loses all the German identity of his birth but keeps his US identity where he has lived for 18 years.*

In associating to the dream, Fritz repeats he has never been himself. He followed his older brother in school and studied to be like him, not to be himself. He also said he never thought about his parents or how they were or their effect on him. He firmly says he was content as a child; nothing was amiss. The dream says he is split between childhood and adulthood, between one country and another. Here the self divides itself into two halves in such a way that a partial self acts as a complete self (Bollas, 1998, p. 159), not needing the other.

In the dream everything is split – his wallet, two boys and two countries representing his identity. They all symbolise a division within the personality and an unconnected self. He has been living as two people, with neither in relation with the other. The boys might represent him psychologically stealing from himself beginning in childhood. It implies he began separating the secret self from the true one when young. Children make bargains with themselves to make it through, hide their truth and disguise real feelings, assessing parents cannot handle them. The dream implies childhood was a difficult time, although he says otherwise. He has worn the persona mask so well no one knows who is real and until now this did not bother him. According to him, nothing bothered him as he was not invested in much.

People want to comfort themselves, assuage pain, cover the hurt, find joy. The persona provides a form of protection. Fritz paints a curious relationship with himself, bolstering the illusion of self-sufficiency and a hedge against any intimacy or relationship to the world, others or himself. Such conception is a form of self-delusion or a learned masking of desire for others. There is a strange laziness within Fritz although he is high achieving, diligent at work, accomplished. The laziness comes out in the denial of emotional neediness, mixed with hunger to possess success, competence and approval – and wanting it to come easily.

Fritz has been emotionally silent; even in childhood he seemed to ask little from the happy family he portrayed. Mother doted and father was unemotional, removed. He accepted both as who they were and does not recall needing or expressing anything else. In denying and repressing any needs, however, he became closed off and estranged from his feelings. His defence was to negate emotion, avoiding the unknown or chaos of intimate exchange. These are murky waters where the 'as-if' person experiences a dilemma. This person seeks closeness, to feel accompanied and, at the same time, distances to protect against the threat of emotional invasion, which they interpret a relationship entails.

The desire for intimacy is denied. These people dwell as if in twilight, non-differentiated, usually anxious and fearful of falling apart, yet they cannot admit the depth of their apprehension, nor find its causes (Seligman, 1986, p. 70). To avoid anxiety, insecurity and conflict, Fritz's mind shuts off. Fritz anticipates his falsity will be discovered and he will be found out as insufficient and an imposter. The 'as-if' person has a fragile emotional framework and lives a sort of double exposure. Uncovering layer upon layer of obfuscations reveals Fritz's continual and unconscious dodging away from anything close.

Although he denies this, there must have been some disappointments or early lack of attention and care that planted the seeds for his emotional absence, for his feeling insufficient and that he needs to hide from himself. Jean Knox, British Jungian analyst, explains this as follows:

> In order to be loveable and loved, she must cease to exist and so must destroy all her aliveness in a constant struggle against being who she is. This conflict and resistance become a kind of self-torture. On the other hand, to experience oneself as a real person, with a sense of self and a capacity to make her own choices brings the risk of violent retaliation … It is an irresolvable impasse, which eventually leads to a state of despair. To love means to exist and to want to have one's independent existence recognized and responded to by the loved other.
>
> (Knox, 2007, p. 544)

Fritz long ago retreated behind a wall of isolation, but he now has a conflicting desire to engage. It is 'through "affection" that the person is involved and therefore feels the full weight of reality … A purely intellectual perception means little, for what is known is mere words and not the substance from within' (Jung, 1968, CW 10, para. 61). Fritz learned to blur the line between truth and fiction. His self-described narrative of being strange, easily rejected, became a substitute for exploring further or finding any other reasons within. He lived a one-track existence. As it began so young, his storytelling techniques about himself increasingly acted as substitutes for any other knowledge. This compensatory adaptation meant he avoided sorrow, emotions, and muted any relational needs. However, it did allow him to maintain the status quo so nothing rocked his world. He is slim, conscious of weight and food, exercises, but all this is arranged to appear one-dimensional and almost nondescript. Although carefully composed and meticulous in his appearance, always dressing in stylish suits, matching colours, rather formal, he reports feeling unappealing and insecure. He wants notice professionally but does little to stand out or comply with professional requirements, like writing papers and publishing. He is highly intelligent but tones this down and wants to be sought after.

Although he does not like to be seen, he often wonders how he is viewed. He walks around as if he is invisible and registers discomfort with others. *He has a dream he is not being real.* He thinks the dream is not significant but does bring it to therapy. Not being real is his usual mode of existence and he needs to understand what that means as the dream also refers to his neglected inner life. As Jung said:

> A certain kind of behaviour is forced on them by the world, and professional people endeavour to come up to these expectations. Only, the danger is that they become identical with their personas – the professor with his textbook, the tenor with his voice. Then the damage is done; henceforth he lives exclusively against the background of his own biography ... One could say, with a little exaggeration, that the persona is that which in reality one is not, but which oneself as well as others think one is.
>
> (Jung, 1969b/1991b, CW 9i, para. 221)

The 'as-if' person only seems invested in others, yet Fritz has few friends outside of work contacts or the women with whom he has affairs. He did not previously question this, and the paucity of his connections went unnoticed for years. His emotions were frozen and his reactivity to life flattened. Nothing amiss entered his consciousness as he registered no emotionality or disturbance. He avoided any recognition of this by being busy and preoccupied with the serial affairs. He recounts these as responding to the overtures of women. He does not consider the affairs mean anything but instead feed his vanity. He does not think of the affairs as expressing hostility to his wife, sadness, emptiness or his belief no one knows or cares about him. With his insistence on being rational, not emotional, the toneless responses, polite but unruffled, I wonder about the full extent of his emotional paucity.

Moreover, Fritz lives in secret. Again, he insists being rational is what counts. He does not talk deeply with anyone nor share himself. He reiterates he never knew or thought about it, and he did not imagine anything else. Therapy opens a different world, and he regards each session as difficult, even with tears at times, much to his surprise. Feeling in distress at one point, he admits to being fearful but does not know of what. He seems to just go where the wind takes him. Life decisions have been arbitrary as he moved from one job and country to another, always initiated by a boss who recognised his potential. Again, Fritz responded with his polite and compliant manner, 'as-if' he was involved but really it meant little.

Fritz gradually begins to realise his mother, although supportive, was unhappy in her marriage. His parents were not affectionate with one another, and his mother frequently complained about his father. His father was removed emotionally from everyone. With his mother, Fritz felt cared for, and she was unconditionally devoted to her children. His memory is that his parents were never emotional or angry and they never disagreed. Their emotional desert became his and the longing for intimacy and love remained undeveloped and unfulfilled in him as well.

With some nostalgia he described childhood as the golden years and a time of no worries when all was predictable and taken care of. However, he recalls an incident when he stopped playing chess at age 12 or 13 because he did not win a tournament and he was ashamed. He just gave up and did not play again or question this response. Even though he liked chess, the pain of the loss was too much. He did not think to tell anyone how he felt. He was shy as a child, and it sounded like Fritz was passively ignored, but this too had to be denied.

As a teen and in his early twenties he did not date. He waited for his first crush for several years. Almost immediately after they married, and he was happy, troubles began. He did not know what to do and remained for years in an unhappy state. He never understood what sounded like emotional turmoil in his wife combined with his lack of response as he neither knew how to address feelings with her nor how to manage a relationship. Relationships were bewildering.

Fritz never gets angry or stands up for himself. He is blandly accepting. He comments that memories are false, not facts, so they cannot be trusted. Fritz has dulled all expression of emotion towards himself and others, and his psychological development is stunted. Emotional absence inhibits the ability of the ego to gain access to the unconscious, disrupting the emergence of a dialogical relationship between them. He has not valued himself and does not believe he is any good, no matter what anyone says. He worries about being flawed and making the wrong decisions. Like the 'as-if' person, he covers the holes in his psyche, but this only works if he remains distant from intimacy with himself and others.

In a dream *Fritz is a fellow at the institution where he works and is taken to a lab. He is attired in jeans and a shirt and thinks he should be more formally dressed. Then he realises he cannot find his way back.* He is lost, as he is in his career and personal life currently. The dream says he cannot go back but, also, he is not ready or correctly dressed for his current job. Being lost means he cannot return to what was, and the only way is forward, but he does not know where it leads. His usually formal clothes are exchanged for more casual dress as he must surrender his measured and formal attitudes that keep him from himself, like a suit of emotional armour.

He mentions movies he watches while exercising. I begin to watch them as well, and in the following sessions it becomes a means for us to discuss who he identifies with and why. The emotional tone of the characters and their life reactions plus the back and forth sharing of impressions is a way for him to be seen. His emotional reactions begin to surface.

Fritz says he is in search of identity and mentions wanting to be a hero like Superman. He reads philosophers who address the tragic and defeated, the person who when he dies had a life people will miss. Fritz says he does not have anything anyone will miss. He sees he can get somewhere professionally but is sensitive to rejection and holds back. One part argues with this desire by saying it does not count. Failure, defeat, the sense of giving up on himself and dull emotions describe his inner world.

He has not wished for much and lacked the experience of feeling anyone would be interested in him. He admits he is hostile and expresses fearfulness of continuing to live this way. Fritz is beginning to recognise the damage to his psyche.

> Whoever looks into the mirror of the water will see first of all his own face. Whoever goes to himself risks a confrontation with himself. The mirror does not flatter, it faithfully shows whatever looks into it; namely, the face we never show to the world because we cover it with the persona, the mask of the actor. But the mirror lies behind the mask and shows the true face.
>
> (Jung, 1969b/1991b, CW 9i, para. 43)

Everyone embodies different masks in different settings, as it is the way to adapt to the demands of society, shaping social roles and how others are dealt with. But adaptation also has its dangers. As Jung described,

> The persona is a complicated system of relations between individual consciousness and society, fittingly enough a kind of mask, designed on the one hand to make a definite impression upon others, and, on the other, to conceal the true nature of the individual.
>
> (Jung, 1956/1972, CW 7, para. 305)

Unable to reveal the truth about themselves, the 'as-if' person acts as someone they aren't. In Jungian terms the psyche cannot transform or individuate if one remains stuck in outer perceived expectations, blocking hearing or responding to the real self. The result can be a shallow, brittle, conformist kind of personality with an excessive concern for what people think. This leaves a person unconscious of any distinction between themselves and the world. Any uniqueness is lost.

In such cases, the ego is almost completely identical with the persona; individuality is repressed, representing maximum adaptation to society and minimum adaptation to one's individuality. This psychological constellation inhibits development. The need for a façade comes at the price of self-discovery.

> One cannot individuate as long as one is playing a role to oneself; the convictions one has about oneself are the most subtle form of persona and the most subtle obstacle against any true individuation. One can admit practically anything, yet somewhere one retains the idea that one is nevertheless so-and-so, and this is always a sort of final argument which counts apparently as a plus; yet it functions as an influence against true individuation.
>
> (Jung, 1997, p. 821)

Fritz's case illustrates an adhesive identification with the persona, clinging to it as if that is all there is. These people appear slick, the outer adaptation seamless, while they live with the nagging knowledge no one knows them, but neither do they. They can play at being a person and pretend intimacy and underneath know it is a forgery. This means dishonesty in relationships, including lying to oneself. The persona is the shield, protecting the hidden heart – vulnerable, fragile and easily damaged. It is clear from this example that it takes a crash in some area of life to alter the rigid protective persona.

With Fritz, the emotional wrong turns happened so early on they could not be stated. Nonverbal interactions carried too much disappointment and were crushing to the personality. Shoving the emotions aside and feeling unacceptable, Fritz donned the mask of a performer to escape psychological distress. As an adult he relied on the persona to mask the melancholy and fragile self, lacking in animation, stuck in routine. He masked himself from himself in his persona costume.

The rigidity of persona develops from the apprehension of being judged, indicating separation between the need for the outer acceptable façade and hiding the inner darkness and shame about any blemish or problem. The mounting disruption of self is accentuated by a persona that acts as a barrier to equip the person for the social and superficial world. It is a perpetual re-impersonation, and unconsciously the 'as-if' person becomes separated from authenticity. The fabrication is an artifice as the real recedes – so far away it could be almost forgotten. The persona or social role takes over. It is as if surface attaches to surface and the person cannot find the way into the real.

The Jungian interpretation of the symbol stretches towards the dimension of the not-yet. Jung commented, 'Fantasies are symbolical in the sense that they represent an attempt to elucidate, by means of analogy, something that still belongs entirely to the domain of the unknown or something that is still to be' (1916/1953, CW 8, paras. 493–5). The symbol anticipates what a person will discover in the course of time and in ways impossible to determine beforehand. Thus, the Jungian symbol has a dimension that is not only individual and subjective but also collective and cultural (Connolly, 2002, p. 365).

The search for the real person is the task.

> However narcissistic it may be, our subjective speculation can no longer seize and appropriate this gaze before which we appear at the moment when, … bearing it along with every movement of our bearing or comportment, we can get over … the mourning of ourselves, I mean the mourning of our autonomy, of everything that would make us the measure of ourselves.
>
> (Derrida, 2003, p. 161)

The conception of the self is something prior to and apart from the social conditions producing it. The influences derive from the ways we are raised and educated, the language we learn, the stories to which we have access, the emotional flow of circumstances. This includes the stories we are told, the expectations from family and culture as well as the restrictions. All these can both create and constrict the self. Like Fritz, even those people caught in rigid and entrenched patterns can find their way into exploring their personality from the surface inwards. Fritz continued ever deeper into self-discovery. 'I feel that strong emotion must leave its trace … so that we shall be able to love our lives through from the start' (Woolf, 1985, p. 67).

Social media – seen and unseen

We live in an era when emphasis on appearance is paramount. Many don't take time to know each other, instead relying on superficial observations, showing off on social media with their words, body, ideas, images.

> We rush impetuously into novelty, driven by a mounting sense of insuffi-
> ciency, dissatisfaction, and restlessness. We no longer live on what we have,
> but on promises, no longer in the light of the present day, but in the darkness
> of the future, which, we expect, will at last bring the proper sunrise.
>
> (Jung, 1963, p. 236)

The singularity and superficiality of the 'as-if' person is emphasised through the social media emphasis on ego, persona and image. The lack of deeper reflection is indicated by how many people are obsessed with the number of 'likes' they get. These actions deflect from the inside self and keep people at a distance. Although able to put out attractive, appealing, intriguing personas, behind those personas is a fragile ego, uneasy and uncomfortable. There often is hardly any contentment or peace inside.

The fractured self is apparent in current personal and social disorientation. A lack of depth in our culture along with its surface mentality is replicated in the 'as-if' personality. This constant adaptation undermines personality development, though it eventually comes to a crashing halt. Rapidly glancing from one topic to another avoids the spaces for deepening, indicating arrest in psychological development. Social media can portray images of the world as real, not as illusion. Technological adroitness becomes the frantic and often manic attempts to believe all is beautiful and nothing amiss.

Social media has become the lens of our experiences, simultaneously shaping and constraining psychic sensibilities, yet we can remain unaware of the scope of its impact. Preoccupation with glitz and altering self-image characterises Western culture. As Jung said many years ago, 'The more successful we become in science and technology the more diabolical are the uses to which we put our invention and discoveries' (McGuire & Hull, 1987, p. 397). Social media platforms often feature inauthentic presentations geared to the amount of hits as a verification of success. Quality and the unique do not seem to count when selves are easily manicured, adapted to the general rather than seen as defining the individual. Interacting digitally with fake representations on the internet can endanger the capacity to cope with complexity and ambiguity and to operate with facility.

Whatever we feel about the tools of technology, the images we generate and the attitudes we have towards them impact us. They can cause a dimming of life, afflicting many in this image-driven world. The defensive adoption of psychic retreat and narcissism hide gnawing anxiety, internal dissociations and fragile self-cohesion. Preoccupation with sleek self-image and prestige indicates an individual life beset by the need to impress social forces. Social media platforms often feature inauthentic presentations with inaccurate information, telling us the world is full of impossibly beautiful people with wonderful and luxurious lives. The shift towards appearances away from feelings and emotions has a cost, however. As British psychoanalyst Adam Phillips said, 'We learn to live somewhere between the lives we have and the lives we would like' (2012, p. xi).

The following is a dream and short commentary about a man in his mid-thirties, Terrell, who is unable to decide on a life focus. He is without a solid career and lacking in self-care, although finally in a stable relationship. Many aches and pains plague his body. He is desultory and spends time playing the video games of his earlier years to delay and avoid his life. He realises this and it causes great distress, but he is stuck. He has openly separated from his original tightly knit family with their religious roots. This was momentous for him and created much internal distress. Terrell is not the person he was raised to be, and this is becoming very clear.

He is on his second marriage and happier but morose within, depressed, his life patterns erratic, his mood mercurial. He becomes lost, afraid and often resorts to drugs to dull the ache inside. He has begun a new life, seemingly different from his original family structure, but his talents and qualities remain unused. Thoughts circle and fire in his brain as quick as the video game, leaving him confused and with little direction. His experience describes many of the 'as-if' personality characteristics – talents unused and scattered lives.

Terrell's dream: *I'm playing some video game about conquering the world. It's a strategy game. This part is a bit more unclear. It's a game I don't really like and haven't played in a while. My mother got me to play it, but she asks me why I'm still playing it if I don't even like it. I tell her that sometimes I come back to games I used to play when I was a kid because they get better or different over time. I still don't think I like this game.*

Here is some of his commentary on the dream:

> I've spent countless hours trying to figure this out, and I keep having the same dreams and the same problems and the same inability to see myself. I think to myself sometimes that might not be that smart or that sensitive or that in tune. Like a French horn out of tune. Maybe I'm just lazy. Maybe I'm just incompetent. Maybe I'm just broken. Maybe I am forever shattered by my developmental scarring.

Fantasy, as defined analytically, has many interpretations and has become increasingly prominent in our lives, accentuated with the loss of body contact through electronic communication. Are we coming to think of psychological space, consciousness and the unconscious as not even located in the body? Jung said, 'The body is a most doubtful friend because it produces things we do not like; there are too many things about the body, which cannot be mentioned. The body is very often the personification of the ego' (1970a, p. 23).

There are so many images of everything nowadays. We compare reality to images, instead of comparing images to reality. Or perhaps we are losing the difference and distinction between them. Screens and all that can be created on them can dull the capacity for astonishment, the experience of surprise and discovery. They can lead to a radical detachment from the world.

There are yet to be uncovered layers behind the persona of pretend. The internet has increased the flow of images duplicating life, and anyone is bestowed with the power to invent and emit them. Social media and a constant internet connection have significantly changed the way people live and perceive relationships, and this also has fostered illusions hugely impacting identity and image construction. This alternative reality acts as a substitute and a valid refuge against the anxiety and shame associated with the idea of presenting oneself in an authentic social context (Favero & Candelleri, 2017, p. 358).

Media technology reduces the body and psyche to adapt to what is popular, gains the most numbers and reflects the superficial quick response. Like the 'as-if' personality, it becomes a world split from the true self. Face-to-face personal relationships are progressively eliminated in favour of various types of web-based social interaction (Favero & Candelleri, 2017, p. 359), resulting in withdrawal and social seclusion. One can make any picture or vision so no one can guess the façades in the virtual world of touched-up and half-seen bodies. Surface counts, not the unconscious. As Jung noted, 'Technology … is based on a specifically rationalistic differentiation of consciousness which tends to repress all irrational psychic factors' (Jung, 1970b, CW 11, para. 443).

On social media, 'defined identities are not so much a prerequisite of interaction as they are in real life and may open possibilities for testing identity' (Roesler, 2017, pp. 376–7). Identity cannot solely be found behind the masks of social media when no complete self is offered or seemingly desired. Instead, the imposter persona houses the identity. One picks up an identity for a while. She becomes the face of the one she imagines looking at her. Air-brushed, tinted, trimmed or reshaped, he becomes an object, needing to hide any vulnerable and sensitive reactions in the search for self-legitimisation. Aiming to be a media queen means packaging herself in the flash of façade, quite like the 'as-if' personality. However,

If she can be encouraged to play with the imagery, allowing it to take whatever form it happens to come up with, the energy locked in the shadow will emerge, bringing with it the buried creative fire. In that new integration, the self brings healing for the soul and energy for the art.

(Woodman, 1993, pp. 100–1)

The intimate and private that are non-existent within the social media platform bring up issues of presence and absence. There is the risk that imagination, imitation and false idealisation substitute for real-life relationships and experiences. Like Terrell, the 'as-if' person is not clear about who he is and who he is not.

The wilderness of mirrors

He continually looks outward, checking to make sure it is safe, but the unease lives inside, thoroughly masked from the view of others. He experiences a form of isolation from his body sensations and from the immediacy of experiences, leaving him devoid of aliveness. He constantly checks his phone and assesses the likes on social media. If there is any issue or not enough approval, depression sets in and builds up with an insidious nature. His good self-feelings depend on what others think, even though these others are virtually unknown. And, how can anyone know the real self through a touched-up image and carefully modulated text?

This man appears 'as-if' real although inhibited in relationship and self-expression. There is an underlying apathy and distrust of the world. This person feels as flat and superficial as the social media screen, yet he does not know how to peel off the layers and find what lies inside. With any hint of negativity, sorrow is ignited, and he begins to slowly shut down and withdraw. He suffers deeply, failing to experience what others seem to enjoy. The same scenario repeats day after day, as he remains glued to the surface, compromising individuality.

The connection to self, to who we are as individuals, is expressed through authentic representation, not false adaptation. At the crux are the psychological tasks linking conscious and unconscious with the physical body. *Embodiment* is defined by the Oxford English Dictionary as 'a tangible or visible form of an idea, quality or feeling', and the concept of a sense of self is an example of an idea – the idea of who each of us is as an individual. People learn about the world and about themselves through their bodies; thus, the body is the basis of subjectivity and persona self-expression. However, for the 'as-if' person the body is subject to constant surveillance and pressure for improvement. This attitude reveals the treacherousness of our fantasies about what constitutes the good life, the ideals that many subscribe to without a second thought but are impossible to attain. Perhaps they are not worth it, but the 'as-if' person tends to cling to them as a means of self-definition and internalised judgement.

Social media itself arouses a sense of isolation as the virtual substitutes for person-to-person connection. Contact with the world is feigned with no real personal or touchable contact. The idealised and illusionary can be used to avoid what the 'as-if' person assumes to be inevitable disillusions, especially when real has been disappointing. Much becomes reduced to the general or the trivial as surface and appearance substitute for being. The reality of the emotions can also be muted, or the opposite and become wildly uncensored. One becomes a plaything, and what is sought is unclear as it is ever-elusive in the never-static image.

Those compelled to check social media seem consumed by a passion for self-exposure, being noticed and stylised for popular consumption. These portrayals, whether true or not, are popular, and the idealised general image is lauded. This does not lead to more authenticity, but for many, it dictates how they should be, providing only a simulacrum of life. The general image is relied upon rather than the authentic. They attempt to attain fascination yet there remains a remoteness without bringing the real person close to themselves.

The self as it is presented in cyberspace brings up identity in the search for an answer to the question, Who am I? Identity conveys a feeling for the uniqueness of one's life and the fact of being different from others. Inner solidity gives a feeling of continuity and uniformity over time, producing the coherence for personality development. As Jung said,

> Inasmuch as a man is merely collective, he can be changed by suggestion to the point of becoming – or seeming to become – different from what he was before. But inasmuch as he is an individual he can only become what he is and always was.
>
> (1935/1954, para. 11)

We have the chance to create our identity and, at the same time, are confronted with a choice of identities, possible ways of living, philosophies of life, ways of dressing and so on. This includes the influence of culture, how we grew up and our living conditions. We incorporate this unconsciously into our psychic structure and it becomes part of our deepest self. Meaning does not emerge from the reduction of complexity, but in personality enriched via our interconnectedness with others.

> Is not the main point in psychotherapy and psychoanalysis to get out from behind our masks and become fully present with our suffering and our anxieties about being accepted in the face of the real other? How can this come about if we can so perfectly mask our deficiencies technologically?
>
> (Roesler, 2017, p. 379)

Social media 'is linked to the need for attachment, proximity and even intimacy with another. It is a technical tool which can collapse the miles that separate us and bring us together in a warm fantasy of contact' (Hauke, 2009, p. 46). Perceptions of what we call reality are not neutral but reflect our individual personality, calling us to develop a conscious and discriminating attitude towards technology as part of our lives. 'The changes in interpersonal interaction brought by technological media are strongly connected with the extent and quality of presence of both partners in the interaction' (Roesler, 2017, p. 375).

Just as it is up to the individual to take responsibility for the partnership between the conscious and unconscious mind, a conscious awareness of social media use is key. The search for personal meaning can be at odds with attempts to normalise human beings' idiosyncratic natures. Technology with its fantasy contact can make us too much the same, allowing the 'as-if' person to evade the existential uncertainty of life. They can become lost in mere image and sacrifice the real and creative.

There is belief in the efficacy of images and their capacity to enrich reality, both inner and outer. Image is defined by Jung as:

> a condensed expression of the psychic situation as a whole ... an expression of the unconscious as well as the conscious situation of the moment. The interpretation of its meaning, therefore, can start neither from the conscious alone nor from the unconscious alone but only from their reciprocal relationship ... [The symbol, on the other hand,] is the best possible formulation of a relatively unknown thing, which for that reason cannot be more clearly or characteristically represented.
>
> (Jung, 1971, CW 6, paras. 745, 815)

A symbol is alive and continually evolves in its meanings.

The dream self

Fritz, referred to earlier, has a dream many months into analysis: *I was with a couple of guys, and one knew me. That one asked to buy my patent. I said no, I will not sell it. You can use it, but I can sit on my roof, drinking my coffee and know it is mine. I do not need to make money on it. The patent is me and I know that.* To Fritz this dream confirms his gradually evolving confidence and surety, a solidity around claiming what is his and not being threatened by another male. The dream declares strength of self, unshaken and secure. The patent could represent what he has made of himself and who he really is.

As one becomes more psychologically flexible, the sources of the self, imbued with authenticity and animation, emerge. Bringing the 'as-if' person into life is a process that requires passing through many gates and learning to stay on the path. The life hidden within the reliance on persona can be narrowly perceived outwardly as acts of isolation although it contains the goal of self-creation. 'What would I say, if I had a voice, who says this saying is me? ... it's not with thinking he will find me, but what is he to do, living and bewildered, yes, living, say what he may ... I wait for me afar for my story to begin ...' (Beckett, 1999, pp. 24–5). The persona must not be minimised, however, for it holds possibilities, potential and value for reaching into the depths of the self.

References

Bari, S. (2020). *Dressed*. Basic Books.
Beckett, S. (1999). *Texts for nothing*. John Calder.
Bollas, C. (1998). State of the fascist mind. In *Being a character*. Routledge.
Connolly, A. (2002). To speak in tongues: Language, diversity and psychoanalysis. *Journal of Analytical Psychology*, 47(3), 359–82. doi: 10.1111/1465-5922.00325.

Derrida, J. (2003). *The work of mourning*. (P.-A. Brault and M. Naas, trans.). University of Chicago Press.

Favero, D. & Candellieri, S. (2017). Analytical psychology: Do the new technologies have an impact? *Journal of Analytical Psychology*, *62*(3), 356–71. doi: 10.1111/1468-5922.12319.

Hauke, C. (2009). Turning on and tuning out: New technology, image, analysis. *Journal of Analytical Psychology*, *54*(1), 43–60. doi: 10.1111/j.1468-5922.2008.01756.x.

Jung, C.G. (1916/1953). *The collected works of C.G. Jung: Vol. 8. The archetypes and the collective unconscious*. Princeton University Press.

Jung, C.G. (1935/1954). *The collected works of C.G. Jung: Vol. 16. Practice of psychotherapy*. Princeton University Press.

Jung, C.G. (1944/1968). *The collected works of C.G. Jung: Vol. 12. Psychology and alchemy*. Princeton University Press.

Jung, C.G. (1956/1972). *The collected works of C.G. Jung: Vol. 7. Two essays on analytical psychology*. Princeton University Press.

Jung, C.G. (1963). *Memories, dreams, reflections*. Vintage books.

Jung, C.G. (1968). *The collected works of C.G. Jung: Vol. 10. Civilization in transition*. Princeton University Press.

Jung, C.G. (1969b/1991b). *The collected works of C.G. Jung: Vol. 9i. Archetypes and the collective unconscious*. Princeton University Press.

Jung, C.G. (1970a). *Analytical psychology: Its theory and practice, The Tavistock Lectures*. Vintage Books.

Jung, C.G. (1970b). *The collected works of C.G. Jung: Vol. 11. Psychology and religion*. Princeton University Press.

Jung, C.G. (1971). *The collected works of C.G. Jung: Vol. 6. Psychological types*. Princeton University Press.

Jung, C.G. (1997). *Visions: Notes of the seminar given in 1930–1934*. (C. Douglas, Ed.). Princeton University Press.

Knox, J. (2007). The fear of love: The denial of self in relationship. *Journal of Analytical Psychology*, *52*(5), 543–63. doi: 10.1111/j.1468-5922.2007.00685.x.

Leonard, L.S. (2000). *The call to create: Celebrating acts of imagination*. Harmony.

McGuire, W. & Hull, R.F.C. (1987). *C.G. Jung speaking: Interviews and encounters*. Princeton University Press.

Phillips, A. (2012). *Missing out. In praise of the unlived life*. Farrar, Straus, and Giroux.

Roesler, C. (2017). Psychoanalysis: The use of media technology and its impact on the therapeutic relationship. *Journal of Analytical Psychology*, *62*(3), 372–94. doi: 10.1111/1468-5922.12317.

Seligman, E. (1986). The half alive ones. In: A. Samuels (ed.), *The father: Contemporary Jungian perspectives* (pp. 69–94). New York University Press.

Sontag, S. (1966). On style. In *Against interpretation*. Dell.

Wilde, O. (1890). *The picture of Dorian Grey*. Project Gutenberg [eBook #174, created October 1, 1994]. www.gutenberg.org/cache/epub/174/pg174-images.html.

Woodman, M. (1993). *Conscious femininity*. Inner City Books.

Woolf, V. (1928). *Orlando: A biography*. Harcourt, Brace and Company.

Woolf, V. (1985). *Moments of being: A collection of autobiographical essays*. Harvest Books.

Chapter 3

The presence of the father's shadow

The following story is about the intricacy and value of following the shadow. The shadow requires attention and notice as underneath are buried the treasures of knowledge.

Tales of the Dervishes

There was a statue with pointing finger, upon which was inscribed 'Strike on this spot for treasure'. Its origin was unknown, but generations of people had hammered the place marked by the sign. Because it was made of the hardest stone, little impression was made on it, and the meaning remained cryptic. Dhun-Nun, wrapped in contemplation of the statue, one day exactly at midday observed that the shadow of the pointing finger, unnoticed for centuries, followed a line in the paving beneath the statue. Marking the place he obtained the necessary instruments and prised up by chisel blows the flagstone, which proved to be the trapdoor in the roof of a subterranean cave which contained strange articles of a workmanship which enabled him to deduce the science of their manufacture, long since lost, and hence to acquire the treasure and those of a more formal kind which accompanied them.

(Shah, 1974, p. 55)

One of these buried treasures might be the father figure who contributes to the development of a conscious, well-integrated and whole human being. Generally, however, the father as a relational parent has been without import, vaguely defined and elusive culturally, emotionally and psychologically. Exploring what has been repressed brings us to what appears in the shadow: complexes and defences. This is also evidenced in the cultural attitudes about fathering apparent in the political, sociological, familial and psychological arenas. The perspective here promotes attention to what has been ensconced in the shadows, shaping the complexes and defences. This has meant 'the sensitive and affirming father, the playful father, the one with many sides and feelings, not the punitive, stern, self-contained or just the weekend or the commander-in-chief father' (Samuels, 2010, p. 248).

DOI: 10.4324/9781003315254-4

Historically there has been a prevalence, and even assent, to tyranny supported by a patriarchal tradition in which the child is expected to submit to the father and his ways. The father often represented and enacted domination, power and control. This dynamic has been taken for granted in the past, yet its one-sidedness remains a widespread norm. Such a dynamic can create a mindset of submission and oppression in which the child must fit with the father's ideals and appear 'as-if' agreeable and compliant.

The 'as-if' personality is formed from early environmental failures, focused here on the dynamics with the paternal figure. The loss of a good and present father can mean a child's talents and possibilities for the future can remain dormant or fade into doubt and contribute to the lack of self-connection. Without a nurturing paternal figure, children are susceptible to invasion by negative images. They might identify with the father's insufficiency and absence, especially as so often he does not mirror a range of helpful masculine or feminine energy. When the father cannot fulfil his child's needs for love and affirmation, self-denigrating habits and moods abound.

The questioning and countering of these former systems, although previously ignored and denied, has now come to the forefront. The father/child dynamic relates to themes of identity, reaching back to infancy and forward into adulthood, and affects how the personality unfolds for present and future generations. Hopefully, the psychological and personal reflections portrayed here can provide support for new ways of relating and promote awareness for expansion of previously limited emotional relationships. Father is not merely the one holding the other parent who holds the children; he can hold the children in relatedness and love.

Shadow

Fairy tale images of wicked kings and evil figures often represent the father in his unconsciousness, absence and neglect. The child is portrayed as innocent and helpless with no power or effect. Outside of the tales and legends a narrow father image has populated the collective and personal mind. The reality of absent, unavailable or unemotional fathers reaches into many past generations with ponderous influences on the present. Here, I emphasise the effects of the ruptures and crises, the deficiencies in psychological space from eroded father love. The child and then the adult suffers, wanting to be loved.

The unconscious father is a burden passed on to the child, leaving a vacuum filled with a negative father figure. 'He wanted to put the sadness in the past and begin his future, and after that it was inevitable that he would make his life as far away from his father as he could, that he would put oceans between them and keep them there' (Rushdie, 2012, p. 21). The inadequate or incompetent father is emotionally absent and passive and his psychological relatedness ranges from insufficient to non-existent. The father may express the shadow through his attitudes and behaviours – emotionless, shady, engaging in affairs and addictions. The child can become confused and preoccupied, the father's voice loud in the child's mind whereas the child's own voice is muted.

A child loses individuality and can become submerged in living out the father's shadow. The danger is in being unconscious of this and its subsequent effect. In its negative ramifications, it is damaging personally and culturally. 'The fact that a man can father a child and then flee from the task of being a father is one of the most frequent and insidious crimes of all time ... the absence of a father bears consequences throughout the whole of life, and even for the following generation' (Zoja, 2001, p. 285).

To become conscious of the shadow requires effort and brings recognition of the unknown, sometimes disliked but human qualities and actions. This includes the undeveloped and ignored, perhaps denigrated yet valuable parts the father does not attend to and then passes on to the child. The shadow effect is substantial as it encompasses more than the repressed and includes the unconscious, both personal and collective. Jung wrote extensively on the shadow:

> When one tries desperately to be good ... and perfect, then all the more the shadow develops a definite will to be black and evil and destructive. People cannot see that; they are always striving to be marvellous, and then they discover that terrible destructive things happen which they cannot understand, and they either deny that such facts have anything to do with them, or if they admit them, they take them for natural afflictions, or they try to minimize them and to shift the responsibility elsewhere. The fact is that if one tries beyond one's capacity to be perfect, the shadow descends into hell and becomes the devil.
>
> (Jung, 1997, p. 391)

The shadow contains what we know about ourselves but try to hide. It also carries those aspects unknown, but somehow feared, as if we are worse than we thought. The impact of denying and disguising ourselves from the personal and cultural shadows keeps us narrow, even ignorant and trapped within walls of our own making. The shadow exerts itself in the 'as-if' person who looks the part and functions outstandingly according to others, yet often feels nothing is meaningful; without meaning the experiences of life are reduced to nothing (von Franz, 2000, p. 148). Descending into the shadows and abandoning the 'as-if' façade for the real is the antidote, something quite difficult for the 'as-if' person to do because it means acknowledging the shadow of the father as distinct from their own.

The shadow produces chaos and melancholy and can be felt as a dark time. It is a difficult task of separation, of facing oneself and the father personally and culturally without covering up, accepting the reality of what is. Although this can be accompanied by moments of despair, encountering the father's shadow is a requisite for self-fruition. The shadowy recesses reveal the parts of the self calling for recognition, accessing the core, resolving the yearning and melancholy. The 'as-if' person often tries to escape the shadow aspects – depression and anxiety – through flights of imagination and grandiosity. The discomfiting but necessary awareness of the shadow represents the coming to earth necessary for actualising creativity and life (von Franz, 2000, p. 128).

For example, a woman insisted her father did his best and said she had already spent enough time on him in therapy so there was no need to discuss him. His demanding ways had become internalised, however, and she still hesitated in the world. She did not want to touch the roots of the issue as she had forgiven him and that was supposed to be it. But was forgiveness enough? Has she been able to wrest herself from the effect of his rule? Analytical psychologist James Hillman (1983, p. 25) described this so-called resolution as a person who is feeling precarious and lacking internal solidity.

For the 'as-if' person, fantasy and reality have become transposed, and there is a manic defence against change that is maintained by keeping the old fantasy alive (Czubinska, 2020, p. 332). The woman who 'forgave' her father did not realise how obedient she was, how held back, her dreams unrealised as she remained compliant with his traditional, authoritarian ways. Especially when the responsible and involved father is not present, the person may recoil from life, lacking the assertiveness to move into the world. The woman remained in limbo, undecided, unsettled, lacking verve to be herself. Her creativity and assertion of life were unconsciously sacrificed, and she was bored, unable to land on anything of value to herself.

Colluding with this type of father suppresses his shadow, perpetuates unconsciousness and excuses him while, unbeknownst to her, she takes on his shadow. 'The most pernicious psychic disorders derive less from the way one confronts a problem than from remaining unconscious of it' (Zoja, 2001, p. 293). The shadow side of the father plunges the child into darkness and chaos. The child is lost in the drama of his unconsciousness and unresolved conflicts. For instance, some fathers will not allow the child to surpass them. The envy of the child who has different and more successful qualities threatens the father. This father tries to keep the child back, undermines talents, does not provide support. His failures fall onto the child who must also fail.

To change and expand our perceptions of the father means we become open to many-sided variations. This includes experiences dwelling not solely on the malevolent power of the father but also on his display of affirmation and warmth. These are the myriad qualities of the father figure extant in the psyche even when insufficiently experienced. This is acknowledged in the following quote: 'The existence and operation of the archetypal father means that some form of internal image may develop even when no external father figure is present' (Samuels, 1986, p. 40).

When there is no well-rounded or relatable paternal model the child is deceived and betrayed, left without. From this lack, the unfolding of the self is both compromised and given impetus, depending on many personal and collective conscious and unconscious circumstances. The father/child dynamics can inhibit or enhance the ability of the ego or the 'I' to access the unconscious, disrupting or enhancing the emergence of the dialogical relationship between these aspects. When ego and self, or the deeper, more encompassing personality, are in communication, the conscious and unconscious learn to access each other. Together they allow us to surmount obstacles and facilitate growth and individuation.

However, the weight of the unexamined father's shadow limits development for him and his children. The personality can become stuck, and the children assume roles that hide the raw emotional absence, the loss and feelings of being unloved. The child might adopt various personas and live defensively, without trust in the world. This false adaptation denies the disappointments, anxieties and lack of eros or relatedness from the father. Bound to the shadow of the father, this accentuates the lack of healthy reliance on and separation from the paternal. When this is not possible, the person remains rooted in the past in a complex way and is tied to the longing for an inaccessible, unreachable and unknown father. The site of these wounds lodge inside the 'as-if' personality and one's expression is limited by the rule of the father.

The fathers I am discussing here are self-absorbed, depressed, preoccupied, isolated, dictatorial and emotionally unreliable. Their children do not have an experience of being well held by a father figure. The 'as-if' person has no relatable father, conscious of their emotions, able to support or give love. To reiterate, for many generations, the internalisation of a related father figure has been unexpected, undefined, overlooked and unavailable.

There is a powerful and negative father–child dynamic in the face of the continuing, omnipresent shadow of patriarchy with its harmful presence impacting life development. With other models absent and combined with pervading cultural and familial influences, the child is groomed to assume the father's way and absorbs his shadow. 'The child was compelled to exist to fulfil the needs of the father. This failed to acknowledge the need for the child to develop an identity of his own, and an eventual separate existence' (Kay, 1986, p. 63). The formation of a separate identity and individual life is frittered away, as if one means nothing. Insecurities around the father result in the lack of self-assertion or solidity, the sacrifice of personal development and emotional vacuity. By escaping oppressive masculinity as well as overcoming the burdens of traditional, restrictive femininity, the child turned adult can differentiate into a real self.

As Jung said, 'I had the whole problem of the father to solve' (Lambert, in McGuire & Hull, 1980, p. 156). Masculine identity, in its various forms, needs to be released and awakened into life outside of previously restrictive traditions. Father as a related and active figure in family life has disappeared into the unconscious, causing psychological disturbances and confusion as he has proceeded to desert his partner, children and himself. The psychic void from this father is experienced depressively as an inner void (Kristeva, 1991, p. 82). Voids stemming from failures in the psychological environment with the father bring discontinuities of the self. This leads to an unremitting emptiness, the place where nothing fills an insatiable need to be.

Self-realisation is embedded in all psychological processes, and the psyche, like the body, strives to keep balance. However, when the father's mental representation as negative, absent and assaultive is internalised, the child and then the adult cannot trust or find themselves in any other (Knox, 2003, p. 156). Deprived of good father care and attention, a schism develops within, and a child learns to hide through persona and façade, denying or avoiding the process of personality differentiation. With numerous obstacles and distress complicating the ability to know what one wants, the 'as-if' person reaches for anything to fill the amorphous something inside, but without adequate focus or intent.

According to Jean Knox, 'Love would be feared and avoided because of the fear of the other who represents the difference that cannot be tolerated' (2007, p. 553). The person cannot manage the tension of the oscillation between themselves and what is different. This means there is no ability to hold the tension of opposites, which is necessary for anything creative or new to emerge. When no tension of opposites is allowed, the child can easily merge into the influential father's shadow. This describes what can be called a 'dictatorial and totalitarian state of mind, keeping the status quo and eliminating any opposition … Being taken over, assimilated or incorporated is the early fantasy of identity-loss and ceasing to exist as an autonomous being' (Czubinska, 2020, p. 333).

Referring to the undeveloped, unseen and ignored aspects of the father, 'the shadow takes over with blurring of the external from internal' (Czubinska, 2020, p. 335), and the child assumes the posture of a psychological extension or accentuated image of the father. The defence against the father's shadow can escalate into the child's inability to function as a total and real personality. Beginning as a coping mechanism, the defence aims to segregate the subjective self from negative experiences and to ensure the survival of the individual psyche. Internalising the father's shadow forms a barrier, preventing the person from relating individually and creatively to themselves and to the world. Too often private experience must be denied in the service of being acceptable to the father. The child accepts the father as dominant and complies but is then unable to access their own way.

The 'as-if' person frequently feels emasculated, particularly in relationships and inevitably in the therapeutic transference. Disturbing memories, including buried desires, tug inwardly as reminders of something forgotten or perhaps never experienced. Dealing honestly with the past with its heavy impact is a difficult task when overlaid by the father's unexplored shadow, bringing awareness of repressed experiences of confusion and conflict, unmet desires and needs.

The composite examples in this chapter portray people who had to avoid being known in many respects, their psychological depths sacrificed, primarily to themselves. Vitality was lost years before as talents and individuality curled up inside. Personal strength was threatened by paternal authority and the psyche was without recourse and began to shut down in childhood. The father wound led to a narrow emotionless existence in the service of an unmeetable and inappropriate paternal agenda. Intimidated by or unconscious of the patriarchal culture and its ideological images, these people internalised violence and anger, as it could not be externalised. In defensive postures, each of these people lived in solitary confinement 'as-if', pretending but not being.

A shattered man

Years ago, Jefferson, then in his mid-thirties, divorced with three teenage children living with their mother, walked into my office. Over many sessions we roamed the landscape of his psyche – delving into his disturbed relation to natural physical instincts, his feeling of duty rather than love towards his children, the distortion of spirit into the dogma of religion, his newly discovered attachment to nature. 'We can get over our mourning of him only by getting over our mourning, by getting over, by ourselves, the mourning of ourselves, I mean the mourning of our autonomy, of everything that would make us the measure of ourselves' (Derrida, 2003, p. 161). The demands raised by the unconscious lead him from attempts at conformity with the collective to comfort with his individual self. Jung commented, 'Psychic processes are balances of energy flowing between spirit and instinct, though the question of whether a process is to be described as spiritual or as instinctual remains shrouded in darkness. Such evaluation or interpretation depends entirely upon the standpoint or state of the conscious mind' (1969, CW 8, para. 407). Jung further contended it is the instinct upon which wholeness of the personality depends. Said another way, alignment with the instincts is a key piece for personality transformation and individual expression. It is also learned with loving paternal connection.

The therapeutic process

How is it possible to lose a self? The treachery, known and unthinkable, begins with the secret psychic death in childhood when the child is unloved and cut off from his spontaneous wishes. Father wants or forces or expects the son to be different. The son's centre of gravity is in the father, not in himself. 'Part of the sluggishness and carelessness of everyday life is its failure to grasp its own experiences, its failure to recognize and take stock of itself ... the mind learns to repossess its experiences from the fog of habit, convention, and forgetfulness' (Nussbaum, 1994, p. 340). This is the conundrum.

In the therapeutic relationship and process we attempt to comprehend emotional issues of all kinds, internal and external, acute and cumulative, past and present. Within the framework of the therapeutic setting, the timelessness of the unconscious becomes apparent. Time is often associated with the linear, the father as logos or the rational. Yet, time is a dimension of the physical universe and equally a subjective matter of the mind and memory – a circular and fungible experience. We may both fear and hate time as the harbinger of limits and mortality, while simultaneously depending upon it for life. Without awareness of time, we might settle comfortably in the status quo. On the other hand, we may live in the illusion of timelessness to assuage the pains of life's limits, our conflicts about and capacities to acknowledge and bear the losses, hurts and disappointments as well as the hopes and possibilities. Central to the functioning of the human psyche is the subjective remembrance of time, the articulating and ordering of mental elements in the act of verbal linking with the inchoate. The susceptibility to overvalue linear time can be a signal of alienation from nature and its cycles.

The timelessness of the unconscious becomes activated by intent, fear, hope or any strong emotion, and this activation is accompanied by a lowering of consciousness. This can be likened to the psychological process where the nuances and the small shifts are noted as each therapist and patient register their reactions. We attend to the words as well as the senses and body feelings as we share and speak to and from the range and depth of the experiences revealed in the therapeutic setting. It takes time for people to recognise what they do to each other and what was done to them through accessing and opening the innermost ravages in the search for repair. Being real comes from examining the despair and dejection the patient has felt and the growth they desire. In the therapeutic holding environment, they can learn to go on being.

Jefferson has always felt a terrible internal deadness, a hopelessness in perceiving only the stains of his personality. He is highly self-critical and easily discouraged. He experienced me, his analyst, as cold and disinterested in him. Any real person is absent from his purview as his real sensations are also absent. There can be no immediate emotional experience, no spontaneity, and he watches carefully to avoid surprises so he will not be caught off guard.

Jefferson entered therapy due to failed relationships. The following relates his story, his disappointments from early in life and his adoption of the 'as-if' image. This held him together so he could manage the inner feeling of being shattered. Because he fears the 'shattering', as he calls it, he must be on, perform 'as-if' all is orderly and abide by the rules although he does not agree with them.

Jefferson recounts he wants to be rigorous about his father who is not so bad, and he has examples where he also walks one or two steps down the same road. However, he adds, father completes the journey. Then, he back-peddles from this statement to be careful and fair to his father. He then counters with saying his father was awful. To be open to this father is neither comfortable nor easy. In fact, with this type of father, who has a very long shadow, it is damaging.

Jefferson adopted strong defences to preserve the security of his being, but they placed him in a double bind. He wanted a father to be close to but there was much betrayal and his father's shadow interceded to make it impossible. When young he had no words for this; he just knew his father was not to be trusted. Jefferson had no father touch. Deprived of this tactile encounter, he lacked the pivotal earliest experiences of self. He had only a negative experience, with massive neglect in his primary relationships, which led to emptiness and a sense of non-being, a person without value. This absence is accompanied by impaired self-representation, and this leads to insecurity with others. The father's presence and loving touch are necessary. He provides the infant with the containment and integration necessary for stabilising impulses that can overwhelm. The infant needs this loving touch to find a body-self, which originates from being related to and held safely from the very beginning.

This all became more convoluted as to the outer world, Jefferson's father was upstanding, but at home Jefferson had to live with his father's silence, strict rules and oppressive personality. THE FATHER, as they were to call him, is still holding forth and contending he did nothing wrong. Jefferson calls him a clever sociopath. Deprived of good father care, a schism occurred within, and this son learned to hide through persona and façade, avoiding, living 'as-if' to protect himself from the duplicitous father. This attitude compromises the ability to fully show up in therapy and to form relationships. Release from the restrictive, ruled-laden negative father complex requires gaining consciousness, trust and self-agency. The wounded self, emotionally put down by parent/father, learns to be alert to the other to calibrate how to respond, although not to oneself as the self is gone now.

Although he did not want to be like his father, Jefferson sought his approval. He admits, which makes him feel nauseous, that his father was seductive and clever. He repeatedly tried to make his father understand through attempts to talk, writing letters to explain, but his father did not listen or acknowledge what Jefferson said or who he was. For example, without explanation, when he was a sophomore in college, Jefferson, an excellent student, was cut off from school funds by his father.

Jefferson reads the German philosophers of the 19th century, specifically Nietzsche, as he seeks answers to a life he considers meaningless. He firmly believes no one can be close or understand him. He is insecure and secretly angry at almost everything, but mostly at himself. He is serious, sensitive and yet detached. Although not outwardly evident, he experiences extreme discomfort with others. Not wanting to be like his father, he backs away from being aggressive or assertive.

Meanwhile, Jefferson finds the timing between self and others disjointed. He has difficulty receiving attention or being physically touched. When he sees a beautiful woman, he turns away as he is apprehensive about getting close because he expects her refusal. He assesses his misery is worse than others' pain and this ensures no one will understand. The loss of contact with an authentic self can result in closing off. Unable to generate meaning, he loses his self even as he is always thinking of himself. No one knows how lost he is in this disorganised place. André Green noted, 'The [fa]ther's blank mourning induces blank mourning in the infant burying part of his ego in the [pa]ternal necropolis' (1997, p. 9).

If the father provides guidance and protection, nurturance and love, respect and a broadening of wisdom, the child can move into life with confidence. If not and when there is failure of the father figure, there will be an unceasing search for father images. If father has the persona of inflation and control, the physical, instinctual and emotional aspects of masculinity sink into the child's unconscious, and the child, like Jefferson, is susceptible to incorporating the father's shadow. As a result, Jefferson took cover to remain unnoticed.

The body in shadow

As a child, Jefferson received no hugs, no touch, no eros and little personal engagement. There was little love between his parents who put up a façade for years. The father's emotional distance, deceptiveness in his marriage, illicit work ethics and irresponsibility created a foundation of distrust and insecurity in both body and psyche for Jefferson. Jefferson grew up in a church community where his father was a highly respected, but duplicitous man. He had affairs, cheated in his business dealings and hid all of it, including his penchant for pornography. Jefferson strictly followed the church's religious teachings until he left the church in his late twenties. He felt his soul was disconnected from the church and its rules; it felt empty, with no relation to his essence.

Quite markedly, this all sorely affected his relation to self and others. 'The separation of psychology from the basic assumptions of biology is purely artificial, because the human psyche lives in indissoluble union with the body' (Jung, 1969, CW 8, para. 232). His authenticity was absent because real spontaneous sensations were disallowed by the father early on. Jefferson lacked confidence and was uneasy socially. His high intelligence allowed him to succeed in his career, but he could not get organised in his home; his relationships began and went nowhere; and he could not commit to anyone or anything. Something was always wrong. He was controlling yet felt out of control and manufactured rules in his head about how to act. He also was oppressed in his flow of speech, always checking to see if he was acceptable. This kept him from spontaneously feeling or expressing any internal experience.

Jefferson did not know about attachment, love, protection, vulnerability, dependence or comfort with others. His interior landscape remains hidden and vulnerable and the outer world mirrors how different and separate he feels from others. When there has been impaired paternal care, a child internalises the deadness and becomes dead and numb, suffering an unrequited emptiness and lack of security. Instead, the child registers anxiety, becomes subsumed with destructive or obsessive drives and persecutory impulses. These reactions developed so Jefferson could survive, as his instincts about people were tragically blunted. These are the psychological holes that create a residue of being unable to love or make the most of one's talents (Green, 2001, p. 176).

It is a risk for Jefferson to be who he is – exposed, human and vulnerable. Jefferson experienced profound early emotional neglect while the need for the other was denied and desperately longed for. 'A novelty which could prove to be even more grave than the absence of the father would be the absence of the search for the father' (Zoja, 2001, p. 287).

Sometimes after or during a session, I would feel hopeless or empty, unable to reach him. This might be what Jefferson also feels in his frustrations and struggles to connect. The therapeutic relationship can offer a kind of repair that involves remembering the wrenching and broken connections. However, this is painful as Jefferson experiences only the burden of despair and low self-worth. While sharing the innermost ravages and co-constructing the patterns and reflecting on them leads to personality development, for Jefferson it mostly leads to shame.

He describes therapy as lancing an abscess in the painful uncovering of disappointments, obscurities, mysteries. Session after session Jefferson addresses the feelings, perceptions, thoughts, ideas and emotions he had not previously addressed or acknowledged with anyone. Together we explore his psyche, populated by things subtle or uneasily perceived, and interpret the interpersonal spaces. We listen carefully and this penetrating look follows a slow but steady rhythm.

Jefferson can handle much physical distress, working long hours, hiking in what could be dangerous territory, not caring if anyone knows where he is or not. Jefferson was trained for self-denial due to the lack of care and insufficient experiences of resonant mirroring. He describes his family as devoid of love and reiterates the dogma of the church with its rather cruel abhorrence of the natural man. His natural impulses were compromised owing to the emotional and physical lack of relatedness to his father, the church and his mother. This created dissociation between body and soul and what he was supposed to be yet was not. It left him immersed in helplessness and impotence, flattened and with few sparks of hope. Until the father complex is understood, he feels incapable, without adequate voice or life direction (Schwartz, 2020, p. 43). Jefferson had taken on the father's shadow to be better than him, but this also meant he was strongly intertwined in a negative father complex, and he became lost.

One of the purposes of therapeutic inquiry is to heal the splits so the personal and collective conscious and unconscious can open. Living as part of the whole starts from the reality that we are already participants, part of the cosmos, interconnected. For Jefferson, his journeys into nature, when he faced the elements, were like a cosmic participation. He gained some sense of self there. However, even in the expansive beauty of nature, he remained hounded by doubt and uncertainty, wondering if he was being true to himself and painfully feeling the longing for love.

Jefferson was oppressed by self-hatred and uncertainty. By negating and rejecting parts of himself, he became unseen, and his sense of strangeness was accompanied by depersonalisation. Julia Kristeva, French psychoanalyst, described this as melancholia ... 'grief about the sadness, aloneness and off-ness' (1992, pp. 12–13). These are the very words Jefferson uses to describe what sounds like an impassable abyss separating him from others. For him, the world was made of edges and shameful spaces and relationships that were false and unreliable.

Jefferson dreams *about being in the airport and with people who are getting stoned. He leaves them and has a big bottle of beer. Then he runs into a security guard who says he is not to carry around beer.* He says the guard is regimented like a soldier and represents the rules. This regulated part of him conflicts with his desire to be free, and his safety is then compromised. He had no guidance from his father and here is his dilemma – to follow rules or be himself and how to bridge the gap between.

The dream reveals the unknown hidden recesses of the psyche, the valuable holder of personal, emotional, psychological and physical issues. Dreams offer insight, messages and psychic realities of which we are otherwise unaware. They present us with the challenges and opportunities for increasing self-knowledge, uncovering truths and answering the question of who one is. Jung commented, 'Transformation processes announce themselves mainly in dreams' (Jung, 1969/1991, CW 9i, para. 235).

There is an inherent impulse towards forming a unified psyche. As Andrew Samuels put it, 'The symbolic process begins with a person feeling "stuck", hung up, forcibly obstructed in the pursuit of his aims and it ends in illumination, "seeing through", and being able to go ahead on a changed course' (Samuels, Shorter & Plaut, 1986, p. 145). Because of this impulse a pathologically disintegrated psyche spontaneously attempts to reintegrate. This requires a willingness to enter a dream and sit with it. It is about being with the unknown and letting the images affect understanding as they guide us. We don't know where dreams come from, but we can find their purpose as they illustrate the steps to developing consciousness. They warn us if we are going astray, encourage us and provide insight. To interpret dreams, we become disciplined and logical but also emotional, feeling, imaginative and sensate.

In another dream *he is in his father's house and in the closet changing. He is naked. A boy of eight years comes in and then a woman, and he covers himself when the boy comes in.* In his associations, he is disappointed he is still in his father's house. The dream implies something sexual and covered up, but he does not go further into it. Rather, he begins this session saying he does not trust I could understand. He is reading *The Death of Ivan Ilyich*, written in 1886 by Leo Tolstoy. Jefferson recounts the character Ivan screamed for three days before he died. Jefferson says he feels similarly but such an outer expression of anguish is not his style, and he would never show so much pain and suffering. He recognises this is what he calls the shattered place where he becomes lost, isolated, out of balance and highly anxious. The shattered space disallows thought and he must hide it by responding 'as-if' it is not there.

Jefferson's sadness represents the nonverbal expression, the dominant feature found to be self-disappearance and disinvolvement (Green, 2002, p. 645). Jefferson does not recognise the splitting or parcelling of self as it occurs automatically and has been happening as long as he can remember. Here is where he goes unconscious, taken over by the father's shadow, denying his self-expression. The traumatic interactions with early caretakers are replicated in an equally traumatic internalised object relationship, leaving in its wake the true self waiting to be found (Modell, 1996, p. 86). Jefferson says his goal is trying not to need people. He is vulnerable and fearful his space or boundaries will be broken, and he will get hurt. One of the results of the retreat from early grief and mourning, hurt and pain, is becoming de-centred and emptied of anything spontaneous.

At times Jefferson sounds terrified when describing the loneliness punctuated by crying or wildly eating chocolate or cakes. When he desperately seeks comfort in food, his actions symbolise himself without the safety of the self and a retreat inside for self-preservation. For a long time, Jefferson seems resistant or unable to get in touch with the psychic reality of these interior places that are distinguished by their lack of structure or organisation (Green, 1997, p. 37). This is not an uncommon occurrence when the outer world is so lacking in protection, guidance and love.

Jefferson is usually in a mental state of self-loathing and dislike for his body. The hole of the paternal absence left him with no healthy male identification but an internal culture of void, emptiness, self-contempt, destructive withdrawal and self-deprecation with a predominant masochistic quality (Green, 2002, p. 644).

This, of course, is enacted physically as well. Jefferson disdains and denies his body instincts while seeking internet pornography and what he calls compulsive masturbation. There he remains unseen and unknown, unrelated and shut off, alone behind a computer screen.

Jefferson remembers an occasion as a child when he laughed with friends but assessed it was too much and strictly instituted a rule to never be free like that again. He felt ashamed. The anxiety and feeling of being destroyed from within is what remained. His self-doubt makes life feel brutalising. Jefferson is often internally bombarded by what he should do when he has free time. Should he read, exercise, have a coffee or work on his home? This is the enactment of what Jefferson calls the shattered place where rules substitute for the spontaneous self.

Jefferson says this shattered place is painful to experience, and he becomes more alone as he often does not have words for it. He frantically defends the preservation of private space, as he experiences the self as fragile and acutely vulnerable to the responses of the other (Modell, 1996, p. 78). For example, he might have sex but does not stay the night, as this is too intimate. Being with any other person is difficult for him because the inner ballast seems off and he cannot be perfect enough. If he stays the night, his vulnerability and real personness might be seen.

Failure in the containing function is another way of naming what Jefferson calls this shattered place where he feels so fragile and alone. British psychoanalyst Wilfred Bion described this as characterised by minute splitting; an experience of fragmentation of mind and objects; a feeling of being trapped; a sense of nameless dread; a sense of disintegration; the inability to bear absence, while experiencing links as being filled with cruelty; being bombarded with sensations and not having time to compose thoughts or reactions; intolerance of suffering; manic searches for a container, which Jefferson calls needing someone to make him whole (Stevens, 2005, p. 622). Jefferson says my comments cause him to lose his thoughts and feelings and focus on being correct or giving the right answer. He becomes internally bombarded by many possibilities and confused about how to respond and this can paralyse his mind. He gets caught in what he thinks is wanted and this separates him from what he thinks and feels.

Green (1997, p. 146) called this psychological situation *blank mourning* and aligned it with the emptiness. It also has the physical response of feeling deadened. A person survives the early emotional neglect and grief, but vast emptiness remains. It progressively and throughout life translates into numbness. Despair sets in. This is a part of the tears Jefferson sheds in therapy, and he can do nothing but let them be. His psyche and body need to weep – maybe for the lack of resonance, the unrequited longing and the neglect and lack of father propelling the search for his self.

Correcting the imbalance

Jung contended what passed for normality often was the very force that shattered the personality of the patient. 'It was a beautiful spring morning, and very still. That brings back the feeling that everything had come to an end' (Woolf, 1985, p.

84). Trying to be normal, like following the collective religion or the family, for Jefferson, violated his inner nature and was itself a form of pathology.

> The situation becomes difficult, however, when the patient's nature resists a collective solution. The question then arises whether the therapist is prepared to risk having his convictions dashed and shattered against the truth of the patient. If he wants to go on treating the patient he must abandon all preconceived notions and, for better or worse, go with him in search of the religious and philosophical ideas that best correspond to the patient's emotional states.
> (Jung, 1966, CW 16, para. 184)

Self-regulating processes within the psyche are activated in attempts to correct the psychological imbalance. Individuality and identity forms to repair the broken chain of circumstances. The realisation was that Jefferson had not mattered, the bond to father was broken irreparably. The search went unanswered for a father who could think of and love him, but this was not to be.

From examining our tragedies, we can find a capacity to live authentically. This means tolerating the frustration and learning to face the emptiness without trying to fill or deny feeling, disappointment, dependence or desire. Gradually and slowly as the realms of the physical body and the psyche are bridged, Jefferson gains liberation from automatism and replaces it with increased sensitivity to his self. He can see his father for who he is and decides to not interact with him. He still carries much of the father's shadow but has also sloughed off much of it. He finds some comfort and ease in being his individual self, but intimacy in relationships is still unavailable. How much Jefferson's life could evolve with another and whether he could create a space for expressing curiosity, play and creativity are still in question.

> In the last analysis every life is the realization of a whole, that is, of a self, for which reason this realization can also be called 'individuation'. All life is bound to individual carriers who realize it, and it is simply inconceivable without them. But every carrier is charged with an individual destiny and destination, and the realization of these alone makes sense of life.
> (Jung, 1944, p. 222)

In other words, how much he can loosen control or address the deep division from within is based on the psyche's defences for protecting the self from dissolution (Solomon, 1998, p. 229).

References

Czubinska, G. (2020). Difference – Is it hated or desired? Reflections on the totalitarian state of mind. *Journal of Analytical Psychology*, *65*(2), 325–44. doi: 10.1111/1468-5922.12587.

Derrida, J. (2003). *The work of mourning*. (P.-A. Brault and M. Naas, eds.). University of Chicago Press.

Green, A. (1997). *On private madness*. Karnac Books.

Green, A. (2001). *Life narcissism, death narcissism*. Free Association Books.

Green, A. (2002). A dual conception of narcissism: Positive and negative organizations. *Psychoanalytic Quarterly, 71*(4), 631–49. doi: 10.1002/j.2167-4086.2002.tb00020.x.

Hillman, J. (1983). *Healing fiction*. Station Hill Press.

Jung, C.G. (1944). *The collected works of C.G. Jung: Vol. 12. Psychology and alchemy*. Princeton University Press.

Jung, C.G. (1966). *The collected works of C.G. Jung: Vol. 16. The practice of psychotherapy*. Princeton: Princeton University Press.

Jung, C.G. (1969). *The collected works of C.G. Jung: Vol. 8. The structure and dynamics of the psyche*. Princeton University Press.

Jung, C.G. (1997). *Visions: Notes of the seminar given in 1930–1934*. (C. Douglas, ed.). Princeton University Press.

Kay, D. (1986). Paternal psychopathology and the emerging ego. In: A. Samuels (ed.), *The father: Contemporary Jungian perspectives* (pp. 45–68). New York University Press.

Knox, J. (2003). *Archetype, attachment, analysis*. Routledge.

Knox, J. (2007). The fear of love: The denial of self in relationship. *Journal of Analytical Psychology, 52*(5), 543–63.

Kristeva, J. (1991). *Strangers to ourselves*. Columbia University Press.

Kristeva, J. (1992). *Black sun*. Columbia University Press.

Mathers, D. (2001). *Introduction to meaning and purpose in analytical psychology*. Routledge.

McGuire, W. & Hull, R.F.C. (eds.) (1980). *C.G. Jung speaking*. Picador.

Modell, A. (1996). *The private self*. Harvard University Press.

Nussbaum, M. (1994). *The therapy of desire: Theory and practice in Hellenistic ethics*. Princeton University Press.

Rushdie, S. (2012). *Joseph Anton: A memoir*. Random House.

Samuels, A. (1986). *The father: Contemporary Jungian perspectives*. New York University Press.

Samuels, A. (2010). The transcendent function and politics: NO! *Journal of Analytical Psychology, 55*(2), 241–53.

Samuels, A., Shorter, B. & Plaut, F. (1986). *A critical dictionary of Jungian analysis*. Routledge and Kegan Paul.

Schwartz, S. (2020). *The absent father effect on daughters*. Routledge.

Shah, I. (1974). *Tales of the dervishes*. Octagon Press.

Solomon, H.F. (1998). The self in transformation: The passage from a two to a three dimensional internal world. *Journal of Analytical Psychology, 43*(2), 225–38.

Stevens, V. (2005). Nothingness, no-thing and nothing in the work of Wilfred Bion and in Samuel Beckett's Murphy. *Psychoanalytic Review, 92*(4), 607–35. doi: 10.1521/prev.2005.92.4.607.

von Franz, M.-L. (2000). *The problem of the Puer Aeternus*. Inner City Books.

Woolf, V. (1985). *Moments of being: A collection of autobiographical essays*. Harvest Books.

Zoja, L. (2001). *The father*. Routledge.

Chapter 4

The refusal of twoness in sexual addiction and pornography

The red shoes

In the story, a destitute young girl is given a pair of red shoes. Much to the townsfolk's consternation, the young girl, dressed in rags, wears the shoes to her mother's funeral, and a rich woman sees her and adopts her. The woman burns the shoes, along with the girl's old, tattered clothing. Later, the girl sees a young princess wearing red shoes, and she becomes obsessed with owning a pair. When she is older and about to confirm at Church, the woman has new clothing made for her at a tailor. The girl picks out a pair of red shoes on display, knowing full well that her guardian has horrible eyesight and is practically colour-blind.

When the woman discovers from members of the congregation that her adopted daughter wore red shoes to her confirmation, she becomes upset. She tells the girl that she cannot wear red shoes anymore and must wear black ones instead. The following Sunday, the girl disobeys and wears red shoes.

A soldier sees the red shoes, taps them with his fingers, and says, "Look! Lovely dancing shoes! Stick tight when you dance!" And after that, it is as if the shoes become possessed, and the girl starts dancing and dancing until she kicks her guardian in the shins, and a coachman pulls the shoes off. The shoes are locked away in a cupboard, but the young girl can't keep her eyes off them. No matter how horrible those shoes turn out to be, the girl is obsessed with the idea of wearing them again.

Her guardian becomes very ill, so the girl puts on the shoes, rationalising that her guardian is dying, so who cares if she puts the shoes on or not? Once again, the shoes cause her to dance and dance. Except this time, she can't remove the shoes. They are stuck on her feet. The girl dances in the fields, in a graveyard and on the highways. The shoes control her completely. The red shoes that she once loved have turned on her. She dances and dances, day and night, without any rest or food.

One day, the girl dances by her house, and inside, she hears singing and realises that her guardian has died, but thanks to the shoes, she can't stop to say goodbye to a woman who cared for her like a mother. Finally, she begs an executioner to cut off her feet. But even with wooden feet and crutches, which the executioner makes for her, the red shoes and feet stalk her. Wherever she goes, the cursed shoes

DOI: 10.4324/9781003315254-5

follow! Finally, she asks God for help, and the red shoes disappear, and finally, the poor girl finds peace.

The fairy tales of every culture are both specific and general as we all take similar yet diverse pathways into ourselves, depending on various personal and cultural influences. The kind of selfish thinking displayed in the story of the red shoes is very similar to an addict's egocentric logic. This fairy tale parallels the narrative of the man in this chapter who had his own demons to learn about and face so he could become free to be all of himself. 'Unlived life is a destructive, irresistible force that works softly but inexorably' (Jung, 1964, CW 10, para. 252).

Moving from oneness to twoness is a psychological process reflecting inter- and intrapersonal relationships. This chapter links the perspectives of Jungian analytical psychology with those of French psychoanalyst André Green on the dead or blank mother and narcissism. The similarities and differences between them describe situations in which the psyche can become narrowed and fragmented, affecting a person's experience of self and others. Each perspective offers unique insights into a dark and often lonely place, elucidated by the composite example of a self-described sexually addicted man named Daniel who had lived 'as-if' real most of his life.

Opening to the addiction

Daniel initially sent an email saying he was sexually addicted, and it was time now to figure it out. He made the first of many appointments, several times a week, and continued what proved to be a complex search for a self and life of inner peace and honesty. There were many layers of sediment that blocked him from an experience of himself. Over time, we both learned how Daniel's addictions, which ranged from prostitutes to internet pornography, alcohol, drugs and lying, drew him into and away from himself. He was like the main character in *The Strange Case of Dr Jekyll and Mr Hyde*, in which the psyche splits between persona and shadow, each having a strong magnetism that becomes more disparate over time as Mr Hyde becomes more seductive.

Daniel's affects and desires for love and affection had been relegated to the shadows and were enacted only in the body; they were without relatedness. In his mind, he believed these encounters were real relationships and justified them as such. Sadly, he did not know the difference. His compulsive behaviours attempted to mask the shadows of melancholy, fragility and lack of self-animation. He became identified with select elements of his personality and was not open to the affect, the fluidity of the unconscious, the voice of the other, the not 'I' or self as different from the ego (West, 2008, p. 371). In this situation the self is in combat with itself, and transformation is disabled as inner resources remain undeveloped.

The shadow from the perspective of Jungian psychology encompasses more than the repressed and includes the unconscious, both personal and collective. It can feel destabilising to face the reality of who we are and the quality of life we have acceded to. As Jung commented:

When one tries desperately to be good and wonderful and perfect, then all the more the shadow develops a definite will to be black and evil and destructive. People cannot see that; they are always striving to be marvellous, and then they discover that terrible destructive things happen which they cannot understand, and they either deny that such facts have anything to do with them, or if they admit them, they take them for natural afflictions, or they try to minimize them and to shift the responsibility elsewhere. The fact is that if one tries beyond one's capacity to be perfect, the shadow descends into hell and becomes the devil.

(Jung, 1997, p. 391)

In *The Poetics*, the ancient Greek philosopher Aristotle (384–22 BCE) noted, 'our pity is excited by misfortunes undeservedly suffered, and our terror by some resemblance between the sufferer and ourselves ... a person ... involved in misfortune not by deliberate vice or villainy, but by some error or human frailty'. The reference to human frailty here represents a person like Daniel, who was encased in narcissism, isolative self-reference, and a generalised fear and avoidance of anyone separate, different or other than himself. Nothing could threaten the fragile hold he had on his ego and self.

Daniel embarked on Jungian analytical psychotherapy because he felt something missing; he could not name his malaise, corrosive but imprecise, that alienated him from himself and others. Although Daniel's addictive behaviours were compulsive isolative acts reflecting inner turmoil, they also contained the unconscious goal of self-creation for accessing his spirit. Compulsions and addictions also arise from the healing depths of the unconscious as they challenge the addict's desired and consciously held image.

Compulsion is the great mystery of human life. It is the thwarting of our conscious will and of our reason by an inflammable sulphuric element within us, appearing sometimes as a consuming fire and at others as life-giving warmth. The efficient and final cause of this lack of freedom lies in the unconscious and forms that part of the personality which still has to be added to the conscious person in order to make them whole.

(Jung, 1963/1971, CW 14, para. 151)

The effect is to transform the personality and liberate the addict from the bondage to unchanging thoughts and actions so they can find release from suffering.

Daniel dreamt, *There is a red stockinged lady outside the bookshop in Zurich, where earlier in the day I had bought Jung's* Modern Man in Search of a Soul. As Jung wrote, 'The image is a condensed expression of the psychic condition of the whole' (Jung, 1971, CW 6, para. 745). This quote addresses the complex issue in Daniel's dream and presents the possible opening from oneness to include the other in a move from the singular to the relational. In addition, the dream and quote demonstrate a way into Daniel's psyche assisted by the feminine. The woman, attired as she was, implied she might be a prostitute, like many of the women he bought for sex. Symbolically and in ancient cultures, the prostitute has been an initiator to the sacred, but for Daniel she represented guilt, shame, insecurity and lack of control. However, no matter how much he acquired or experienced, his needs, insistently clawing at him, remained unsatisfied. The addictive search temporarily assuaged his psychic distress, but the underlying separateness of disconnection and disillusionment quickly set in. Disconnection from self comes at a cost – long-lasting shame and self-loathing, difficulty self-soothing, internal conflicts and struggles, and complications in relationships. Without internal coherence or compassion, such fragmented individuals are extremely vulnerable and defended.

There are any number of unconscious fears. There is dread of anticipated disappointment that the experiences will turn out not to be as good or as fabulous as expected. Addicts do not trust the inner world or feel it is empty and sterile. Because it is unknown, it might not be good enough. The inner world might contain forces so dangerous and destructive that addicts must camouflage them. They fear evoking ridicule and dismissal rather than admiration and praise. Fear of the unknown leads to domination and adherence to routine patterns. Yet, there can be neither change nor rebirth without confusion, risk and pain.

To avoid any threat to his system, Daniel's life was bounded by addictions to food, drink and sex, all serving to disconnect him from his body and psyche. The addictions were misguided attempts to fill the internal void, eradicate the emptiness and, in effect, turn him from the self. The dream places him in the centre of a city, or symbolically at the centre of himself. Daniel's addictions allowed him to live in an illusory world where he could escape the heavy shame and guilt they perpetuated in his mind. Focused on the glare of personal inadequacy and insufficiency, he was uncertain of his worth or lovability. He felt the hollowing of loneliness, of not belonging to anyone or anything, yet he was ambivalent about being seen, known or revealed. Because he avoided intimacy, his secret but real self and his emotional longings remained in separate and inaccessible compartments.

The word *addiction* originates from the Latin word *addīcō* and is a compound of *ad* (to, towards, at) and *dīcō* (say, affirm, tell). According to Roman law, an *addictio* was a person who became enslaved through a judicial procedure. When debtors could not repay the debt, they became slaves so creditors could recover their losses. Today the addict denotes a person who is bonded, enslaved to a substance or any activity from which they cannot turn away.

Addiction in its many different and unique manifestations is a growing issue, regardless of ethnicity or social or economic class. Addiction is complex and multidimensional and involves individuals as well as their environments. The American Society of Addiction Medicine defines addiction as a primary, chronic disease of brain reward, motivation and memory with an intricate and related circuitry. Dysfunction in these circuits leads to biological, psychological, social and spiritual manifestations as a person quite compulsively pursues reward and/or relief through substance use and various behaviours.

This coincides with Jung's description of the Western person: 'Western man is held in thrall by the "ten thousand things"; he sees only particulars, he is ego-bound and thing-bound, and unaware of the deep root of all being' (1966b, CW 12, para. 8). There exists a widespread crisis of cultural sterility, materialism and superficiality. Today many people experience a sense of psychic deadness, disembodiment, inner deadness and the feeling that they do not really exist (Connolly, 2013, p. 638). There is precariousness to these defences and without the mask in place, there is nothing, no inner representation of face or body. This emptiness fosters anxiety, despair and loss of meaning. Something is needed to combat the pall of emptiness, and that is often an addiction to erase the psychic pain and distress. Addiction can be interpreted as one outcome of the derailment from self and others, exacerbating apathy and lack of connection.

Minor adjustments and adaptations initially served as a shield preventing access to the kernel of the issues. What endures is a dull psychic pain characterised by the incapacity to connect emotionally; the affects become blunted. As Jung noted, 'It is through "affection" that the subject is involved and therefore feels the full weight of reality … Psychologically, you don't own what you haven't actually experienced. A purely intellectual perception means little, for what is known is mere words and not the substance from within' (1959, CW 5, para. 61). Without feeling there can be no connection.

Although Daniel did not realise it, his addictive behaviours were forms of stealing and deceit enacted towards himself and others. They were expressions of his controlling nature and a fundamental attack on intimacy. They also made him feel less rather than more. His retreat to oneness was based on his fragile self, the continuity of being replaced by the need to maintain singularity and safety in a world secluded from others.

'As-if' personality

A malady of the soul absorbs the 'as-if' personality. The self remains hidden, intrigued by fantasy, unable to tolerate reality. 'One does not become enlightened by imagining figures of light, but by making the darkness conscious. The latter procedure, however, is disagreeable and therefore not popular' (Jung, 1967, CW 13, para. 335). The person is acutely tuned into capturing the signals of others and reacting accordingly and solely to achieve their own gain. Relationships are manipulations for attention and approval. It took years for Daniel to begin his inner journey, as his road was littered with restlessness and addictive behaviours orchestrated to hide his real self. Daniel's internal conflicts propelled him continually to defy societal and family conventions. His sexual addictions represented the division between an outer compliant and good-guy façade and the interior, accusatory gaze of his shame and guilt: 'Individuation and collectivity are a pair of opposites, two divergent destinies. They are related to one another by guilt' (Jung, 2014, CW 18, para. 1095).

Daniel used addictions because he could not hold the tension between psyche and body, grief and memory. The addictions indicated the other within was ignored, separated, as if a stranger. 'Impoverishment of the self is due to the effects of dissociation from traumatizing experiences with an original and longed for other' (Solomon, 2004, p. 638). The absence of the other, referring to early experiences and those replicated through Daniel's life, both left behind and re-created the emptiness at his core. Emotional wounds were secreted into the shadows. Integration was difficult for Daniel, who lived in a state of singularity, needing to appear perfect. To the world, he presented a façade and illusion rather than his real self. He 'retreated into a dream world without notice of actual dreams, perpetuating the timelessness of his fantasies' (Steiner, 1993, p. 99). A talented actor, Daniel did not fully inhabit the role or the stage on which he found himself. Addictions allowed him to misrepresent reality and perpetuated a romanticised, idealised and distant worldview from which he was aloof and untouched.

Every attempt to understand this type of person hits a wall. The addict does not emotionally invest in people, places or objects, anticipating the lack of satisfaction or care, nor do they know how to care for others. There also is the issue of damaged connection to the body as the instincts are off, the spirit dampened and without genuineness. Daniel felt erased, flawed, lacking. He was motivated by the sense that something dire needed to be addressed and given expression to but what that was remained unclear.

The personality I've described here is emotionally removed. Daniel admitted he was fraudulent and living a sham existence. Although false, his survival suit allowed him to blend in, so nothing suggested any disorder about him. He did not know anything other than this façade and was without the tools for intimacy with anyone, most of all with himself. This defence of the self is a protective mechanism preserving the fearful ego rather than permitting it to be annihilated. Eventually a psychological crisis occurred as his outer façade and the inner reserves collapsed, revealing the issues at the centre.

André Green and the dead mother

André Green brought attention to the concept of *maternal deadness*, referring to an emotional lack in the maternal realm. His themes reflected French culture and states of absence, negation and nothingness (Kohon, 1999, p. 5) combined with the idea that classical psychoanalysis was founded on mourning (Ogden, 1999, p. 142). Green described maternal loss as lack of presence or aliveness, leaving fractured attachments and internal discontinuity. He described the 'absence of memory, absence in the mind, absence of contact, absence of feeling all – all these absences can be condensed in the idea of a gap … instead of referring to a simple void or to something which is missing, becomes the substratum of what is real' (Kohon, 1999, p. 8). A depressed, emotionally unavailable, preoccupied, anxious and emotionally deadened mother is introjected or taken into the psyche. Interactions with her were empty where they should have been alive. Although physically present, due to emotional and energetic lack, she was perceived as unreachable and unable to satisfy the child's emotional needs.

As this was his experience, Daniel learned to ignore feelings so his life repeated the early absence of sufficient attachment. 'I have always loved desire. Certainly not that desire which believes itself to be determined according to a lack which raises up and upon which it depends, so much that it cannot get over it' (Cixous, 1994, p. 29). This arose from emotional disappointments, from not being held in the parental mind, from lacking parental resonance. Daniel did not have an accepting and loving mother caregiver who could nourish him into himself. According to Green this 'constitutes a premature disillusionment and ... carries in its wake, besides the loss of love, the loss of meaning, ... of no explication to account for what has happened' (Green, quoted in Lussier, 1999, p. 150).

Established early on, patterns of thinking, feeling and acting are designed to navigate an unfriendly, unsafe or oppressive environment. These become solidified with repetitive use and are resistant to modification with time. The patterns are held in place by automatic, unconscious physical and physiological habits. From a young age, Daniel's investment in himself became dismantled, leaving behind what seemed like psychic holes. These were composed of the wounded places, regrets, abandonments and betrayals. Daniel avoided all these feelings with his addictions, which increased in intensity as time went on. Alongside this, his inner discourse was critical, preoccupied with judgements, with self-erasure of thoughts and feelings. Underneath was a pit of emptiness like 'a psychic ruin that seizes hold of the subject in such a way that all vitality and life become frozen, where in fact it becomes forbidden ... to be' (Green, 1986, p. 152).

Daniel was unable to access much less repair the mourned object or awaken the lost desire. The weight of unacknowledged grief and despondency kept him emotionally separate from others. His zest or passion for life was compromised; the self was folded in on itself, excluding others. This is an aspect of what has been called *anhedonia*, or the inability to derive pleasure from anything. It parallels the situation of *anomie*, meaning a lack in the usual social or ethical standards, leading to Daniel's sense of emotional precarity. This not only indicates social instability but also parallels the psychological breakdown of standards and values resulting in desperation, internal poverty and diminishment of prosperity.

Consumed with tenacious sorrow, attachment forms, not to the parents who are without sufficient attachment, but to the gap or the absence. Life is dimmed; dissociation occurs between body and psyche from the lack of love. Daniel was frozen in a state of psychical pain and alienation, of disappointment; he felt incapable and had no confidence. The thing that endured was 'an essentially conflictual, ambiguous nature of desire, which is conceivable as the desire of the desire of the Other' (Green, 1979, p. 69).

Daniel's internal narrative illustrated the despoiling effects of his self-feeling. Emptied of energy or enthusiasm, an emotional morass developed, falsely buoyed by his addictive behaviours. To hide all this, Daniel pushed people away, lied to make them happy, deceiving them and himself. His efforts were oriented to please others and perform, so he had to act 'as-if' real when he felt only a fiction of himself (Sheehan, 2004, p. 420). The problem was he did not know how to do otherwise.

'I do it too much', he said. A range of emotions, angers and frustrations disappeared into his daily rituals of pornography, masturbation, drugs and excess drink and food. All were mechanisms to hide. Is pornography the problem or does it reflect the more severe issue of the lack of connection, distance from self and others, a seeking to remain unseen?

'The fear of there being nothing or no one worth obeying' (Phillips, 2015, p. 77) drove his addictions. Daniel could not control his tendency for sexual boundary breaking and tried to get every woman he encountered. His need to control the feminine, the woman and everyone represented his lack of control. His desire in the guise of lust represented his incessant need for love and attention. Even when Daniel got the craved objects, they all felt tenuous.

The adaptation of mimicry, the protective fictions and the imposter role began early in his life. 'The reality of the person's self was eschewed by his important others, the other experienced as poisonous to the self' (Solomon, 2004, p. 644). Mother was anxious, depressed and preoccupied and Daniel's *object cathexis*, or investment in those outside himself, became disturbed. Instead, his self became buried within, and he could not summon the energy to make a full attempt at life. He developed distrust in the world, exacerbated by the cult-like claustrum of the family and religion. From a young age, he was supposed to attest faith and belief, but he could not. This fact had to be hidden, so he put on a happy face and pretended while the roots to his self became increasingly untethered. Unable to fit into the family or group, he defined his real self with forbidden thoughts and feelings, yet he had to dissociate from this as it was an unacceptable reality to others.

Daniel dreamt, *I apologise to the Black woman housekeeper I ran out on when I discovered there was work to be done. I ask her if she will help me be responsible and she says she will. As I awaken, I am struck by the fact that I am a liar, and that the truth is not in me. I wonder if I have become a compulsive liar, and if there is any hope for me since I have been untruthful for so long. I am struck by how much I lie and deceive for fear of being found out for who I really am.*

This dream illustrates the complexity of Daniel's attitudes. He wants help from his psyche in the form of the Black woman housekeeper, but he also notes he is a liar. Daniel lived in 'a solitary confinement of the self ... There was fear of opening to another at the risk of psychological annihilation' (Solomon, 1998, p. 228). The total self was missing, and he was able to acknowledge his fears of disintegration. Having felt so different from others as a child, Daniel used his isolative routines to maintain the hegemony of his façade and the singularity of omnipotence. Like the 'as-if' personality, alienated from relational aliveness, Daniel was run by helplessness, embittered desire, by something withheld (Meredith-Owen, 2008, p. 462). Making these attitudes conscious through dream imagery allowed him to naturally revivify contact with his personality aspects. He would have to perform housework with attention to the basics as the dream so clearly stated.

The shadow

Jungian analytical psychology acknowledges the value of integrating the shadow qualities often projected, undeveloped or deemed unpleasant. 'The meeting with oneself is, at first, the meeting with one's own shadow. The shadow is a tight passage, a narrow door, whose painful constriction no one is spared who goes down to the deep well. But one must learn to know oneself in order to know who one is' (Jung, 1959/1968, CW 9i, p. 2). Collecting the dissociated fragments and bringing them into relationship eliminates the opposition between self and non-self. 'Dissociation is a survival necessary to keep the self safe from the toxic experience, which may include the absence of the other' (Solomon, 2004, p. 638). Daniel's pull to women, drink and food represents the split-off shadow perpetuating the 'as-if' personality, singularity and his desperate need to control. This causes psychic numbness, loss of passion. In the need to maintain certainty, spontaneity is sacrificed.

One cannot individuate, that is, become the person one is meant to be, without relating to the shadow. It was the shadow to which Daniel was both addictively drawn and from which he equally fled.

> The shadow is a living part of the personality and therefore wants to live with it in some form. It cannot be argued out of existence or rationalized into harmlessness. This problem is exceedingly difficult, because it not only challenges the whole man, but reminds him at the same time of his helplessness and ineffectuality.
>
> (Jung, 1959/1968, CW 9i, para. 44)

Meanwhile, Daniel through his addictions was seeking the feminine and the masculine as well as the mother and the others unknown within. Later in therapy Daniel said he went on chat rooms disguised as a woman because he felt more comfortable than when he felt he had to uphold what he considered the male image of brawn. He felt weak, uncomfortable in his body, not male enough and needing constant reassurance he was noticed and valued.

Jung noted the body, like the psyche, is a symbolic communicator of wounds, dissociations and unconscious contents. As he said, 'Don't run away and make yourself unconscious of bodily facts, for they keep you in real life' (Jung, 2012, p. 66). For Daniel, a lifelong attitude of distance from his body and ignorance of its needs became the defensive structure he relied upon. However, it was precarious – like living on a foundation of sinking sand.

The 'as-if' person characterised by both omnipotence and impotence avoids the shadow. This leads to affective immaturity and a defensive impenetrability, obscuring the underlying fraudulence and precariousness. The person experiences a disjointed sense of reality due to underlying anguish, panic and void. Physical and psychological dissociations become buried in a contrived, mechanistic and sterile world. Self-esteem and self-worth dependent on maintaining superficial images do not support authenticity.

Daniel dreamt *he had a tray of small cakes and is handing them out to others at a party. One has a bite out of it, and one is damaged, and he turns each around, so no one sees. They will think the cakes look all right from the front, but the reality is the hidden flaw.* Daniel associated the cakes to his mother and the madeleine to French novelist Marcel Proust, memorably associated with the desire for his mother in his book *In Search of Lost Time*, published in 1913. Daniel interpreted the dream to mean he received damaged goods from his mother whereas the better food was given to others. The dream illustrated the early unmet needs for warmth and love, the lack that sent him into a life of isolation, fear and separateness ruled by addictions. Daniel said he did not know how or why he was drawn to these addictions. His personality had been lost so long ago, he didn't know what he was trying to resurrect. Daniel only felt guilt about his behaviours. He presented with a mild demeanour yet had a voracious side. Or perhaps this was the desire for the self, hidden within the fear of being real.

Addicts can become enamoured of fantasy images of themselves and others as addictions provide a distorted mirror. Meanwhile, Daniel defended against the shadow with the image of himself as someone extraordinary. 'The essential factor is the dissociation of the psyche and how to integrate the dissociation' (Jung, 1966a, CW 16, para. 266). The addictions were retreats to prevent contact with his depressive pain and anxiety. These avoided parts of the self were split off and projected onto other objects. There, they remained welded together, making significant parts of his personality unavailable (Steiner, 1993, p. 54). Hidden dependencies, the disjunction from affect, loneliness and depersonalisation resulted in Daniel's psychic retreats, which he enacted through the sexual addictions. He retreated to hide and protect as a means of avoiding the intolerable anxiety in all aspects of his life (Steiner, 1993, p. 12).

Daniel was neither an experiencer of life, nor had he learned to be an internal participant in his mental life. As Jung commented, 'As long as it is a provisional life, your unconscious will be in a state of continuous irritation against you' (1997, p. 194). This provisional life denoted the lack of investment in reality. Daniel resorted to grandiose fantasies to anesthetise and compensate for what he felt as a dark shadow over him. The shadow represented the very parts Daniel could not accept, but the addictions were also the shadow controlling him, reinforcing the secret spaces that separated him from others. Even though the secret also carried the hope that one day he could emerge, be found and met, Daniel instead was subsumed in it (Khan, 1983, p. 105). There was no other within who spoke or objected, but there was the one inside who accused him and was guilty. He had to escape that one and did so with the women he bought, convincing himself they were not only sexual partners but also friends. He could not admit he was using them.

Daniel's veneer, honed from years of façade, could obfuscate the therapeutic transference he verbally established from the first session as intellectual. This reassured he would not break the boundaries, as he was wont to do. But it was also an unconscious fear of recurrence of the original relational detachment and loss of love. 'Behind the defenses were a terrified infantile part of the self, a devious and cunning tempter and seducer' (Colman, 1991, p. 360). The seductive parts pulled him to hide the chaos and emptiness from our therapeutic relationship. This was equivalent to the wall erected between him and the world and paradoxically contained his pent-up wish to merge.

There are 'acute conflicts with those who are close … an impotence to withdraw from a conflictual situation, impotence to love, to make the most of one's talents, to multiply one's assets, or when this does take place, a profound dissatisfaction with the results' (Green, 1986, p. 149). Daniel could not sit with emotional emptiness, the painful state of loss or desolation. Encounters with others were quickly rendered null and void. However, feelings of being fake, unseen and worthless were tangled up with feelings of entitlement as Daniel strove to suppress his dimly felt despair. Such attitudes can escalate to a crushing of personality and self-annihilation. This arouses a disturbing netherworld of psychological oppression and a need for release from its mutilations.

Daniel's addictions were 'defenses against separation and loss while offering the illusion of omnipotence and manic excitement' (Knox, 2011, p. 147). He could not give up the fantasy of fusion with the other, a defensive and aggressive dynamic in his internal world enacted through addictions. Never satisfied, he always needed more but never knew what was enough. When he divorced, quit the religion and retired, the ties to his former life were severed and his addictions simultaneously ramped up.

The crime

For years Daniel *had a repetitive dream of killing someone.* Upon awakening he was upset and did not understand. The dream immediately bothered him but then he forgot it. He had no idea who he killed. He was not conscious of the crime. The dream image repeated his avoidance of personal ethics and responsibility, his self-betrayal. The unconscious was trying to get his attention, but he resisted, not listening to the voices within. Trying to remain unconscious was part of the killer and the killed referred to in the dream.

He wanted to hide from the dream. He felt it referred to his compulsive thoughts, and he would be found out. He did not consider the killed and killer was himself obliterating him from his life context. For him, 'the affects take on a primitive, powerful, archetypal form until they are known, humanized and managed by the ego or they can wreak havoc on the personality' (West, 2008, p. 378). Daniel had been acting against his self and ran internally from discovering the severity of the betrayal. He could not chance exposure of the real and frantically compensates through keeping himself 'as-if' because this is all he has known. Running so hard kept him unconscious, anxious, unable to relax, needing to resort to drugs, food, alcohol and sex.

In another dream *the pharmacy will not fill a prescription for pain because he lacks the correct government identity. He wonders if he has ever been himself, what his self is, who he is. Behind him is a voice saying the shadow knows and repeats this phrase.* The dream is quite direct about what he needs – an identity including the shadow. And it also implies he cannot avoid pain through medication.

In therapy the subjective relation to the interior world with its symbols informs the capacity to create meaning, connect to others and engage with life by listening to the language of the unconscious. Jung stated, 'The confrontation of the two positions [the opposites] generates a tension charged with energy and creates a living, third thing ... a movement out of the suspension between opposites ... a quality of conjoined opposites. So long as these are kept apart – naturally for the purpose of avoiding conflict – they do not function and remain inert' (Jung, 1969, CW 8, para. 189). Daniel was caught in this inert place.

Narcissism and the 'as-if' personality

Daniel nullified his loving dependent self and identified almost entirely with his destructive, narcissistic wounded parts. This provided a kind of negative inferiority/superiority of self-admiration for his cleverness, but also a denial of his total being. It was overlaid by the obsessive desire for sameness while erasing the other to maintain the status quo. 'As individual attention is habitually and excessively focused on the façade of the persona, the deeper, neglected aspects of the personality continually sabotage the individual's conscious intentions' (Jung, 1959/1968, CW 9i, para. 221). Narcissism indicates a narrowed capacity for experiencing emotions. It eliminates opposition, retains singularity and a strange form of certainty while the power of desire for the other secretly remains.

'This self-protective mechanism had become an addictive and self-referential activity with a ruminating quality' (Solomon, 1998, p. 234). Arrested in emotional development, Daniel rejected the instinctual – body, earth and time. Daniel's early emotional losses had formed into internal and unmanageable disillusionments. 'The narcissist strives to keep everything of value within the compass of himself because, paradoxically, he is plagued by doubt as to whether there is anything of value within himself' (Colman, 1991, p. 365). He lived in the illusion of no others sharing his world while imagining he had control over his existence, albeit in a rather empty universe.

Daniel went through the world as if life was real when he felt it wasn't. 'The self has yet to face the long repressed but often suspected, underlying internal reality, a hauntingly ever-present background sense of living in a void or facing a vast emptiness' (Solomon, 2004, p. 636). The psychological residue denies time and makes change unimaginable. In the throes of his addictions, Daniel was even more absent from himself. Not being present promoted the search for the ideal but was counteracted by an ever-present tension cutting off pleasure. This impelled him to chase his addictions, and the feelings aroused from them became even more prominent. This brought dissociation from self and circumvented psychological movement while thwarting any internal harmony.

Life has no permanence or meaning while its impermanence is also denied. Like Daniel, those who fail to go along with life remain suspended in mid-air. They hang onto youth, negatively anticipating life's descent. With age they look back, clinging to the former glory days and fear decline. 'They withdraw from the life-process ... and remain fixed [in nostalgia] with ... no living relation to the present ... The negation of life's fulfilment is synonymous with the refusal to accept its ending. Both indicate not wanting to live, and not wanting to live is identical to not wanting to die' (Jung, 1969, CW 8, para. 800). For example, Daniel had a reminder on his Apple watch that he would die, sent five times a day, to remind him of life.

Narcissism is associated with solipsism, egoism and pathological self-return in an enclosed circularity. Nothing comes in or goes out. Sexual addiction, which originates when there are disruptions in the process of forming a healthy and stable self, is also a defence against vulnerability.

Narcissus could not live if he knew himself. The refusal to accept unknown, strange, uncontrolled and disturbing feelings and thoughts brings psychological dissonance. This happens when a person's behaviour does not match their self-image, or the image they think or want others to have of them. When they project their shadow, they refuse the self and there is distancing and losing of themselves. Jungian psychology is founded on the recognition of the dissociated parts, the unknown and the splits in the psyche that lead to or obstruct knowledge of self and other. A question is whether the narcissist can learn to engage with the other when trying so hard to deny imperfection, depression, vulnerability or dependence. Instead of individuating, the narcissist maintains a static, false and illusory self-image at the cost of being real.

Arrival and erasure, promise and excuse constitute two sides of self-cancelling that escalates into self-hatred. To be freed from the shackles formed from the 'as-if' façade requires a significant working through of deep-seated vulnerabilities. The encounter with the other is crucial for overcoming narcissistic defences. 'The narcissistic omnipotent object relations are partly defensive against the recognition of the separateness of self and object' (Colman, 1991, p. 359). The 'I' can never become truly present and spins away from itself in a process of continual self and other alienation. Shedding the armour of 'as-if' means recognising there are subjectivities distinct from one's own. Yet, the person feels anxiety and apprehension, and they become increasingly impenetrable. The psychological walls are high, and no one gets in or out. Daniel's personality was punctuated by an intolerance of difference or change, and he was lost in the narcissism of small things while a sense of powerlessness plagued him.

His self-image was distorted in a negative way, reflecting little of his true being (Jacoby, 2016, p. 158). Residing in the alcove of his mind Daniel's grandiose phantasies came from feeling inferior while remaining dependent on outer approval. Yet, he felt that if he was like everybody, then he must be nobody. For example, his goal of being a millionaire by a certain age fostered a 'frenzy of activity compensatory to the internalized depletion from self and other alienation' (Jacoby, 2016, p. 156). Although Daniel thought he cared about others, he displayed a superficial social adjustment to hide his chronic uncertainty, dissatisfaction and envy.

Daniel needed notice but did not know intimacy. 'To recognize desire for what it is, dependent on others and also disallowed reveals him as unacceptable to himself, to be in conflict, too much in danger, disturbed by his own needs' (Phillips, 2013, p. 35). Although at this point in therapy he was in a monogamous relationship, his dreams of other women continued. In one dream *he is with a much younger woman who seems to be with a man in a corridor. The man leaves. Daniel says he will help her. She says no I will help you. He puts a hand on her arm, and this feels good. She puts her arm on his.*

Delusion is the word he could not remember while discussing this dream. He said the actual affair with the woman in the dream was a delusion. In this comment he attempted to cancel the former addiction and negate its intensity. The persistence of what he called evil thoughts kept telling him he was bad even as they lured him in. This psychologically conflicting situation appeared in the dream. Daniel began to understand this dream situation as indicating when he went unconscious, because he had no idea how or why he was there. He decided he would not lie to his partner and often in dreams like this realised he must tell her. Yet, years into the relationship he struggled to reveal the full extent of his vulnerability and felt easily rejected.

His emotions were so submerged he often hardly noticed them. Daniel spent his life avoiding feeling by maintaining control and now realised how rapidly he left his body, like in the previous dream. He said he needed conscious intention to remain present, as he previously only knew sneaking and hiding. The current emotional intimacy with his partner brought up the extent of his narcissistic defences as he realised the problem was worse than he thought. Daniel inhabited what he called separate mind compartments populated with sexual encounters like those depicted in the dream and they were on his mind frequently. These signify the solitude of the 'as-if' adaptation that filled his world, leaving no room for anyone but himself.

Daniel dreamt *of a woman in the back of a bus who had rough sex with a guy. Daniel was in the front of the bus looking at the woman next to him and her lips. He felt no concern for the one in the back who was with the edgy and perhaps dangerous guy.* In the next dream that night *he was with people and trying to find a place but did not know why he was with them or where he was going and just seemed to be floating along.* He felt empty in both dreams. They point to dissociations from self, other, body and emotion as well as the dispassionate attitude to the feminine. Unbeknownst to him, Daniel was lonely and wanted someone to love him. He said the compulsive thoughts were there a lot; self-doubt abounded, drawing him to the lewd and despicable. So driven by his actions to erase the pain, all he could register was a sense of difference that felt unfavourable to the self (Colman, 1991, p. 364), making the addictions more insistent to escape such uncomfortable feelings.

Daniel's addictions substituted for the natural and instinctual self. André Green surmised it was 'a destruction of the psychic activity of representation which creates holes in the mind, or feelings of void, emptiness' (Kohon, 1999, p. 290). The sexual addiction does not fill but perpetuates the need to reveal the emotional secrets and find self-worth.

The symbolic emerges for healing

I dreamt *Daniel was an imposter, and it was worse than he thought.* In the next session he admitted to having sexual encounters in his mind all the time. I wondered how his partner could trust him. Was he lying in therapy and to himself as well? Was he still putting on a front? In the psychological work and through the transference and countertransference the former sterility, lack of intimacy to self and others gradually had become apparent. The images and symbols in dreams exposed the transformative aspects of the personality. 'The symbolic capacity signifies the possibility for integration and the symbolic life through the holding together of the opposites and the creation thereby of a third thing' (Solomon, 2007, p. 159). They help a person move out of the one-sidedness of addictions tied up in their defence systems. Yet, there was my dream, and it hinted that all was not finished. Daniel's trust in his inner source was still unformed, and he was unable to manifest its guidance for individuation.

Jung said, 'In this world created by the Self we meet all those many to whom we belong, whose hearts we touch; here there is no distance, but immediate presence' (Jung, 1973, p. 298). The acknowledgement of vulnerability and incompleteness is the psychological work of filling in the gap. James Hillman, archetypal psychologist, conceptualised

> what individuates is not us, but our passions, talents and places of wounding. Our complexes need to shake off their infantile associations and find maturity, reality and the physical connection with psyche. Then the personality becomes a rich, multidimensional canvas.
>
> (Slater, 2012, p. 30)

For Daniel, the relation to his interiority and the symbolic gradually evolved over time as his psychological restlessness led to recovery of his spirit. He became able to find internal supplies for self-esteem rather than seek continual external gratification. Accepting the disowned and split-off others in his personality meant neither his nor women's bodies were objectified. In the psychological work and through the transference and countertransference the former sterility, lack of intimacy to self and others gradually diminished. Clinging to oneness opened to twoness as an internal couple formed within his personality and gradually emerged. Abandoning the former singularity and isolation meant accepting the shadow and finding place for self and inclusion of other. 'Then the conjunctios of various sorts can begin to happen, where, it might be said, the internal couple can be allowed to come together and generate conception and rebirth' (Meredith-Owen, 2008, p. 389).

Over time, accepting the disowned and split-off others secreted in the shadows of addictions opens relatedness to self, soul and world. This represents the phoenix rising from the ashes, the melancholy in narcissism explored rather than denied. The discovery of what is meaningful counters existential meaninglessness. Jung explained individuation in the following way:

I use the term 'individuation' to denote the process by which a person becomes a psychological 'individual', that is, a separate, indivisible unity or 'whole'. It is generally assumed that consciousness is the whole of the psychological individual. But knowledge of the phenomena that can only be explained on the hypothesis of unconscious psychic processes make it doubtful whether the ego and its contents are in fact identical with the 'whole'.

(Jung, 1959/1968, CW 9i, para. 490)

This process requires the capacity to gather the multiple personal and collective threads. The tension between ego and self, surface and shadow, are part of forming an identity in which the various selves can co-exist in the open. Conscious awareness of emotional wounds is restorative to this process. Hopelessness and impasse shift to openness to the unknown and unfamiliar. The personality of the 'as-if' becomes more relaxed and freer. The addiction arises from the healing depths of the unconscious, transforms the personality and liberates the internal bondage from unchanging thoughts, actions and meaningless suffering.

Our subjective relation to and relationship with our interior informs the capacity to create meaning, connect to people and engage life in fulfilling ways. The relationship within evolves over time and demands we face ourselves in authentically honest and confessional ways. Even if it can seem like a burden to our preferred conscious image, we find ourselves in the real and present, not as we might wish.

To bridge the tension between what was and what will be is basic to the regulation of the psyche and the emergence of new attitudes.

Why do you want to shut out of your life any uneasiness, any misery, any depression, since after all you don't know what work these conditions are doing inside you? Why do you want to persecute yourself with the question of where all this is coming from and where it is going? Since you know, after all, that you are in the midst of transitions and you wished for nothing so much as to change. If there is anything unhealthy in your reactions, just bear in mind that sickness is the means by which an organism frees itself from what is alien; so one must simply help it to be sick, to have its whole sickness and to break out with it, since that is the way it gets better.

(Rilke, 2001, p. 93)

The innate restlessness of the psyche seeks more than the here and now and longs to be refined, the spirit and life force embodied and aimed towards conscious awareness. For the person caught by addictive behaviours and secrets this means facing the emotional emptiness and letting go of the façade. By attending to the inner world, the self can heal and unify body and mind. One can engage and be active in the external world with a renewed sense of purpose and meaning in life, not based on isolating oneself but relating with others. Our living on demands inclusion rather than foreclosure on whoever or whatever is different in ourselves and others. 'Relationship to the self is at once relationship to our fellow man, and no one can be related to the latter until he is related to himself' (Jung, 1966a, CW 16, para. 445). Through the therapeutic relationship and its process over time Daniel began to trust and become more consciously embodied, intentional and self-aware.

References

Colman, W. (1991). *Envy, self-esteem and the fear of separateness*. *British Journal of Psychotherapy*, *7*(4), 356–67. doi: 10.1111/j.1752-0118.1991.tb01141.x.

Connolly, A. (2013). *Out of the body: Embodiment and its vicissitudes*. *Journal of Analytical Psychology*, *58*(5), 636–56. doi: 10.1111/1468-5922.12042.

Green, A. (1979). *The tragic effect: The Oedipus complex in tragedy*. Cambridge University Press.

Green, A. (1986). *On private madness*. The Hogarth Press.

Jacoby, M. (2016). *Individuation and narcissism: The psychology of self in Jung and Kohut*. Routledge.

Jung, C.G. (1959). *The collected works of C.G. Jung: Vol. 5. Symbols of transformation*. Pantheon Books.

Jung, C.G. (1959/1968). *The collected works of C.G. Jung: Vol. 9i. The archetypes and the collective unconscious*. Pantheon Books.

Jung, C.G. (1963/1970). *The collected works of C.G. Jung: Vol. 14. Mysterium coniunctionis*. Princeton University Press.

Jung, C.G. (1964). *The collected works of C.G. Jung: Vol. 10. Civilization in transition*. Princeton University Press.

Jung, C.G. (1966b). *The collected works of C.G. Jung: Vol. 16. The practice of psychotherapy*. Princeton University Press.

Jung, C.G. (1966a). *The collected works of C.G. Jung: Vol. 12. Psychology and alchemy*. Princeton University Press.

Jung, C.G. (1967) Collected Works 13. Princeton: Princeton University Press.

Jung, C.G. (1969). *The collected works of C.G. Jung: Vol. 8. The structure and dynamics of the psyche*. Princeton University Press.

Jung, C.G. (1971). *The collected works of C.G. Jung: Vol. 6. Psychological types*. Princeton University Press.

Jung C.G. 1973. Letter to Mary Mellon, *Letters, Volume I, 1906-1950*, Routledge & Kegan Paul , p. 298.

Jung, C.G. (1997). *The vision seminars [1930–1934]* (C. Douglas, ed.). Princeton University Press.

Jung, C.G. (2012). *Nietzsche's Zarathustra: Notes on the seminar given in 1934–1939*. Princeton University Press.

Jung, C.G. (2014). *The collected works of C.G. Jung: Vol. 18. The symbolic life*. Princeton University Press.

Khan, M. (1983). *Hidden selves*. International University Press.

Knox, J. (2011). *Self-agency in psychotherapy: Attachment, autonomy, and intimacy*. W.W. Norton.

Kohon, G. (ed.) (1999). *The dead mother: The work of André Green*. Routledge.

Lussier, A. (1999). *The dead mother: Variations on a theme*. In: G. Kohon (ed.), *The dead mother: The work of André Green* (pp. 149–62). Routledge.

Meredith-Owen, W. (2008). *'Go! sterilise the fertile with the rage': Envy as embittered desire.* *Journal of Analytical Psychology,* 53(4), 459–80. doi: 10.1111/j.1468-5922.2008.00741.x.

Ogden, T. (1999). *Analysing forms of aliveness and deadness of the transference-countertransference.* In: G. Kohon (ed.), *The dead mother: The work of André Green* (pp. 128–48). Routledge.

Phillips, A. (2013). *Missing out.* Picador.

Phillips, A. (2015). *Unforbidden pleasures.* Farrar, Straus and Giroux.

Rilke, R.M. (2001). *Letters to a young poet.* (S. Mitchell trans.). Modern Library.

Slater, G. (2012). *Between Jung and hillman.* Quadrant, *Xxxxii, 2,* 14–36.

Solomon, H.F. (1998). *The self in transformation: The passage from a two- to a three-dimensional internal world.* Journal of Analytical Psychology, *43*(2), 225–38. doi: 10.1111/1465-5922.00022.

Solomon, H. (2004). *Self creation and the limitless void of dissociation: The as if personality.* Journal of Analytical Psychology, *49*(5), 635–56. doi: 10.1111/j.0021-8774.2004.00493.x.

Solomon, H.F. (2007). *The self in transformation: The passage from a two- to a three-dimensional internal world.* Karnac.

Steiner, J. (1993). *Psychic retreats: Pathological organizations in psychotic, neurotic and borderline patients.* London: Routledge.

Susan Sellers ed. 1994. *The Hélène Cixous Reader.* London and New York: Routledge.

West, M. (2008). *The narrow use of the term ego in analytical psychology: The 'not-I' is also who I am.* Journal of Analytical Psychology, *53*(3), 367–88. doi: 10.1111/j.1468-5922.2008.00732.x.

Chapter 5

This is a love story
Echo and Narcissus

Exhausted from the hunting, the boy sought relief in a field crossed by a river, a *locus amoenus* close to where Echo was hiding.

Is there anybody
here?' Echo answers:
'Here!'

He is astonished.
He casts his eye in all directions and,
in a loud voice, cries:

'Come over here!'

She calls back to the person calling her.
He looks around and, when no one comes out,
he shouts again:

'Why run away from me?'

He gets back all the words he has called out.
Narcissus stands there, misled by what seems
a voice which answers his, and calls again:

'Let's meet here together'.

She could not reply
more willingly to any sound

and cried: 'Meet here together'.

Echo came out and ran to Narcissus, who aggressively rejected her:

'Take your hands off me! Stop these embraces!
I'll die before you have your way with me!'

DOI: 10.4324/9781003315254-6

All she replied was:
'Have your way with me'.

(Ovid, Metamorphoses, 359–401)

But Echo was not the only one he scorned, many before received the same treatment. One of them, a young boy, after being rejected cursed Narcissus, and the goddess Nemesis agreed to it. Moved by the thirst, Narcissus laid down next to the river and while drinking he glimpsed at his reflection in the water. He got so enchanted by his own image that he couldn't leave anymore. The figure he was gazing at was so lovable that it took a long while for him to realise he was falling for himself.

> Without a sense of shame,
> he desires himself. The one approving
> is the person being approved, and while
> he is pursuing, he is being pursued.
> He kindles fire and burns at the same time.
> How often he kisses the devious spring
> without success! How often he reaches in
> to clutch the neck he sees in the centre of the water,
>
> and yet his arms cannot
> embrace himself! What he is looking
> at he does not recognize,
>
> but what he sees …
> sets him aflame, and the very error
> which deceives his eyes excites them.

(Ovid, Metamorphoses, 402–436)

This chapter is a partial perspective on why the narcissistic aspects of the 'as-if' personality make it hard for this person to love and be loved, even when that is what they desire. Narcissism is a complex part of this personality structure. This person stumbles and is awkward in loving. They do not easily reciprocate; they feel stunted within, easily anticipating wounds and rejections. With a sense of inner confusion and cut off from others, they are unable to respond, or their response is insufficient, self-focused and lacks connection.

All of us begin life wanting love from others and loving those who love us. The 'as-if' personality, however, is made up of many complexities, particularly around the tender topic of love. There are numerous reasons the narcissistic aspects of this personality type lead to challenges in love. The 'as-if' person has difficulty in any relationship, even with their own self. As perceived in the 'as-if' personality, this person circles around but does not easily enter into the intimacy, feelings and emotions of love. This desire for love is often frustrated, and intimacy stutters in the continual movement into and then away from love. The 'as-if' person fears welcoming others in and into those spaces not linear, uniform or homogeneous.

Beyond the slick and assured surface these people present, in this chapter I present various examples of the inner conflict and psychological distress the 'as-if' person experiences through the narcissistic response. The issues become apparent through dreams, illustrating, among other aspects, the influence of early parental absence and mis-attunements. Also included in the narcissistic response is the Jungian concept of puella and puer, a term often applied to those with difficulty growing up, actualising potential and being intimate and committed to life. I weave in additional concepts from Jungian psychology on shadow, body and image with reference to the French philosopher Jacques Derrida. His writing on Narcissus and Echo includes the French concept of *différance*. Its multitude of meanings parallel the internal and external relational continuum between self and other. There has been growing interest, in proportion to its current increase personally and culturally, in understanding the 'as-if' person with narcissistic qualities.

The conundrum of narcissism

Narcissism has been described as a grandiose sense of self with exhibitionism, insistence on uniqueness and disturbed object-relationships. *The capacity to kid oneself is huge and arises from* the decay the person vaguely feels lying just beneath the surface. This person struggles to establish an integrated sense of self. *They are living on illusions, and paradoxically, the illusionary is based on the avoidance of being thoroughly seen and known.* The overriding question is: If I am not seen as exceptional, what am I?

Although Jung makes few references to narcissism in his *Collected Works*, his thinking about how people can fall into states where they avoid embracing life pertains to this very concept. Often appearing as a shiny object, adored and idealised, the 'as-if' person seems to live on the projections of others to feel alive and avoid collapsing into what feels like an abyss of interiority.

Love is basic. A need? An instinct? A life force? Spirit? Love is all of these and more. Our lives involve us in a series of images individually and collectively about love. The mythology and psychology of love reveal the conscious and unconscious elements of relationships. Jung called the contents of the collective unconscious *archetypes*, referring to a prototype or a model after which other interpretations are patterned. Love itself can be viewed as an archetype with its movement towards uniting spirit and instinct, self and other, body and psyche. Archetypal love patterns are endless and intriguing, catalysing numerous and unexpected encounters uniquely constellated for each person.

Each of us is drawn to different forms of love derived from our unique wounds and needs. Recognising the mythic dimensions at the basis of our personal experiences unites us in the universal nature of what it is to be human and to love. Myths are metaphorical representations; following their narratives allows us to gain insight into the sources of our reactions, behaviours and perceptions. They illustrate the blueprints for handling situations experienced at each stage of our lives. As Jung exhorted, find your myth and live it to the fullest (1963b, p. 195). In this chapter I explore the myth of Narcissus and Echo and what it reveals about the singularity in the 'as-if' personality. The obstruction of love and relatedness, which is prevalent in narcissism, is a feature indicative of the 'as-if' personality.

Love constellates positive, negative and challenging elements in the personality. Love opens us to the truths about the delight, pain and confusion in relationships. Love leads us down alleyways we might otherwise avoid. It takes us into ourselves; shakes our foundations; is rude, shocking and enlightening. Love rocks our world and sets us on the path of the unexpected.

Love is transformative. It reaches into the places we thought we would never go and requires that we grapple with them. We cannot control love. Love requires us to face the many insufficient and sufficient ways we give, receive and need. Love and the search for love keep us on an edge of self-development. It is like a precipice from which we might fall as well as a dark cave for emergence into renewal. This is the fear of the narcissistic part of the 'as-if' person who does not like change. Anything touching on the area of love and relationship brings unknown issues to the surface. For the narcissist, love is a difficulty, not a pleasure, because relationships carry threat and anxiety. Normally it is love that makes us feel alive – love for other people, love for activity and nature, for quiet. However, because 'as-if' people cannot deeply love, they feel deadened and numb.

This is apparent in the myth of Narcissus as it reveals the disturbances in the self-connection. This can be seen with the 'as-if' person marked by the need to be admired by others, who observes the world with a sense of superiority, looking at others with disdain and exaggerating their own achievements. The narcissist's experience of uncertainty is felt as unbearable. Centred on themselves, they have difficulty seeing how their actions harm others. At least this is how it appears. Underneath is a personality quaking, insecure, frantic to cover the psychic holes with a fantastic series of personas.

Were I to devote my attention solely to the psychopathology of narcissism, I run the risk of neglecting or obscuring the urge for self-connection embedded in this personality type. As with the 'as-if' personality, the narcissist can seem beyond reach because of their level of self-involvement. This is too pessimistic and negates the considerable benefit psychological work can have. The wider relevance of the narcissist's suffering and disillusionment applies to the conundrum of relating to anything outside themselves. These are the very situations open to self-discovery.

As well as being a study in self-deception, narcissism is defined by the singularity and one-sidedness of existence. The narcissistic drama plays itself out at the expense of real life. This person looks at themselves too much to see anything. Jung noted, 'To the degree that he does not admit the validity of the other person, he denies the other within himself the right to exist – and vice versa. The capacity for inner dialogue is a touchstone for outer objectivity' (1969, CW 8, para. 187). In addition, and at cost to the wholeness of the personality, this singularity occludes relationship to the unconscious as it is also a form of the other – different and unknown. This is a type of oneness that has difficulty integrating or expanding to include twoness. The narcissist does not easily see or take in the existence of any other. Instead, an insistence on sameness becomes a defence against feeling inferiority and shame, as they resort to protection behind the narcissistic wall of impenetrability. A central question is whether the narcissist can learn to engage with the other.

As Jung said, 'Your vision will become clear only when you can look into your own heart. Who looks outside, dreams: who looks inside awakes' (1973, p. 33). In the myth of Narcissus, the blind seer Tiresias told his mother Narcissus would not live if he got to know himself. The message in this myth is present, to some extent, in the unconscious of us all. It implies knowing oneself, opening to the other, and this involves not only death to what was but also change.

Yet the imposter/narcissist is a composite of outer appeal while reflecting inner absence. This person lacks connection to self, and the life of the soul seems unignited or even refused. In a typical scenario, she presents a calm demeanour, an aura of ease and cool aloof distance. She might show up late, only talking of herself, with no commentary or interest in anyone else. Although seemingly focused on herself, she is distracted, her attention drawn elsewhere. Nothing seems sacred or special and all is brushed off with a light comment or laugh, as if it were of no import. So what does count to her?

She remains unknown, an enigma, but also not so interesting. There is a flat predictability, a lack of effort, and she lies. The narcissist is not where she says she will be; she pretends. Who is this vapid person? Is she appealing? What draws people to her? She puts out a seductive veneer and tender fragility, a perfect image, delicate, unflustered, with no apparent shadow. Is there even an opening to the psyche? Can any of the walls come down and can she trust or garner trust from others? She is charming, compliant, a cold and sparkling gem but what lies within?

She presents as untouched, without effect from others, has few reactions to them and appears lacking in genuineness. The analytical process is meant to touch the hurt and pain, the defensive wrappings enfolded around her early damaged heart. It is a relational damage from which she can heal if she dares enter the process. The responsibility and trust in others and in the integrity of the analytical connection must be made. This imposter type clings tightly to the idealised mirror and the status quo. To do otherwise is to risk losing much. So, although she says she desires change or growth, when it comes to it, she might turn away. Or the relationship in the analytical process may grab her and hold sway.

Why mythology?

Mythological stories, with their wealth of symbolism, parallel psychological processes. The mythological is a way of being, thinking and expressing the various life pathways, the obstacles along those paths and how to get through them. Discovering the language of myth is part of a return to the basics of being a person. As a therapeutic and life tool, it is a psychological experience of entry to the unconscious, both personal and collective. Jungian psychology is based on becoming who one is, truly. This aspect of Jungian psychology helps us investigate the depths of the personality, expanding beyond yet relevant to the daily round of existence.

The various interpretations of a myth reflect a particular era, person and society. The myth expresses a need, whether we are conscious of it or not, and its content connects us to those through the ages. We can feel the thread of this personally and collectively. A myth's subject matter is not literal but symbolic and serves the psychological need to access and connect the unconscious with conscious existence.

Jung believed mythology was the projection and expression of the collective unconscious (1969, CW 8, para. 325). The figures and motifs found in the collective unconscious are images, symbolic and impersonal, revealed in the intricate plots and story lines of the numerous myths and fairy tales worldwide. They express a uniformity over time and space and are meaningful to the individual and the culture. More than a fantasy story, a myth is a way of experiencing the world and portraying a worldview. A central function of myth is to reveal the psychological with its links to the outer, creating meaning and relevance for the person.

Mythology and its symbolism weave narratives that bring the divine and natural realms together. Mythic narratives are antidotal to our daily anxieties and fears while exposing age-old knowledge and paths towards consciousness.

> The primordial experience is the source of creativeness ... it requires the related mythological imagery to give it form ... for it is a vision seen 'as in a glass darkly' ... Nothing is missing in the whole gamut that ranges from the ineffably sublime to the perversely grotesque.
>
> (Jung, 1966, CW 15, para. 151)

In the ancient Greek myth of Echo and Narcissus, each figure represents in different ways the self searching for affirmation and intimacy.

The myth of Narcissus and Echo highlights the desire and denial of attachment, loss, love, life and death. Narcissus and Echo each express body and psyche disintegrating from lack of love. The devouring nature of narcissism in relationship to self and other focuses on the following themes. The ancient Greek writer Ovid portrays Narcissus paying a price with his life for rejecting as a lover anyone other than himself. Echo invites connection with her voice and emotional response, yet she has been largely ignored culturally and in psychological writings.

Any story or myth contains a multitude of interpretations fundamental to its effect. In a chain of meanings there is not one interpretation but the interweaving of many and only some can be noted here. These conceptual frameworks have been collected through the ages to expand horizons, rather than bending into a narrow frame. The force or impact of the mythological symbol needs to have a local and ethnic quality through which it can be allowed to act on the soul (de Koning, 1998, p. 565). The myth of Narcissus and Echo is Western and may not have the same relevance to other cultural traditions. Its cross-cultural aspects and various disciplines are integral to unpeeling the layers of the Narcissus and Echo story. A point here is also to move from a solely male-dominated story to one that brings forward the role of Echo and what she means for the modern psyche.

For example, French philosopher Jacques Derrida's creative contribution to philosophy and post-modernism exhibits a crucial element through the concept of *différance*, a French word that refers to 'differ' and 'defer' (indicated by the 'a' in *différance* instead of *différence*) and to the difference between being and being-of-being (de Koning, 1998, p. 563). Applied to the concept of narcissism, Derrida's use of the term *différance* means there is not one centre, and each presumed centre yields to another. Derrida's thought on the text and words is very close to Jung's conceptions of the image and symbol, in which there is no ruling monotheistic paradigm or theory (de Koning, 1998, p. 559). Symbols and archetypal meanings are expressed through many different images, personal and collective, unfolding like an accordion.

The singular

Narcissism in the 'as-if' personality type reveals the structure of a singular, isolated and lonely self, covered by an outer show of grandiosity and ignoring others. Narcissus represents the disconcerting process of inverting one's gaze. He neither looks outside himself, nor does his turn inwards recognise who he is. Narcissus cannot see himself, and this is the very point of his tragic ending. 'Why try / to grip an image? He does not exist – / the one you love and long for' (Ovid 3.432–3). This line of Ovid's draws our attention to the plight of Narcissus and Echo, who both died, failed to love and be loved, leaving the self unfulfilled. And this presents the conundrum and struggle of the 'as-if' personality as well. 'Passionate desire has its two sides: it is the force that embellishes everything and, under certain circumstances, destroys everything' (Jung, 1967, CW 7, para. 165).

Narcissus's death was punishment for being unable to engage in love with anyone but himself. Likewise, the narcissist is doomed to suffer pain for being unable to love anyone outside themselves. Even as it works to protect, self-love can sabotage by denying the needed love of others, the love that self-love alone doesn't provide. Narcissism can push us to love others in a complex interweaving of self with other. We see ourselves in the other, mirroring and separating at the same time.

American philosopher Pleshette DeArmitt (2013) reconfigures a kind of narcissism that is 'open to the other as other'.

> That is, an experience in which the self is formed by a relation to the other, and in which the other prevents the self from closing onto itself, a relation in which the love of self and love of the other can no longer be thought of as mutually exclusive but must be understood as inextricably intertwined.
>
> (Oliver, 2015, p. 37)

Said another way, this indicates movement from one aspect transported or carried over to the other, and from this action the personality evolves and transforms. In this interpretation of bringing self and other together, we love others because we find a reflection of at least some part of ourselves in the form of the other. Thus, healthy narcissism searches for the familiar in the other but does not exclude the other. To be recognised occurs not alone but is intertwined with others as well. In effect, the self is restructured and expanded through this experience.

Connecting this perspective to Jungian psychology, the process involves the ability to manage the tension between opposites that characterises healthy psychological structure (Schwartz-Salant, 1982, p. 67). Attraction is the mystery of one for the other, remaining separate and connected but without cancelling each other out. This is a basic concept of Jungian psychology, handling this push and pull between what seem to be opposing forces. From struggling and holding we regain balance; we are changed. The tension of opposites can be interpreted as self and other, what is same and what is different, what is comfortable and what is challenging, and so on. By holding these various views, feelings, emotions, reactions and beliefs, we can make something else happen from their combination. In the process, we facilitate growth and development away from our old patterns.

Likewise, the longing for merger and feeling at one with the other is a feature of falling in love as both partners vie for attention and swing from one to the other. One of the paradoxes is a threat of loss of one's boundaries and identity as a separate person. Sameness threatens our distinctive and separate identity and our sense of self because it brings us back to a less differentiated, narcissistic state of functioning (Czubinska, 2020, p. 330).

This becomes apparent in the 'as-if' personality's relationships, which revolve around them. From their narcissistic response, anyone else is perceived as an object to use, to fill needs and shore up their fragile self-esteem. As part of this personality, the narcissist is contempt-prone, looking down on others. This establishes emotional distance so no one can perceive the associated fragility. Although surprising at first, the link between contempt and fragile self-esteem can be explained by the vulnerability of narcissism. Narcissists can be so sensitive to hurt, it causes inattention to others' emotional needs and relationships go awry.

In addition, shame is a significant factor of the narcissist's inner reality. This emotion represents the deep pre-verbal wounding when one begins to feel unlovable and unacceptable. This early and ineradicable felt hideousness must be covered with the 'as-if' façade. This can take the stance of overweening pride, inflationary projection of oneself, flagrant flaunting. Narcissists are exhausting with all their frantic energy focused on hiding their deeper inadmissible feelings of shame. A protective shell grows to protect the internal fragility, but it is inflexible, and no one can get close enough for love or loving. The shell remains in place.

Narcissists feel superior to others yet depend on them to reflect a positive image. In this way many narcissists are co-dependent. They are hypersensitive to any challenge to their illusion of being the best, often reacting to perceived slights where none exist. They avoid their shortcomings being revealed, opinions or authority questioned, or self-esteem and pride tarnished. They will do what it takes to prop up their image and block any negative feedback.

Although narcissistic injury commonly appears, even in therapy, the extent of its painful effects can get missed. The narcissist is a master illusionist, insisting on needing no one yet desperate for attention. This person is oddly unsatisfying to be around, and after a conversation others feel empty. Were they posing? Their separate existence denies others, allowing for no differences in the need to preserve sameness.

Narcissism seeks validation, being seen, but when made conscious can be used for expressing healthy self-worth. The person who speaks enthusiastically about their latest project may not be bragging or asking for undue praise as much as trying to share what is meaningful to them. They are not necessarily driven by self-interest, but rather by social interest through communicating about their inner world. They are talking *to us, not at us*, and they will be only mildly disappointed, not violently enraged if we interrupt, disagree, grow bored or change the subject. We are neither at the mercy of their self-adoration nor captive to their envy. This person is seeking empathic and real responses. We can feel the difference between this kind of exchange and one driven by the compulsive need of the narcissist for admiration as confirmation of their value.

For many years, narcissism has been one of psychotherapy's core concepts and its treatment remains a theoretical focus. Narcissism represents the injured psyche and questions arise about how it can be healed. Narcissism can be described as a disturbance of self-connection, as self-loathing, having difficulty self-soothing, being fraught with internal conflicts and struggles and complications in relationships. In the cult of self-adoration, narcissistic devotion to the body beautiful involves paradoxically an ascetic attitude to life, crippling the psyche with the need for perfection, rigid rules, tight and anxious limits, creating a spiritual vacuum.

Needing to be seen in the eyes of others the 'as-if' person holds onto a precarious sense of self. It is 'as-if' this person can only exist if seen by another. There is insufficient access to their insides. Clinging onto others becomes a survival mechanism, but it does not allow them to be their own separate person, capable of moving and developing in space. 'If the experiences and feelings that underpin the terrible feelings of dissolution are not investigated and transformed, clinging may become an addictive behaviour, a malevolent attachment that works against development, based on a delusion' (Cavalli, 2014, p. 560).

The narcissist feels anxiety and apprehension about life. This is hidden by developing an idealised persona and rampant grandiose posturing. It is quite perplexing when the person presents as a star, basking in the light, mesmerising to others. Like today's narcissist, in the myth Narcissus only sees his beauty as it is the ideal. Narcissus's self-identity is inflated, unrealistic, incomplete and cannot recognise any shadow as his vision is one-sided. The narcissist seems to want to keep it this way. To become whole complex human beings, according to Jungian analytical psychology, we must accept the disowned and split-off parts, those parts secreted away, the unexpected, residing in the shadow and the unconscious.

The narcissist is the part of the 'as-if' person who appears to be confident, assured, self-centred and satisfied. This pose is a cover for the fragile and vulnerable ego of one who cannot mature, feel the entire self and who exists in stasis, unease and insecurity. The reality is a person alone with low self-regard, a nagging comparison to others and interior isolation.

Early attachment deficits

Whether nurturing or toxic, childhood relationships have formative influences on later adult relationships. Insufficient childhood experiences indicate the presence of distant, toneless, practically inanimate, emotionally dead parents. When internalised, such relationships leave feelings of misery and a lack of satisfaction and despair, expressed in terms of a void, emptiness, futility and meaninglessness (Kohon, 1999, p. 290). Narcissism becomes a defence against relatedness and arises from the apprehension of replicating the earlier and painful objects experienced as associated with absence and loss.

To respond for real or to be real means to show a dependency checked early on with these inadequate parental figures. The possibility of relating to a good object was denied. The early physical and psychological disappointments form into cycles of disillusionment and withdrawal. There is a deep well of loneliness if the person ever takes time long enough to stop and feel. She is arrested in development, rejecting the instinctual, the physical, earth and time. Jung referred to this as associated with inertia, low self-worth and depressive moods. 'She started out in the world with averted face ... and all the while the world and life pass by her like a dream – an annoying source of illusions, disappointments, and irritations' (Jung, 1959, para. 185).

Or this person was determined by their parents to be most special, the darling, made to show off, pressured to shine for their pleasure and to brighten their lives. This is conveyed through verbal and nonverbal messages. To mistake the imaginary for the real, and to further not even recognise the imaginary as mirror, as visual echo, of one's own self: 'Unwittingly, / he wants himself; he praises, but his praise / is for himself; he is the seeker and / the sought, the longed-for and the one who longs; / he is the arsonist – and is the scorched' (Ovid 3.425–6). Early, very early, the child learns there is no choice but to be good, make their parents happy, achieve, be the best.

Detrimental effects occur when the child must please or save the parent to obtain a semblance of parenting. Emotional wounds come from loss and feeling unlovable. 'Narcissican melancholy is fundamental sadness bound with immemorial loss' (Oliver, 2002, p. 129). The narcissist develops object hunger, a need to fill the emptiness with people, places and things to compensate for the void and the sense of being unsafe and uncared for. Life is precarious. Defensive postures are erected and linked to early developmental lacks. British psychoanalyst Donald Winnicott said, 'the [parent's] adaptation is not good enough. The process that leads to the capacity for symbol-usage does not get started or else it becomes broken up ... in practice the infant lives, but lives falsely' (1960, p. 146).

Who is in the mirror?

Identity comes from the Latin term *idem et idem*, which literally means 'the same and the same', or 'repeatedly, over and over'. The notion of identity is understood in opposition to otherness. However, Narcissus's refusal to separate does not allow for otherness as it is too threatening, and he seeks to be mirrored himself rather than what is seen in the other (Schwartz-Salant, 1982, p. 91). This person can recognise the need for no other – 'What I desire, I have' (p. 91) – and the grandiose self takes over. A combination of inadequate self-love fighting with self-hate describes the dissociated states abiding in narcissism, occluding a deeper relation to the unconscious. There is a deep-seated belief there is nothing within and nothing of value, and the narcissist is afraid to plunge into the unconscious (p. 65). The narcissistic conundrum characterised by non-love signifies lack of connection with the self and other, with effects felt both personally and culturally.

The narcissist seems to have too much pride, motivated by their inadmissible feelings of shame. They experience a peculiar feeling of unreality and defend against depression and suffering; so preoccupied with managing the fears and anxieties of those around them, they do not develop an inner core of their own. They are social chameleons who never had a chance to just be, as they are constantly acting, putting on impressions, worrying, staging performances in the public eye, socially constructed.

Lacking the capacity for self-observation indicates an inability to tolerate interpretation. This also represents the other and therefore is threatening. Like a mirror, analytical and psychological processes reveal the inner self and inescapable truths. 'That which you hold is but the shadow of a reflected image ... with reflection interpreted as the soul or vital center' (Schwartz-Salant, 1982, p. 88). Being drawn to the mirror day after day can represent obsession with inflation and superficial vanity. It might also reflect loss and negation, contributing to self-destructive feelings, the self divorced from the body. It might also be the search for the self.

Therefore, acts of reflection and mirroring are psychologically complex. To perceive oneself in a reflecting surface is also to recognise the shadow, or the dark underside. 'Some words are doomed like lilacs in a storm. And some are like the precious dead – even if I still prefer to all of them the words for the doll of a sad little girl'.[1] These are opposing yet integral to the shine on the surface and the natural occurrence of light coming through the depths. If these depths of being have remained unexplored, the narcissist's reflecting surfaces do not reveal anything. The world seems threatening, and they conceal their precious areas.

The narcissist's outer arrogance and omnipotence hide very real feelings of emptiness, formless terror and dread (Fordham, 1986, p. 159). These people think they are special, and envy forms when they cannot attain what they desire. Narcissism, describing those who are self-absorbed, arrogant, exploitive, has long been associated with envy (Mollon, 1994, p. 34). Although they may not like it, narcissists are vulnerable, their egos fragile, and they tend to be internally self-conscious, passive, shy and emotionally introverted. 'Envy is related to the psyche's early functioning with an implicit aversion to separation and difference' (West, 2010, p. 460). The denial of the Self and the need to hide lies at the core of the problem. The discomfort of the narcissist and the fragility of the ego manifest in anxiety, and feelings of emptiness disappear into the overt actions of entitlement. They seek the limelight to hide the feeling of inadequacy, inferiority and being one step from failure.

As Julia Kristeva commented, 'Depression is the hidden face of Narcissus: that countenance which – although it carries him off into death – remains unperceived by him as, marveling, he contemplates himself in a mirage' (Kristeva, 1992, p. 5). The defence focuses on survival while attempts to grow and individuate seem dangerous. The narcissist looks but cannot find themselves in their need to possess the self and its archetypal potency and beauty as well as its otherness. In the myth this attitude leads Narcissus to his death (Schwartz-Salant, 1982, p. 91).

In instances where the ability to distinguish self from other is impaired, attempts at self-protection may create the painful and damaging conditions the system attempted to avoid in the first place. To compensate for the fragility of ego and self, there is pressure to have complete success assured always. Intimacy is difficult. In the unease and discomfort with closeness, although desired, this 'as-if' person reacts from pseudo affectivity and without access to the full range of emotions. 'The more extreme traumatically engendered condition is that in which any capacity to represent self-experience is ruptured: a state of paralysis in which even the blank impress is lost within a void' (Connolly, 2011, p. 5). The present is erased in the look to the imagined future.

Wounds

Julia Kristeva depicted the wounds of the narcissist as follows: 'I hate it, because I love it, and in order not to use it, I imbed it in myself; but because I hate it, that other within myself is a bad self, I am bad, I am nonexistent' (Oliver, 2002, p. 186). Suffering arises because of missed attachments. The narcissist becomes an observer of life, removed, standing outside and unconnected, the self impoverished. The ramifications can remain unaddressed for years.

The internal and external worlds become separated. The narcissist is poised between what the person fears in their mind and in the world. 'The inertia of libido, which will relinquish no object of the past, but would like to hold it fast forever … a passive state where the libido is arrested in the objects of childhood' (Jung, 1956, CW5, para. 253). The feeling of damage signals the person cannot afford to experience reality, as it is expected to be devastating and horrifying. This is expressed through refusing either complete introjection or projection of the other (Britton, 1998, p. 61). A complexity of intricate challenges confronts the narcissist. Although gifted, intelligent and unusual, over time it becomes evident these people are trapped in predictable repetitive responses and often internally self-deprecating thoughts.

The psyche and body are bombarded with defeat; there is no point because nothing will be perfect enough. No matter how it seems, the narcissist has little natural relation to their body. It is something to make over, to objectify, to distance from. In secret the narcissist turns on themselves in a war against the body and this, of course, blocks love. Yet, these are the 'as-if' people looking like they are fine and ignoring their maladaptive life reactions. They end up living in neverland, a place of infinite postponement and half-identity (Solomon, 2004, p. 639). Again, dissociation from the real develops as a survival attempt and illusions compensate for anxiety and emotional vacancy.

Julia Kristeva refers to the notion of alienation or splitting of the self as the result of the repression of feelings. She said when instinct turns self-destructive, the ego, from early in life, lacks cohesion and falls into bits (1992, p. 19). The self is divided between the inner agonised aspects and the external upbeat façade, expressing the dissonance between the drive to achieve and the despair of loneliness and withdrawal.

> The self – wounded, incomplete, empty, is felt to have a fundamental flaw, a congenital deficiency. Such logic presupposes a severe super-ego and a complex dialectic of idealization and devalorization, both of self and other. It is an identification with the loved/hated other – through incorporation, introjection, projection – that is affected by the taking into oneself of an ideal, sublime, part or trait of the other and that becomes the tyrannical inner judge.
>
> (1992, p. 6)

Sorrow becomes the object of attachment, a substitute to which one clings, cultivating and cherishing it for lack of any other.

Closer observation reveals the compulsively driven unconscious drama within. Closed, adept at covering up, yet full of sorrows, there is an absence of solidity. The person goes through the world 'as-if' real but feels, without their own identity, like a puppet, managed by strings and not free to choose. There is a mechanistic quality to their performance although they pretend 'as-if' life is amazing. The inner life feels barren, the external shell too firm, too brittle, too susceptible to breaking. Their armour cannot bend, nor can they grow or breathe. Something intangible and indefinable obtrudes between this person and others, leaving them with the question, 'What is wrong?'

Echo

In the Greek myth, Echo's dramatic appeal for connection, attention and love was composed of Narcissus's statement and her echoed question and answer, which can be likened to the dialogue of therapeutic inquiry occurring on conscious and unconscious planes. The therapeutic crucible of comment and repeat evolves in a rhythm based on difference yet predicated on the sameness of being human. 'In the last resort we must begin to love in order that we may not fall ill, and must fall ill if, in consequence of frustration, we cannot love' (Freud, 1949, p. 42). In therapeutic work, the verbal and nonverbal speech between participants draws out the self from the unconscious.

Echo interrupts Narcissus's soliloquy of self-absorption and solitary auto-affection stirred by seeing his reflection. Her words reach out to him as the other (Oliver, 2015, p. 35). Echo enacts the search for the other, but she suffers psychologically and physically from being refused. The myth recounts the hunger for love as Echo's body disappears into the modern-day anorexic, the ignored, the body as unnoticed and unwanted. Narcissus wants sameness and Echo difference. The need for inner union is expressed in the tale, and it also notes the fatal destruction that occurs when this is unmet.

Echo has been discussed little in relation to Narcissus, except as a mere repeat. Yet, she represents aspects beyond the self-sameness of Narcissus who cannot recognise any other as an equivalent centre of being. Echo enacts the need for interaction with otherness, and this is part of what creates her subjectivity. It is through her love that Echo transforms her reiteration of the words of Narcissus from mere repetition into her response (Oliver, 2015, p. 37).

On the other hand, Narcissus cries '*Emoriar, quam sit tibi copia nostri!*' ('May I die before I give you power over me!') (Ovid 3.391). He can't comprehend any other consciousness than his own. Like many 'as-if' people, Narcissus is 'caught in a hall of mirrors or an echo chamber, both mourning and celebrating that we are always and only chasing an illusion of self-sameness, an illusion of stable identity, an illusion of some unified we' (Oliver, 2015, p. 36).

Echo embodies the self in the mirror of the other (Oliver, 2015, p. 36). She repeatedly declares her aliveness and emotional and physical desires, names herself and declares her subjectivity through her voice. By speaking she defies the divine punishment placed upon her in the myth by Hera, the jealous wife of Zeus, king of the gods who was a continual philanderer. Echo is punished by Hera for witnessing Zeus's deceptive actions and not telling her. Quite bravely and independently, Echo listens, responds and answers to what she sees and hears and does not turn away.

For Echo the relationship between voice and image communicates through her repetitions, and although unable to initiate, this does not mean a complete removal of choice. Her tone, inflection and so on are still hers. And although she repeats what others have said, she can choose what she repeats. Echo doesn't merely parrot what she hears, but instead establishes place through emphasising and repeating her desires. Even to the end, Echo's voice has life. 'So she is hidden in the woods / and can never be seen on mountain slopes, / though everywhere she can be heard; the power / of sound still lives in her' (Ovid 3.401–4). Her desire does not wane, and she continues to pursue the object of her love throughout the myth.

The myth demonstrates Echo is a self through her desiring of the other and through her insistence of being heard by the one she loves.

The death of the other rips out her heart, silences her lips, and undoes her sovereignty, if she ever had any. What if the philosophical subject is not the man in love with himself, but rather the woman – wood nymph, or perhaps even disembodied voice, ghost or revenant of one – who loved another.

(Oliver, 2015, p. 37)

The figure of Echo illustrates more than mere repetition as she signs her name through declaring her love. 'She models a way we come to ourselves through others … Speaking our hearts and minds, like Echo we are indebted to the other' (Oliver, 2015, p. 43). Echo is no passive object, but is the pursuer, following Narcissus to the pool after he has violently rejected her and even following him towards death by also wasting away. The prolonged extent of her mourning, loss and unmet desire results in her gradually disappearing. Echo's agony, with the gradual wasting away of her body, symbolises the psychological effects of not being received or seen. These are the emotional ingredients essential for development and growth.

Jacques Derrida expanded on this theme, describing the situation when 'the defenses turn and suicidally destroy itself through the very act of defending its self' (2005, p. 123). He contended Narcissus hears himself through the resonance of Echo (p. 164). Her words draw out Narcissus as he hears her and responds. Echo invites dialogue and connection and presents a way out of the impasse of sameness and lack of intimacy. Contained within love is connection and loss, and within each self exists a multitude, not just self-same. Echo speaks the language of love and desire and is active, persistent, unfailing, determined.

The cultural and psychological lack of attention to Echo reflects the negation of the feminine, the physical body, of longing and desire as aspects of relationship to self and others. In needing all to be the same and predictable, the narcissist avoids the multiplicity characterising a healthy psychology. Likewise, these people have beauty and gifts but can be idle, indolent, isolated, withdrawn, surrounded by a few admirers who flatter them. Narcissists do not have the coping skills necessary to deal with anything perceived as negative. They inwardly tend to be gloomy and depressed, unhappy, critical of others, anxious, envious, competitive and have extreme reactions to perceived slights or criticism.

Narcissus portrays the illusory, unable to include the other or the feminine, and his passion remains unrequited. His personality protects against the vulnerability relationship entails. Existing in the bubble of narcissism, self and world become disjointed, as the narcissist hangs onto youth and fantasy, video games, anime, Instagram and Photoshop in an effort to keep forever young and promote an 'as-if' reality that attempts to escape time.

The process of Jungian analytical psychotherapy opens a gateway through agony and loss towards aliveness and love with self and others. Jung called this holding the tension of the opposites. It can be interpreted here as listening and responding to the voice of Echo rather than remaining in the singularity of Narcissus.

Puella and puer

The 'as-if' personality, narcissism and what Jung calls the puella or puer archetype share similar traits: the façade of cheer, garnering attention but refusing intimacy and a bewilderment about growth and maturity. The puella or puer differentiates feminine and masculine, respectively, especially when the concept in Jungian psychology was originally conceived. The inner world is difficult to access. This is a personality characterised on the one hand by a failure to set stable or realistic goals, to make lasting achievements in accord with these goals and a proclivity for intense but short-lived attachments and experiences. On the other hand, remarkable talent is also a characteristic.

Jungian analyst James Hillman described the puer as:

> narcissistic, inspired, effeminate, phallic, inquisitive, inventive, pensive, passive, fiery and capricious, addressing the call to the spirit. This is a call that involves not just the beginnings but requires staying power. Caught in activity; an eternal becoming is not realized and then is reduced to possibility and promise only.
>
> (Hillman, 1989, p. 27)

The problem is that the puella or puer representing the excitement at the beginning soon peters out and cannot manage the methodical plodding needed for continuing development. They do not easily age, and as Hillman contended (p. 25), 'the puer spirit is the least psychological, has the least soul'. The task is to find connection to the continuum of life rather than living in ageless and timeless one-sidedness and illusion.

The veneer of the puella or puer presents as aloof and untouchable and seems to avoid confrontation, anticipating hurt. There is self-focus, denial of the need for others; even if negative there is avoidance of intercession of the other. Based on outer appearances those identified with the puella or puer are often regarded as successful performers and achievers, whereas their inner life remains deficient, without an interior support system or confidence. These people might seem happy, but they are run by a hungry empty self with little enjoyment. The focus on surface and ego keeps the inner life undeveloped. The person attaches through sameness a fusion allowing for no differences. They are too busy worrying about being unlovable and feeling that love could be false (Hillman, 1989, p. 57). They do not risk much and hold back emotionally (p. 69). Often their body cannot feel its own physical responses.

Narcissism is a portrayal of the psychic state of the singular, a life without feeling alive and the self divorced from the body. The foundation is insecure, and the mirror is a narcissistic one without the various subjectivities of the world. In other words, life narrows to find safety and eliminate otherness. Desire and excitement quickly dissolve. All becomes dead, unable to be revived and the fantasy becomes dust. As Jung stated:

> If you contemplate your lack of fantasy, of inspiration and inner aliveness, which you feel as sheer stagnation and a barren wilderness, and impregnate it with the interest born of alarm at your inner death, then something can take shape in you, for your inner emptiness conceals just as great a fullness if only you will allow it to penetrate into you.
>
> (1963b, CW 14, para. 189)

Despite his frustration and suffering, Narcissus cannot leave the spot at the pool, mesmerised by his own image, and there he wastes away.

The Mirror

The myth goes:
He knows not what he sees, but what he sees
invites him. Even as the pool deceives
his eyes, it tempts them with delights. But why,
o foolish boy, do you persist? Why try
to grip an image? He does not exist –

Ovid, Metamorphoses (1993)

In the poem's concluding stanza, Ovid tells us that even in the underworld, after death, Narcissus continues to stare into the pool of the river Styx, fixated forever on his own image.

Narcissism, as I refer to it here, reflects the places where the wounds exist. To avoid suffering the person arrests the processes of life (von Franz, 2000, p. 151). The loss of contact with an authentic self results in closing off from others in antici-pation that the inner spaces will be wrongly broken into. For narcissists, to expose what seems like the tattered shards of themselves endangers the false solidity of their world. This effort is to mitigate becoming depressed, sinking into despair and the anticipated loss of control. Being receptive to the other requires the ability to accept the tiny narcissistic disappointments when attunement is lacking. This leads to either growth when the disappointment is small enough or pathology when the disappointment is more than can be managed.

For the puella or puer, the realities of limits and mortality can hardly be faced. Time is fungible, anything becoming possible in the rebellion against limits. Defined by a wandering nature, personally and psychologically without attachments, life with others is difficult. The flashy appeal is a necessary cover, fostering idealising projections, and meant to maintain emotional distance. The narcissist is hurt, cut off, afraid, and feeling damaged so they engage in flights from reality into grandiosity. Yet they describe feeling like ghosts, unseen, without substance.

Unable to access their psychological foundations, they feel flawed, making the changes required through life seem even more daunting. This is a narcissism that has to do not with self-love, but self-hate (Schwartz-Salant, 1982, p. 24). The inter-nal emotional distance forms a vacuum; feeling unlovable brings emotional and physical alienation, escalating into various forms of numbing.

Forays into the past impose themselves on the present and reach back to the original wounds. The lacks, the estrangement or disintegration of selfhood, the con-flict between ego and self, surface and shadow propel the fundamental search for identity. As life unfolds, so does confrontation with the shadow, erupting through projections. There is chaos and melancholy. Confrontation involves engaging with the wounds, reclaiming the damaged parts and integrating the shadow. For the narcissist, it can feel like the disillusionment has no end.

It is insufficient to simply rely on outer adulation or putting on the many pretend façades. The puella or puer represents one of the anxieties of our era, not breathing deeply while being emotionally disconnected. The focus on youth limits and adversely affects achievements and intimacy and promotes idealisation. Life is based on denial. The puella or puer resists the flow from youth into ageing with energy, honour and respect, inclusive of life's entirety. However, by breaking down the need for the ideal, the narcissist can access the self, not only the ego, and can engage with being rather than solely achieving and doing.

The powerlessness of narcissism

A man in his mid-sixties, Jake, enters my office; he's slim, quick thinking, anxious, yet dolorous. 'Some are overflowing with feelings of their own importance … others give up all sense of responsibility, overcome by a sense of powerlessness' (Jung, 1967, CW 7, para. 222). What is he about? I wonder, as I sense a secret walled-off place. Is it from hurt, shame of being? I sense all this at the beginning though it is uncorroborated, covered up as the 'as-if' person is wont to do. Jake recounts the several therapeutic modalities he has engaged in. They all worked, but only to a point. Jake recalled they helped over the many years previously when he quit drugs and alcohol. He is now very fit and focuses on this.

Jake prides himself on being number one. He works hard but despairingly and roughly comments his artistic side remains in a box. He cannot return to it as it is not good enough and he mourns this loss but insists it must be so. It is not clear why he dropped creating sculpture, or whether he really gave it all his effort. Jake talks like he is speaking to himself. Assuring himself his art can go nowhere, he will not consider otherwise. This soliloquy often occurs in the analytical sessions as if he is alone and no one else there. Or he has the answers, and nothing will alter his firm beliefs. It seems that whatever he has loved, he leaves or suddenly stops investing energy. Jake drops out and away. James Hillman (1989, p. 25) described this person as unable to find belonging, or the right niche, always feeling precarious.

He has moved across the country many times in his life, wanting to be in one place or another and then abruptly needing to leave for somewhere else. All this is driven by some force or desire, but it is amorphous. Jake is self-deprecating; nothing satisfies; he cannot accomplish enough. Sadness is part of his narcissistic enclosure. No one can accompany him there as he is now alone. This silent and withheld part is tenacious, and Jake holes up inside. The emotional switch is an inward movement slicing the other away. He comments his third wife is too fat, not introspective and does not understand him, but he says none of this to her. I am not sure how clear his communication is with her. Or whether she represents aspects of himself he cannot accept. Or whether anyone will ever satisfy as intimacy sounds difficult and seemingly has not even been attained.

There was early, deep wounding from a brutal father who Jake described as unfeeling, physically abusive and verbally demeaning. Jake became angry and defiant in response and knew not to trust. He assumed he was unlovable with a central, congenital, ineradicable hideousness. This is what his father told him quite often. Public failure might show this weak spot, so he exposed little publicly, uncertain of complete success. He pushed away whoever tried to get close. The emotional gulf between himself and others deepened, without ever filling up, and he felt hollow.

Having been so shamed as a child by his father, he had to avoid shame. This aspect of narcissism only wants or can handle perfection. Jake cannot be average, so he does nothing. Here is where he suddenly quits, even if on the brink of a success, and implodes. His need to cut himself off from the world takes over and Jake is left alone with his narcissistic ruminations and loneliness. His unrealistic expectations that all must be fabulous make any creative space fraught with conflict and self-doubt. Jake admits he feels a fraud and inadequate; he worries he is not up to the job or his marriage or his ability as a father. He can become quite discouraged, flat, and goes into decline. He says it is ego, but it seems a more massive pull to inner destruction and singularity. Stuck inside and miserable, telling no one, he describes coasting and then determines he is lazy.

He frequently dreams *of being guilty of not doing something.* He has never discovered what it is or why these dreams repeat periodically through his life or what he is supposed to do. He does not proceed further into the dream mystery, halting as usual either because he dreads the answers or feels he cannot answer the demand of the dream. For example, he wanted to have his own business but never did. He wanted to continue his art but never did. He wants endlessly but never does.

A childhood of violence left Jake with a shattered self, and this led to a shattered world. He internalised the experiences and identified with the violent father, so he now inflicts the violence on himself. He hated his father, and this hate became his own internalised hate, his fault and badness, even when he knew otherwise. This father was his only model for masculinity.

A child's emotional development is shaped by parents who are the original models for trust and love. Jake got none of these, but he did get betrayal. There was no safe place for attachment, except with his equally traumatised brother. They were both belittled, told they were no good and blamed for numerous infractions whether they did them or not. All this left him insecure, rageful, isolated, lonely, desiring connection but unable to communicate his heart or find self-love. His mother did not protect herself or her children. Jake experienced emotional betrayal by both parents with their neglect and violence.

One of the results of this kind of trauma is shame and rage. The world becomes divided into me versus them and is overlaid with loneliness and separateness. Each day Jake plays the same inner rant, telling himself he amounts to nothing. He became solitary as a child with private spaces no one knew about. He feels fortunate to have made it through the chances he took with his life yet fears he is like his violent father, loaded with bitter, vicious hatred. His anger and self-deprecation allow no one close, and he seems unaware of the comfort of intimacy and is estranged from the unconscious, its shadow elements, unused potential and his core self.

The process of hate began early as he could not express it outwardly to parents who were the perpetrators. No one knew what he experienced, felt or the tenderness he had to bury to survive. He could not find a sense of belonging as something was always off. He was embarrassed and shy of his needs, and his low self-esteem made it almost impossible to reveal himself. Shame kept him isolated.

Jake learned to ignore feelings, and life repeated the early absence of sufficient loving attachment. The investment in self became dismantled, leaving behind psychic holes. Recognising the wounded places, regrets, the abandonments and betrayals, big and small, provoked troubling, deeply challenging losses. The grief around this has remained, although resisted and unmourned. He unconsciously avoided it as it seemed too large, but this also led to debilitating anxiety and a sense of inadequacy.

He dreamt *of a great white shark and before this thought to move to California.* The shark is the part that attacks; he fears it, but it takes over and kills anything good. He conceives the world as dangerous. The continual chatter inside is like a ticker tape. He cannot do it, so why try? He does not have what it takes. Jake says he is always angry, like the dream shark with his killer thoughts, and does not talk things out, commenting others are distant, but he seems even more so. No one knows him completely and he prefers that.

He wants to be creative again but pushes down the excitement and stops any movement in this direction. Uneasy, he wants to know how to live. The inner battle wears him down and ruins anything creative, killing life itself.

Jake says he is a fraud and childish, but this is said in a destructive, angry and defeated tone. These are the self-denigrating places, ripping at the self he hides from others. On one hand, he can be naïve, saying he gives his ideas away without taking any credit. On the other, Jake isolates from people, viciously turning from the world. He has trouble expressing his emotions and gets stuck inside the words when they cannot come out. He can get by but does not want to and yet he is lazy. He struggles with the narcissism of perfection where nothing can be average, so in defeat he often does nothing.

Over time, slowly, Jake begins to trust and be more open about his inner misery. He does not have to be or pretend to be successful and can bring into the therapy sessions his reflections and distress. He had not imagined he could do this and dreamt *of me in a session with him, but it took place 30 years ago. At that time, he said he was in therapy with a woman who had faith in him. She encouraged him and it was a big time of change.* Jung said, 'We expect to find in dreams everything that has ever been of significance in the life of humanity, just as human life is not limited to this or that fundamental instinct but builds itself from a multiplicity of instincts, needs, desires, and physical and psychic conditions' (1969, CW 8, para. 527). In fact, the positive transference implied in the dream is often the nature of the psychoanalytical sessions. They tend to honesty and truth in relating, as much as he can reveal. There is enough good relationship so the attachment can hold and the challenge to open the psyche and some of his secrets can be met. I am allowed into his usually shut-off world.

As time went on, the therapeutic relationship becomes a place where he feels met. He says I know him best and he has said more about himself than ever before. I feel there is much he still holds back, but he can be more of who he struggled to be inside. He is writing in a journal daily and feels more centred. He keeps up meditation, and his solo bike riding is important as well. Jung said: 'The only way to get at [unconscious contents] is to try to attain a conscious attitude which allows the unconscious to co-operate instead of being driven into opposition' (1946/1966, CW 16, para. 366).

He dreamt *of modules about a foot wide and three feet high and they fit together. He almost bypassed them as the voices in the dream put him down and said they are nothing unusual. But they are practical and made from recycled plastic and are arranged in squares and circles like snowflakes.* They sound mandala-like, imaging a sense of wholeness, a good building material and with the strength for holding together. These shapes fit, are organised, and he is now making order out of the internal chaos. Finally, there is some inner repose, reflective thoughts and a return to himself as the singularity of narcissism opens to include the other.

On the other hand, the dark sides return periodically, draining his energy and wrapping him in the bubble of narcissism and aloneness. Jake reports body disgust as he gained a bit of weight and wants to be thin again. His physical appearance counts greatly but it never satisfies. He recounts an argument he had in his head with the almonds on his desk. He decided against eating them and this was a victory. But what does it mean to engage the mind in such a restrictive way? What does it detract from life? There is a regulated amount to be taken in and it is done so rigidly. For him it represented a bit of triumph against the inner negative voices. Might it represent increasing self-care? Might it show the rules lording over his creativity and expended in small things?

Analysis is a kind of echo chamber through which, like Echo, the analyst opens the space with the analysand to hear themselves. For Jake, this means perceiving himself, listening, and both of us being more attentive to what could arise from the therapeutic relationship. By this time, Jake is less rigid and more able to move towards rather than away from. This happens because the relationship is strong enough to make space for him to trust, feel he is heard and can reveal himself. This occurs as an analyst returns to the analysand his or her own words, the ends of sentences, fragments of a story, to facilitate development and knowledge. It is a process as Jung acknowledged. '[T]he factors which come together in the coniunctio [or the coming together] are conceived as opposites, either confronting one another in enmity or attracting one another in love' (Jung, 1963b, CW 14, para. 1).

Possibility

Narcissism holds the potential, the charm, the energy and the possibility, if one can open to being vulnerable, accepting the shadow and what it means to be real with others. 'The beginning of conscious life was the end of illusion, the illusion of non-being, and the eruption of the real' (McEwan, 2016, pp. 2–3). This is part of the task in learning to love. It can be the crossroads for growth and development, the phoenix rising from the ashes, the melancholy explored rather than denied.

There is an oscillation between longing for transformation and escape from constriction combined with the need to cling to the images presented to the world. Casting off outgrown selves and overused façades leads to nakedness and renewal. Jung said this about maintaining balance of the psyche:

> This is how you must live – without reservation, whether in giving or withholding, according to what the circumstances requires. Then you will get through. After all, if you should still get stuck, there is always the enantiodromia from the unconscious, which opens new avenues when conscious will and vision are failing.
>
> (Jung, 1987, p. 156)

Learning to love self and others means unwrapping the personality layers and living the raw truths of oneself.

At the end of the myth Narcissus is undone by love for his own image and withers away by the pool gazing after his image longingly. He does not realise it is himself. The dramatic ending moment is one of sorrow and grief. Echo is in the distance watching, alive but without body, unseen and unnoticed, but still with a voice. Where Narcissus died is found a flower, its yellow centre circled by white petals. Known as a narcissus or daffodil, the flower blooms in spring, often around Easter, and is associated with rebirth or resurrection. Love brings self-awareness, the challenge of a depth of feelings and propels a unity for including the other. 'The proximity of otherness within the self … both constitutive of the self and at the same time destabilizes any self-certainty, self-sameness, and self-unity' (Oliver, 2015, p. 42).

> And that is not done without danger, without pain, without loss – of moments of self, of consciousness, of persons one has been, goes beyond, leaves. It doesn't happen without expense – of sense, time, direction.
>
> (Sellers, 1994, p. 43)

We are made of many, not one, coming to ourselves through others.

Note

1   Alejandra Pizarnik's "This – Night," the poem (1969) is from a collection of uncollected poems written between 1969 and 1971, in a 17-page manuscript entrusted to the poet Perla Rotzait.

References

Britton, R. (1998). *Belief and imagination: Explorations in psychoanalysis*. Routledge.

Cavalli, A. (2014). Clinging, gripping holding, containment: Reflection on a survival reflex ad the development of a capacity to separate. *Journal of Analytical Psychology*, *59*(4), 548–65. doi: 10.1111/1468-5922.12101.

Connolly, A. (2011). Healing the wounds of our fathers: Intergenerational trauma, memory, symbolization and narrative. *Journal of Analytical Psychology*, *56*(5), 607–26. doi: 10.1111/j.1468-5922.2011.01936.x.

Czubinska, G. (2020). Difference – Is it hated or desired? Reflections on the totalitarian state of mind. *Journal of Analytical Psychology*, *65*(2), 325–44. doi: 10.1111/1468-5922.12587.

DeArmitt, P. (2013). *The right to narcissism: An impossible self-love*. Fordham University Press.

de Koning, A. (1998). Beyond his story: From interpretation to impact from different cultures. *Journal of Analytical Psychology*, *43*(4), 559–70. doi: 10.1111/1465-5922.00053.

Derrida, J. (2005). *Rogues: Two essays on reason*. Stanford University Press.

Fordham, M. (1986). *Explorations into the self*. Routledge.

Freud, S. (1949). On narcissism: An introduction (J. Riviere, Trans.). In: E. Jones (ed.), Collected papers: *Vol. IV* (pp. 3–59). The Hogarth Press.

Hillman, J. (1989). *Puer papers*. Spring Publications.

Jung, C.G. (1946/1966). *The collected work of C.G. Jung: Vol. 16. The practice of psychotherapy*. Princeton University Press.

Jung, C.G. (1956). *The collected works of C.G. Jung: Vol. 5. Symbols of transformation*. Princeton University Press.

Jung, C.G. (1959). *Four archetypes: Mother, rebirth, spirit, trickster*. Princeton University Press.

Jung, C.G. (1963a). *Memories, dreams, reflections* (A. Jaffé, ed.). Collins.

Jung, C.G. (1963b). *The collected works of C.G. Jung: Vol. 14. Mysterium Coniunctionis*. Routledge.

Jung, C.G. (1966). *The collected works of C.G. Jung: Vol. 15. The spirit in man, art, and literature*. Princeton University Press.

Jung, C.G. (1967). *The collected works of C.G. Jung: Vol. 7. Two essays in analytical psychology. Collected works 7*. Princeton University Press.

Jung, C.G. (1969). *The collected works of C.G. Jung: Vol. 8. The structure and dynamics of the psyche*. Princeton University Press.

Jung, C.G. (1973). *C.G. Jung Letters: Vol. 1*. Princeton: Princeton University Press.

Jung, C.G. (1987). *C.G. Jung speaking: Interviews and encounters* (R.F.C. Hull, ed.). Princeton: Princeton University Press.

Kohon, G. (ed.) (1999). *The dead mother: The work of André Green*. London: Routledge.

Kristeva, J. (1992). *Black sun*. Columbia University Press.

McEwan, I. (2016). *Nutshell*. Knopf.

Mollon, P. (1994). *The fragile self: The structure of narcissistic disturbance*. Jason Aronson.

Oliver, K. (Ed.) (2002). *The portable Kristeva. Columbia University Press*.

Oliver, K. (2015). Psychoanalysis and deconstruction, A Love Story. *Journal of French and Francophone Philosophy*, *23*(2), 35–44.

Ovid (1993). *The metamorphoses of Ovid* (A. Mandelbaum, Trans.). Harcourt.

Schwartz-Salant, N. (1982). *Narcissism and character transformation: The psychology of narcissistic character disorders*. Inner City Books.

Sellers, S. (1994). *The Hélène Cixous reader*. Routledge.

Solomon, H. (2004). Self creation and the limitless void of dissociation: The as if personality. *Journal of Analytical Psychology*, *49*(5), 635–56. doi: 10.1111/j.0021-8774.2004.00493.x.

von Franz, M-L (2000). *The problem of the puer aeternus*. Inner City Books.

West, M. (2010). Envy and difference. *Journal of Analytical Psychology*, *55*(4), 459–84.

Winnicott, D. (1960). The maturational process and the facilitating environment: Studies in the theory of emotional development. *Karnac*.

Chapter 6

Blank, void, emptiness

Hansel and Gretel are the young children of a poor woodcutter. When a famine settles over the land, the woodcutter's second wife tells the woodcutter to take the children into the woods and leave them there to fend for themselves, so that she and her husband do not starve to death. The woodcutter opposes the plan, but his wife claims that maybe a stranger will take the children in and provide for them, which the woodcutter and she simply cannot do. With the scheme seemingly justified, the woodcutter reluctantly is forced to submit to it. They are unaware that in the children's bedroom, Hansel and Gretel have overheard them. After the parents have gone to bed, Hansel sneaks out of the house and gathers as many white pebbles as he can, then returns to his room, reassuring Gretel that God will not forsake them.

The next day, the family walk deep into the woods and Hansel lays a trail of white pebbles. After their parents abandon them, the children wait for the moon to rise and then follow the pebbles back home. They return home safely, much to their stepmother's rage. Once again, provisions become scarce, and the stepmother angrily orders her husband to take the children further into the woods and leave them there. Hansel and Gretel attempt to gather more pebbles, but find the front door locked.

***

Although often presenting with a coat of entitlement, expecting grandeur and exaltation, the 'as-if' person is consumed with sorrow and loss despite appearances to the contrary. This person lives on illusions and the need to continually re-establish these illusions, which requires much effort and self-avoidance. However, the deleterious effects of this personality adaptation are mitigated by the inherent capacity of the psyche to repair. Dreams, relationships and symbols appear in daily life as the life force seeks to reignite out of the emptiness, an ego state of painful loss or desolation.

André Green, with his concepts of blank, void, emptiness, absence and negation expands the descriptors of the 'as-if' personality. 'Psychic abandonment affects access to the self ... setting up internal world attack, time frozen, investment in self dismantled and void occupying the mind' (Green, 2011, p. 193). These ideas

DOI: 10.4324/9781003315254-7

plus the clinical examples in this chapter are mixed with references to Jungian ana-lytical psychology and portray the sombre nature of this subject. The fairytale of Hansel and Gretel exemplify many aspects of children left to fend for themselves, abandoned, without sufficient sources of love. It illustrates their resilience and abil-ity to survive nonetheless.

The situation

Ethan spent his life shaping himself and his body to be primed for adulation and admiration by others. This was his lifeblood. He needed to be noticed but had not realised how much until the attention was not as forthcoming as it had previously been. Somehow, as he got older, it seemed harder. Ethan had always been able to put on the charm. What had happened? Was he losing the spark he used to rely on? He dressed for others, made his career for them, wanted their gaze on him. All those years he put on a show. Even as a child he wanted centre stage. He strove for it. And it seemed to come easily. He now had to reluctantly admit to himself that more drugs or alcohol were required to maintain the effort.

> This is allegory, as lavishness of that which no longer is, but which regains for myself a higher meaning because I am able to remake nothingness, better than it was and within an unchanging harmony, here and now and forever.
>
> (Kristeva, 1992, p. 99)

He wondered if this was a bigger problem than he realised. Ethan's dreams became more intense; *something frightening was chasing him while he was half dressed, panicked and didn't even know where he was running to or what he was running from.* These felt like the nightmare dreams he had as a child of a wolf coming after him. Not only did the dreams make him distressed but he was lonelier and afraid he could not manifest his professional desires or find love. He basically did not know what was wrong.

He was facing the clash between desires and fears and the psychological conun-drum in drawing back from wanting, reaching or getting. He was overcome with uncertainty and disappointment, and he could not yet see a larger vision or other options for his life. These disturbed musings brought him to Jungian analytical psychology. Inside, his self was frozen, blank and vulnerable. He avoided intimacy and felt numb. 'Part of the person remains too young; experienced as "the child", while the true self remains hidden deep within the personality. [He] becomes an "as-if" self' (Wilkinson, 2003, p. 241). The malady of the soul appears in this 'as-if' personality based on façade and illusions that mask needs, traumas and self-despair. In therapy, the coping adult self appeared in contrast to his obscured and abused younger aspects.

Ethan was now at middle age and noticed anxiety in his chest along with aches and pains. He worried about his age and how he could retain his allure. He was used to knowing he was attractive to others, but now he was between relationships.

His past relationships had been easy but sporadic, mostly short term, dissolving due to his boredom, unease and not wanting so much intimacy. He could hardly handle it. He felt a bundle of nerves. He was at a crossroads. Who was he? He was not going where he wanted. Life seemed fleeting, to be passing him by. All these doubts hounded him. For the first time he could find no easy answers.

Ethan was suffering in many ways; he was disconnected, uneasy, confused. Not an unusual feeling for so many with the 'as-if' personality type. They live on the food served from the outside, but the inside starves for nourishment. They feel empty and dry. There is a struggle to find an integrated sense of 'I', as British Jungian analyst William Meredith-Owen noted (2011, p. 674).

The words *blank*, *void* and *emptiness* describe some aspects of the internal disconnections experienced by the 'as-if' person, who often has an attractive personality and is well liked. This is a major defence. Ethan knows there is something he needs but anticipates there will only be hunger and unmet desire. This kind of person may dream of being in space, unmoored, floating, scared about being so alone, yet they attempt to eliminate the vague realisation there is nothing at the centre, as the self seems void and unable to hold.

The sense of nothingness is covered by many layers. Years ago, Ethan developed a secret fantasy world for inner soothing, privacy and containment. His relationships have an adhesive quality, but only for a while. The 'as-if' person connects by melding into the other to please but remains unknown, their history unexplored and their fragile sense of self undisturbed.

The symbolic for healing and filling in the blank

Gradually in the analytical treatment Ethan began to recall his dreams, honour the synchronicities in his life, the reasons for his thoughts and even to empathise with how far removed he was emotionally from his world. He began to journal more frequently and shared these writings in analysis. Through this sharing we were able to connect to the symbols that emerged in his dreams, synchronicities, thoughts and ideas as they evolved through relationships and the analytic process.

'Symbols [like those appearing in dreams and life] are embedded in a context of communication and can only develop in the context of a relationship' (Colman, 2008, p. 275). A symbolic attitude enhances life and creates value and self-worth. The ability to symbolise relates to finding meaning, connecting life events, bringing conscious and unconscious together to form something creative out of what has been unknown. The analytic relationship opens the old wounds of emptiness so new forms of relating can emerge. The symbols contain life and are ever changing as a person unravels the inner world, coming in touch with their own mystery. 'We can consider symbolization as true imaginative play. It promotes the capacity to fantasize as well as organizing psychic space' (Gibeault, 2005, p. 297).

Although sometimes misunderstood and perhaps confusing, symbols arise out of the relationship between inner and outer, past and present in an unfolding, emerging process. With the ability to symbolise the psyche comes alive. Symbols form from accepting the former painful absence, mourning the losses and opening to other personality developments. 'This emergent, relational aspect of the symbol enables it to take on a living reality in the imaginal world and… restore faith in creative living' (Colman, 2008, p. 293). This can take many forms and leads to creative endeavours that had been formerly blocked.

As Jung described, 'The symbol… will change itself into a starry and riddling image, whose meaning turns completely inward, and whose pleasure radiates outward like blazing fire, like a Buddha in the flames' (2009, p. 249). The ability to symbolise is dependent on the development of an ego sufficiently able to engage with the unconscious. Symbols help widen restrictive paths and open us to larger visions of the psyche and a fuller life. 'Transformation leads people to become more deeply and completely who they are and have always potentially been' (Stein, 1996, xxiv). Throughout the narratives recounted here, you will see examples of the symbolic and how these people used the material to expand the personality and benefit from the resulting widening of consciousness. You also read of those shut off from this process.

Lonely

The following narrative is not unusual in its depiction of the 'as-if' person as very lonely. A woman named Vala, age 42, had been in a relationship for more than ten years but never told her partner the significant details and traumas of her life. And her partner never asked. It was as if, for expediency, they had an unwritten agreement to not go into anything painful or beyond daily life. It was not that they did not have moments of joy, but the mountain of unexplored material kept growing. Eventually Vala left. She did not know why. Nothing had really changed but she could not remain. She felt choked, restricted, uneasy and angry. She began analytical work because something was missing, and although she had no idea what this meant, she knew she had to find out.

Vala had a recurring dream that began in her 20s, and it has come back in the last few months. *She is in a house with a secret room upstairs. She is in another room and sleeping. Then she hears someone. She goes to the top of the stairs. There is a person in a hoodie. Her heart is pounding. Vala goes to bed and the person comes to the bed. She wakes up with a start.* The dream raises many questions. Who is the person? Why are they standing at the bed? What does Vala fear? Is that person a part of Vala? She has not looked into herself for years. What has she been afraid to acknowledge? The person in the hoodie might be the hooded parts of herself now coming to her at a vulnerable place where the unconscious can emerge – in the bed.

The analytical work begins with a rhythm, a consistency, filled with her many dreams, images, wonderings, questions and symbols. After years of poor sleep, in fact since childhood, several months into the analytical treatment she begins to sleep. The more we explore the psychic depths, the calmer she feels. Yet, things had happened she is unwilling to touch or explore as those feelings were long ago put away and nailed shut.

Defence mechanisms, of whatever form, have a protective function. The psyche seemed unable to be penetrated earlier. No one had known her loneliness, the days of childhood spent rooting around in the backyard by herself for hours, and where she internally, quietly and methodically created her own world. It was not just fantasy; she was in a place free of constraints. Her expressiveness was without restriction or critique from parents or siblings. She was making her own life raft of sorts, a boat for survival in a house with many rumblings under the placid-appearing surface.

Vala has found the process of relationships hard, sometimes boring, and she avoids intimacy with sex. In other words, she has been quite free and experimental sexually but not intimate. Under her carefree exterior she is worried about everything and is unsure what she wants. Usually, she does not say what her needs are, but she makes sure she is acceptable to others. She now wonders if this is like her mother's lack of passion. She fears making anyone mad or encountering their disapproval. Otherwise, a nameless anxiety comes over her, and she feels sick. Needing her parents' approval dulled her passionate nature and ability to make independent decisions. She had to hide her wild side. She often dreams of being alone in a hotel, and the feeling is one of impersonal sterility.

Vala automatically learned to hide the details of her personal thoughts. Her parents expressed no empathy, and there was no space for play with them. Over and over, she felt deceived by her parents and never learned it was safe to communicate emotions or honour them. Her fears of abandonment resurface when she gets attached as she begins to worry. Parental absence resulted in her isolation; becoming aware of its desolation is to grieve.

There was no way for her to be thought about or carried in the mind of her emotionally absent mother, a blank personality who did little to care for her and conveyed no expressions of love. Mother was vacant, taking pills for her nerves, engaging in little interaction and doing nothing to teach, give guidance or support. Busy reading travelogues and going nowhere, Mother ignored her. Vala knew to fend for herself and not disturb her. Father was a patriarch, dictatorial; his rules were to be followed, and she was to obey without question. He discouraged independent thought, so she would remain under his thumb.

Her siblings taunted her as her interests were different and more creative. They argued and fought with each other. Safety was not to be had and intimacy was unavailable. She grew up with the fear of someone intruding into her psyche and interrupting her thoughts and feelings.

Richard Mizen, British Jungian analyst, referenced Ester Bick, 20th-century Freudian analyst, on the development of what she called 'psychic skin'. This term means 'the embodied sense of a psychological self. It is the sense of having an inside and outside which exist over time and in tandem' (Mizen, 2014, p. 315). When there is lack of mind/body skin, to compensate, a shell or carapace forms over the centre of the self. Adopting roles is a way to survive and to hide. Defences are erected as a way to feel contained, but they are pasted on and lack solidity. The psychic skin is needed as part of the self.

This psychic skin allows for emotional responsiveness and being present for the experiences of the self. It is a protective mechanism against disintegrating feelings and anxiety (Mizen, 2014, p. 329). In other words, this is how individuals feel cohesive, securely held together, and it comes from being appropriately responded to and appreciated, well mirrored by caregivers. Rather than security, Vala constantly worried whether anything would work out. As a child, she worried whether Santa Claus could find her; as she got older, she feared she wouldn't make the team or find love.

She did not sleep well as a child and used the time to dream and make up stories. Her inside and outside self continued to be unacknowledged by her parents. They took for granted that she would do well in school. Although she was bright, her father limited the books she could read, and she had to sneak into his reading shelf when he was not looking. Even being as strict as he was, she looked forward to his homecoming every day, but after the functional hug he retreated into his own room, too busy to play or interact with her. He required almost militaristic compliance with his rules. He was cold and distant, focused on status and money. Formidable and forbidding, he did not play with his children and was always preoccupied.

Mother was lethargic, disinterested in much besides her children being quiet. She was an icy shell, unable to show warmth or affection to anyone. She was a half-alive woman, without personality and little expression of pleasure or joy. She resided in her psychological cavern, hardly attending to her children, hiring people to get things done, so she herself would be left alone. Vala could not understand until well into the analytical work how vacant and absent her mother was. For so long, no one seemed to notice the blankness of this mother, who assumed the roles of mother and wife without expressing maternal feeling, reactions or interest. Mother was social but never emotional, warm or intimate. No one spoke about this and there was no hope for anything different. Vala was left with having to accept her mother's lack of presence or aliveness.

At issue was the blank mother, absent of emotion or response. André Green's concept of the dead mother complex applies to this mother and her effect on Vala. 'The mother is not actually dead but rather psychically dead, that is, transmogrified from a source of vitality into a distant figure, toneless, practically inanimate' (Green, 2001, p. 170). Vala said, 'I feel like the fog again'. This has come to mean she is frozen, without feeling, a bit dizzy even. These sensations often come up around being spontaneous, having enthusiasm, listening to herself, doing something her mother would never do. And over time it was clearly connected to a mother who, in Green's theoretical concepts, is blank.

Mother seems to be there, but the child is confused. Her body is present, but the rest of her is an empty space.

What is necessary is an actual person to absorb the projection, not a two-dimensional flat production that cannot interact … the undeveloped core of the patient's self [needs to be] allowed … to emit itself from its incarceration

> inside the 'black hole' ... to counteract the massive power of the absence at the heart of the abyss.
>
> (Waldron, 2013, p. 106)

This mother does not realise the harm she causes. She goes to meetings, plays cards, unaware and unavailable.

> Without the felt experience of existing (which is at this stage equivalent to existing in the mind of the other), there is no possibility of representing that which is missing since there is no subject to whom it could be represented.
>
> (Colman, 2008, p. 277)

The psychical non-presence of the mother leaves an indelible mark on the child's developing psyche. The absent object (mother) begins a process whereby, in a desperate attempt to thrive, the child splits off and becomes its own parent.

André Green commented about people suffering from the dead mother complex and experiencing images of black holes. When the possibility of a real relationship emerges, like the analytical one, the dead mother zooms in and a black hole opens (Green, 1986, p. 162). Vala had previously had no place from which to be interpreted, nor did she expect to be acknowledged, much less seen. The possibility of real intimacy was unavailable.

Green described depression from the mother's bereavement as loss and perhaps a deception resting on a secret (1986, p. 149). The father could provide a substitute attachment, but Vala's father remained inaccessible. Anxiety, poor sleep and nightmares can result when neither parent is able to put their heart into a child. Another effect is the loss of self-meaning when childhood is devoid of nurturing and empathy. To surmount dismay at the parental loss, the child develops a 'compulsion to imagine, to think, to master the traumatic situation and to mask the hole left as well as the edge of the abyss of emptiness' (1986, p. 152). A person is left with unremitting and painful loss.

Yet, Vala had kept up a relationship in her mind with a mother who was absent, and she could not let go of what she never had, mourn the process or replace the space. As a result, her life had halted emotionally, and she remained unknown to herself while stuck in the familiar spot of avoiding her mother's dislike. Any movement from this position would involve mourning and relinquishing the former dulled self for the one still unknown.

An interior symbolic world that is valued becomes constructed through experiences of optimal connection and separation (Feldman, 2002, p. 399). Vala did not experience this connection, however, as her parents showed no affection to her or to each other, but neither did they fight. Mother was just not available for any emotional or related responses. With this mother, no real human connection was formed. Father was angry – a man to stay away from. Family life revolved around a mechanised order that masked the emptiness. In fact, Vala does not recall her parents being together except during large family occasions. She did not like these events when she had to wear something she did not want to and usually found herself wandering around alone or sitting in the corner by herself. She muses about the influence of an unresponsive mother and how her body accommodated and responded to this form of intrusive and controlling energy. She knows it affected how she sought security as she approached many life situations.

Vala's fears of abandonment emerge when she gets attached. She does not know her value or why people like her. She keeps trying to fix whoever she is with, but of course she never can. Who is she trying to repair and make better? The focus is too much outside herself. She worries she will burden others, so she does not verbalise her needs or depressions. Habitual defensive responses are associated with a wide range of rigid patterns governing the self and other and the rather empty experience of relationships. These cement the feelings of shame, guilt, grief or anxiety while inhibiting and repressing other feelings such as anger, curiosity or aliveness.

How do children learn to defend against the blank spaces from parents? When feelings are split off and a pseudo maturity takes over, they feel they either lack a solid identity or have a fluid sense of self (Mizen, 2014, p. 316). The inner world remains undeveloped and its riches unplumbed. This is not apparent to the outer world as already in childhood people like Vala become adept at hiding reactions and are self-reliant, leaving dependency needs unexpressed as they learn no good can come from expressing them.

The body reveals nonverbal and somatic aspects of the psyche. The wounded places, subjective language and wisdom are expressed in a split-off body complex that holds knowledge about the requirements for psychic balance. Whenever its needs are denied or its messages ignored, it speaks. Jung commented,

> Whatever has an intense feeling tone is difficult to handle because such contents are associated with physiological reactions, with the processes of the heart, the tonus of the blood vessels, the condition of the intestines, the breathing and innervation of the skin.
>
> (Jung, 1935/1977, CW 18, para. 148)

To become embodied is to risk being overwhelmed by intense feelings of anguish over the loss of bonding and subsequent lack of mirroring. Vala experienced what could be called 'life nausea', an existential dread; she lacked security. She took calming over-the-counter medications for years before coming to this realisation, but she was still unaware of the cause or what she was defending against.

In childhood, Vala retreated to the void as it became a solitary place for confinement of the self (Solomon, 1998, p. 228). She felt estranged from others, except her nanny and aunt. With no reliable parent for connection or attachment, she created a self-to-self world in her play and in her mind. Vala locked herself within this interior world, blocking entry to anyone else. There, alone, she could be herself and she knew how to become enriched. Otherwise, the need for safety and security remained paramount but unmet.

Engagement with others was often experienced as non-engagement. Many mechanisms had been set in place to defend against this disturbing feeling. Because it is so painful and occurs so early, the child adopts defences for protection against anticipated harm. Yet, the micro-moments of hurt, disillusionment and disappointment are repeated as life goes on until they are valued and subsequently transformed.

Vala's initial dream opens her world. Its repetition keeps her engaged and she gradually unpeels the layers of her personality, stuck together like glue for so long. It is frightening at times, disconcerting and brings tears. Yet, she persists and her journey both inward and outward brings rewards she could not have imagined at the beginning.

The 'as-if' person attains a modicum of security when others are pleased or not depressed or somehow the situation is restored to a form of equilibrium. At some point, the person will eventually have to face the void – a vast emptiness – as well as the primary existential anguish and panic repressed for survival. Vala lived in a frozen state for many years. 'Early experiences of internalizing the presence of an absent object, create the sense of an internal void at the core of the Self' (Solomon, 2004, p. 635). For many, desire is killed, and this impedes psychological transformation. Yet, the self naturally evolves as the seeds of identity are there from the beginning. Vala's psyche remained underground until it finally began to emerge and develop, leading to synthesis and transformation.

For Vala, psychic reality rested on a precarious ledge, as she lived in a state of suspension, dread, as if walking a tightrope. The predominant impression is of internalising an empty, lifeless void, and the question is how to survive this bleak and often life-threatening experience (Solomon, 2004, p. 642). Defences are erected, blocking the readiness to defend against the impact of others as they felt threatened in the past. Vala comments about not learning how to be, to trust, to let in, to show emotion, to be real. There were no models. Rather, annihilation could happen at any time, like when her beloved nanny was dismissed suddenly and without explanation. Her questions were met with nothing – no answers, a vagueness. Vala was left with sorrow and mourning for the one person who cared for and understood her. The parental reaction was to move on, and Vala's emotions were ignored and unaddressed, as always. This was the pervasive message. She translated this to mean she had to be in complete control because the outer world was unreceptive and even denigrating to her feelings. It became foreign for her to realise interdependency, to be intimately known by another, without her assuming artifice. She had to be totally self-reliant and manage others.

There are numerous interpretations of the 'as-if' person who is hard to reach (Proner, 2017, p. 568). All these interpretations and descriptors are an attempt to understand and ground what seems elusive. The person exists within a protective shell, living within their own invented reality. This is a safe place that protects from the assumed threats, insecurities and dangers of the outside world. The fragility of the ego, or the I part of the personality, is strongly and often unconsciously defended against basic anxieties about the ability to survive. On some level, existence is always at stake. This manifests as the self in conflict with itself, attacks through harsh inner talk, destructive food habits, body disconnect as the 'as-if' person lives a solitary existence in an empty universe (Solomon, 1998, p. 232).

Relationships are difficult as the 'as-if' person is shaped by the underlying river of feared yet anticipated abandonment (Proner, 2017, p. 569). Sharing has become fraught and internally forbidden. Distrust prevails, rampant from the inside but unseen and unimagined to the outside world. Helene Deutsch, who in the 1940s came up with the concept of the 'as-if' personality, described their inner experience as completely excluded (1942, p. 302). Not only is it excluded from others, but the person is so busy creating an image and deflecting energy away from the painful areas they remain oblivious to what they are doing or feeling. The person avoids and evades, even though they seem to cooperate and comply with what is wanted or desired by others. All is aimed at keeping the unknown and needy parts of the self at bay. This can occur through concrete thinking and being so busy there is no time to think.

Various descriptors have been applied to this personality type such as the *impostor syndrome* used in current pop psychology; the *false self*, noted by Donald Winnicott; and the *'as-if' personality* more recently described by Hester Solomon. Attention to the 'as-if' personality in psychoanalytic literature has been mostly associated with women. However, fraudulent feelings and the fear of being found insufficient are not gender-based but indicate broader issues of misconnection with self and others.

In analytical work the 'as-if' person is compliant, follows what they think is expected, looking for rules, wanting approval, trying to be correct and doing it right. If anything is off or they sense they are not accepted for something, shame spreads over the psyche. The transference might be set up as a sameness with the analyst or therapist so nothing new emerges. This creates a strange twinship, unconsciously symbiotic, defensive and without differentiation. Internally the person remains untouched so nothing can shake the system. Shifting this fragile house of cards is threatening.

There is a tendency to be secretive about everything personal, painful or close to the bone of their being. There is a rumbling undercurrent of falling apart, and this must be prevented. Therefore, the world becomes quite narrow and tightly contained. Any movement out of the old routines is stymied, the imagination shallow and compromised due to an inner feeling of hollowness, an echo chamber with little else in this arid landscape (Proner, 2017, p. 571). Superficial adaptation and social successes are necessary, and creativity compensates, however it is accompanied by feelings of fraudulence and an inner loneliness admitted to no one.

Disembodiment

With the 'as-if' person, there is loss of investment in the body – even though it looks like they pay physical attention to the body or try to make an outstanding impression. However, the act is based on maintaining detachment, needing adulation and remaining an outsider. A negativity fills the body. Any form of subjectivity that reduces, simplifies and renders a person as surface is already a form of annihilation and a wilful disappearance of the body. This can occur through many forms of disembodiment. Some who have the 'as-if' personality become preoccupied with pornography, affairs, compulsive sports, diets. Sometimes there is a flood of energy but then the person is drained and carries a sense of heaviness and life is again without meaning. States of overwhelming affect and the attack on the spontaneous psychosomatic being of the self occur with this form of self-hatred and self-division (Colman, 2008, p. 351). There also is an apathy to self. Why care? A haze comes over the person and then it does not matter.

This psychic deadness manifests in states of disembodiment (Connolly, 2013, p. 636) and relates to loss of body ownership and body imagery so that inner and outer are dissonant. 'Growing older is mainly an ordeal of the imagination – a moral disease, a social pathology…' (Sontag, 1978). It is the body that connects us to the world and where we feel real. However, the 'as-if' person neither feels close to their body nor do they feel alive. The body is rather an object to be adorned, fashioned and artificially shaped. It is a body image 'involving an abstract and partial representation of the body in perception, thought and evaluation emotionally and one attends to one body aspect at a time' (Connolly, 2013, p. 638). The body is in pieces and separated from the mind. They feel disjointed, in pieces, not a whole; the impression of oneself is 'as-if' removed. Internal physical states are cut into bits, reduced to minute, tender body feelings. They no longer sense much and therefore can easily disappear, seeming to be without meaning or affect. 'The body is simply a body, an object that has nothing to do with me' (Connolly, 2013, p. 639).

An example of this disembodiment is a patient I will call Sophie. She described herself as engaging in years of what she called debauchery. She just did not care and needed heightened danger and distant and elusive partners to feel anything. It took several years in analytical treatment to discover the reasons. As a child she was continually told to settle down, be quiet, not be so active, that she was too much. Her physical energy was upsetting to parents who only wanted decorum. They were not just distant; they were removed, not only ignoring but also discouraging her body movements. Temperamentally, they were at odds, and Sophie lacked physical or psychological mirroring. As a result, her 'body image was external to the self, something mechanical, inanimate, and even dead at times' (Connolly, 2013, p. 645). As an adult she remained distant from herself, engaging in sexual affairs, not really caring but seeking something, a connection, a feeling, but this too remained elusive. Usually, she was detached and kept herself in shape to be attractive to others and to look appealing. There was no thought of health or well-being, however, and she was not sure she even cared. Getting in touch with the natural truth in her body might provide a sense of aliveness but she had no experience of this. All of us contain information within the body to connect us to earth and a solid reality. Sophie's harsh experiences and conditioning disconnected her from the wisdom of her body.

To become embodied was to risk being overwhelmed by intense feelings of anguish over the loss of bonding and lack of mirroring. The body expresses non-verbal and somatic aspects of the psyche. It becomes split-off, but it also holds the potential and necessity for psychic balance. The body does not forget, and neither does the psyche. Whenever physical needs are denied or its messages ignored, it speaks – maybe constructively if we listen and destructively if we don't. As Jung said,

> Whatever has an intense feeling tone is difficult to handle because such contents are associated with physiological reactions, with the processes of the heart, the tonus of the blood vessels, the condition of the intestines, the breathing and innervation of the skin.
>
> (Jung, 1935/1977, CW 18, para. 148)

Sophie lived removed from herself. She kept all the painful early hurts as secrets inside. All energy went towards surviving, finding security, being self-reliant, depending on no one, never how she felt. Julia Kristeva poignantly described what goes on underneath and is kept unconscious. This is 'the feeling of falling into pieces that may be caused either by non-integration impeding the cohesion of the self, or by disintegration and anxieties that provoke psychological splitting' (1992, p. 18). Sophie became absorbed in work, found friends who were not intimate, kept busy while life felt unreal, lived at a distance. She was not attached to anything inside and had closed those doors firmly long ago. She felt terror about opening them. She had no way to cope with the emotions and no models for handling any of the old, repressed feelings. She did worry about rejection and worked hard to make sure no one really knew her well enough to find the flaws.

She kept trying to gain some relationship with family, but each time she visited she came away disappointed, unhappy and depleted. She always lost weight. She felt her very presence was irksome to them. She wondered what she did wrong, why they did not like her and determined she would be better next time. There was little thought it might be them, that they were the ones who were emotionally deadened and distant, unable to connect or show love and warmth. Over and over, she excused them and their behaviour towards her, assessing she was the problem.

What happened to Sophie? She chose partners who replicated not only her parent's marriage, but also a quality of unavailability experienced in both mother and father. The parents' own ways of relating, both conscious and unconscious, were internalised and became part of the child and then the adult fantasy world.

Sophie focused on her body and style but as a shield for invisibility and distancing. Internally all remained unexplored, blank and empty. She controlled her food as a way to remain emotionally deadened. This took the form of starving or eating a lot, then starving again and engaging in intense exercise. Especially when anxious, she turned to thoughts of food, either to binge or to deprive herself, exercising often or worrying about her body. This submerged any focus on herself, the inner non-feeling, the blank and overwhelming thoughts that she was nothing and going nowhere.

It is through the unity of psyche and soma that we access the key to the feeling for life. This is what Winnicott called 'the feeling of real' (1971, p. 80). But Sophie spent her childhood responding to the intrusions of others who were not in rhythm with her, and the continuity of her being was unreinforced. Sophie had yet to cope with the non-representation of life, the anguish, the nothingness and the terror there was no one there. Early in life she learned to ban the show of feelings. With an emotionally abusive father and preoccupied mother, everyone in the family strove to just survive. Food was sometimes there and sometimes not. No one checked to see if she made it to school. She recalls being close to her sisters but was uneasy with her harassing brother. There was nothing steady or predictable except each day she knew to be on high alert.

The emotionally and physically unstable situation, although filled with chaos, was also filled with the type of absence described in the following quote:

> Here external absence is also and at the same time internal absence because it is an absence of and from the self, a dissociation. The psychic trauma of absence then transmutes into 'something', while the absence itself becomes marked as 'nothing', a nothing which in fact operates as though it were 'something' with a profound and deeply intrusive impact on the vulnerable self.
>
> (Colman, 2008, p. 277)

A person hardly realises the full impact of this absence. Some have said it is like a dread, a terror that is always present and lurking.

Sophie dreamt of houses repeatedly over several years. In the latest dreams she recognised their import but not exactly what they meant. Here is the first dream:

> There is a shaky looking house, and it does not look good. I knew it was me and I did not want it to be, as it was decrepit and did not look great. The next scene was a strong, double story house with a vineyard around it. It was going to be painted pink, but this has not yet happened. The old house has been taken apart, deconstructed, and was now reconstructed as the new sturdy house. Nothing was lost from the old to the new house.

Sophie awoke knowing nothing was lost from the past difficult experiences and was being reused to create a better house. She previously felt as desolate as the shaky house and now in the dream she had the energy to reconstruct the big and beautiful new pink house to live in. Sophie was pleased she had the house rearranged – bigger, classy, pink and feminine. Each beam had been moved from the old to the new as it was being transformed. She said the house was like her and she could now safely make herself different with a more elegant and stronger style. She wanted to live in the second house, and it appealed to her. We talked in some detail about the house symbolising the self and the beams as her bones. All the old material was being reused, taken apart and put together in a sturdier way.

Sophie further associated to the dream in the next session. She realised it represented two parts of her life. One she called 'I am no longer' and the other 'I am'. She said the latter part was unfinished. She recalled being lied to by her parents, her feelings being negated, or told she had to keep family secrets. Like the time she told mother that father was drunk, an alcoholic who drank each night. Mother denied this and told Sophie to tell no one. The real was rapidly denied.

The daily sabotage to the system illustrates something crucial was not fed, held or seen. She faced 'disconnection from the body, or not being fully "embodied": the presence of an idealized, dynamic and potent – but elusive – self; and of a weaker, passive version of self, which was disregarded in a shadow sense, or even despised' (Goss, 2006, p. 681). Sophie commented she spent years drifting, unable to find anyone to understand, love or give any guidance. She had been afloat and confused.

In a much later dream *she was in a haunted house. She was forced into the upper attic where she was abused as a girl. A ghost was there but there was a man who said he will pray with her and protect her. The room had been cleared out and was no longer cluttered. It was painted white, and she was not afraid anymore. The ghost had been exorcised.* She was pleased because she was connecting the dreams and not so afraid. She knew she had not wanted to go into that room but then went in. Although scared at first, she had to go into the old fear. As she went in, she was not alone, and a priest was with her. He represented a better father figure, and his energy was transformative to the story. He could protect, had spiritual knowledge, and she knew he cared about her. The room was no longer dark but white, a darkness turned into light, just as the helpful father changed from the previously abusive one. She called the dream one of release. The priest performed an exorcism to eradicate the evil. She was beginning to recover from the bad energy received from her physically abusive father and the traumas that trapped her for years in confusion and despair. In the dream figure of the priest, a man from the spiritual world, she had a good inner figure to guide her. Her personality was shored up and with it her creative endeavours as well. She began speaking about her experiences through art, podcasts and presentations, no longer hiding or feeling unsafe, trapped in a dark frightening room.

As we continued discussing the dream I recalled its similarity with the Bluebeard fairy tale, a common motif in which the husband, in the form of the negative and destructive masculine energy, kills the wives and locks them in a secret room to which only he has the key. The female heroine must get the key and outwit this malevolent male force, hateful to the feminine and a destructive killer of all forms of the female. In the end of the fairy tale, the heroine amasses the fortitude, and realises she has the strength, to kill the bad male energy, which is replaced by a different figure with a compatible and caring love.

Later Sophie dreamt:

> *It started with a face-off with a man. We were about 10 feet apart from each*
> *other in a room, both carrying shotguns. I was shooting him in the chest over*
> *and over, but he wasn't wounded. His shots at me weren't working either and*
> *I ran out of ammo. I needed to reload and ran to the bathroom even though*
> *I had no idea how to reload a gun. My eye was bleeding, one single drop of*
> *blood running down the tear duct. I don't know what my next move would be.*
> *The scene changes and I am approaching a large old gravesite decorated with*
> *growing vines. A man was sitting on the tombstone watching over it. I had no*
> *desire to approach him. The gravesite had a strong presence I don't know how*
> *to describe but felt a lot stirring up.*

As we talked about the dream, more memories were stirred up, things long buried. For years she had been fighting like in the beginning of the dream with the man. She had been in a power conflict with him and males like him for so very long, driven by being intimidated by male power. This she associated with her brother harassing her, calling her names, bullying and degrading her. It seemed she might also have been sexually abused by him, but this was heavily veiled. She also has sorrow as shown by the tear drop of blood. This she associated with no one understanding her, her parents wanting her to get along with her brother and remaining ignorant about his terrible bullying and her upset and fear of him. Sophie had no clue how to load the gun or what led her to the gravesite where she encountered yet another man. Yet, she discovered she was a brave warrior, using her abilities and qualities for her protection, asserting herself. She was no longer helpless. All this was in the dream, mirroring an unconscious situation now brought to consciousness.

To add a classical and controversial term in Jungian psychology, this man could be termed the *animus*. He takes several forms in this one dream, each representing various forms of the masculine energy. Sophie is beginning to access this male energy by facing him and realising she has the ability, courage, strength and power not only to fight him but also to be herself and fully engage with life. Until now she has succumbed to males, giving in sexually, not developing her talents or taking herself seriously. Males have encroached on her body, and she has simultaneously diminished her intellect. In the dream she is more able than she thought and can now accept these qualities and use them. She can utilise her own male energy rather than be overtaken by it, either within herself or in the outer world.

Her relationships mirrored the distance and coldness in her family. She was content to not reveal herself as she learned early on that was safer. Her unmet emotional needs left her with a gnawing hunger. The impasse in her life, like confronting the man in her dream, indicated the necessity 'not only for the way we establish secure and loving relationships, but also for the repetition of maladaptive and destructive patterns of relationship' (Knox, 2003, p. 82). She chose partners who replicated the relationship her parents had with each other and the relationship with her bullying brother, but there was also a similar quality of unavailability experienced with both mother and father. The parents' inner lives of absence and lack of appropriate protection, support and affect were internalised, becoming Sophie's world. The emotional silence deepened around her. She forgot the pain, busy with partners who would not go deeper or understand her. Life was lived by the old agreement to exist on the surface, ask few questions and just accept. Sophie dulled herself down and became absent to herself. Although the wealth of her personality went unnoticed, just like in her family, Sophie began to realise how much she ran from the intimacy she so desired.

Sophie could be alive in small doses, mostly in performing at work or sexually, but not in her soul. All this was familiar to her and so was the need to not alter anything but remain in stasis. But then something began to emerge from within. She felt a vague discomfort, was irritable and began to seek other relationships, yet these were also not emotionally intimate. She did not realise fully but was gaining some awareness of the dehumanisation of herself as it had solidified over time. In analysis we explored this through dreams, images, poetry, books and the analytical relationship itself. All became catalysts for her continued personality development.

In the analysis she began to respond to my responses. My facial expressions, tone of voice began to register, and she started to feel herself as a person by seeing herself being responded to. It was a process of meeting not only in words but also with nonverbal reactions for creating safety. The shell of her stoic façade began to crack and what felt like a void inside opened to a wealth of material. Her books, reading of poetry and love of art appeared in dream after dream. Slowly the old secrets and loneliness emerged. These also were revealed in dreams. It was as if her whole self began to find a receptive place and, in that soil, began to flower. This included affirmation of her vitality not only physically but also emotionally; neither had been experienced previously. The analytical relationship and its process honoured her personal images and way of being. This included examining and making room for the secret places and emotional freedom of expression. No longer did she consider herself too quirky but could respect how different she was from what she was told she should be.

Feeling an empty label

The term *emptiness* can describe various states. Each 'as-if' person's experience is unique, poignantly laden with meaninglessness and self-alienation. The emptiness is accompanied by disassociation, or deadness. *Disassociation* is the sense of detachment and lack of connection to oneself and outer reality. Some register floating, an uncertain ground, or a lack of sensation, a feeling of nausea – all enacted through myriad forms of psychic numbing.

By avoiding, a person cannot recognise what is hindering their life. Internally isolated and frozen, the 'as-if' personality appears in the need for outer order, even success, but not in one's own aliveness and being. Getting by, making no waves, asking for nothing and trying to not be disliked stymies growth and movement. It becomes so ingrained, shaping everything to not expose fear, anxieties, needs and dependency. In fact, little is safe to share. These are the psychological voids stemming from failures in the environment and causing discontinuities of the self. The lack of good internal representations expresses itself in terms of a void, emptiness, futility and meaninglessness (Kohon, 1999, p. 290).

In the analysis of all these people, we together marvelled at the resilience to survive and sought to awaken desire for a fuller and freely imagined life. Being able to symbolise and find the expansiveness in the personality is what the 'as-if' person has struggled to learn and use. 'The alternative to being is reacting, and reacting interrupts being and annihilates. Being and annihilation are the two alternatives' (Winnicott, 1990, p. 47). This had been restrained by the void, emptiness, and for some there is no way to break the vice. For others, personal space and trust does evolve. Through the analytical and relational work, the valuable resources of the symbolic and the unconscious are accessed. Through the exploration and experience of the earliest origins of the self, there is the possibility for the repair of a faulty relationship to the self, and the individuation processes can be nurtured and set in motion (Feldman, 2002, p. 405). 'It struck me, on my walk yesterday, that these moments of being of mine were scaffolding in the background: were the invisible and silent part of my life as a child' (Woolf, 1985, p. 73).

References

Colman, W. (2008). On being, knowing and having a self. *Journal of Analytical Psychology*, *53*(3), 351–66. doi: 10.1111/j.1468-5922.2008.00731.x.

Connolly, W. (2013). Out of the body: Embodiment and its vicissitudes. *Journal of Analytical Psychology*, *47*(3), 636–56. doi: 10.1111/1468-5922.12042.

Deutsch, H. (1942). Some forms of emotional disturbance and their relationship to schizophrenia. *Psychoanalytic Quarterly*, *11*(3), 301–21.

Feldman, B. (2002). The lost steps of infancy: Symbolization, analytic process and the growth of the self. *Journal of Analytical Psychology*, *47*(3), 397–406. doi: 10.1111/1465-5922.00327.

Gibeault, A. (2005). Symbolization and creativity: The analytical adventures of Mr. A. and Sabrina Spielrein. In: L. Cowen (ed.), *Barcelona 2004 – edges of experience: memory and emergence: proceedings of the 16th international congress for analytical psychology*. Daimon.

Goss, P. (2006). Discontinuities in the male psyche: Waiting, deadness and disembodiment. Archetypal and clinical approaches. *Journal of Analytical Psychology*, *51*(5), 681–99. doi: 10.1111/j.1468-5922.2006.00617.x.

Green, A. (1986). *On private madness*. The Hogarth Press.

Green, A. (2001). *Life narcissism, death narcissism*. Free Association Books.

Green, A. (2011). *The tragic effect: The Oedipus complex in tragedy*. Cambridge University Press.

Jung, C.G. (1935/1977). Tavistock lectures. In *The collected works of C.G. Jung: Vol. 18. The symbolic life*. Princeton University Press.

Jung, C.G. (2009). *The red book: Liber novus*. (S. Shamdasani, ed.). W.W. Norton & Co.

Knox, J. (2003). *Archetype, attachment, analysis*. Routledge.

Kohon, G. (ed.) (1999). *The dead mother: The work of André Green*. London: Routledge.

Kristeva, J. (1992). *Black sun*. Columbia University Press.

Meredith-Owen, W. (2011). Jung's shadow: Negation and narcissism of the Self. *Journal of Analytical Psychology*, *56*(5), 674–91. doi: 10.1111/j.1468-5922.2011.01939.x.

Mizen, R. (2014). On the capacity to suffer one's self. *Journal of Analytical Psychology*, *59*(3), 314–32. doi: 10.1111/1468-5922.12080.

Proner, B.D. (2017). The latency complex: The dead hand of anti-development. *Journal of Analytical Psychology*, *62*(4), 567–84. doi: 10.1111/1468-5922.12337.

Solomon, H.F. (1998). The self in transformation: The passage from a two- to a three-dimensional internal world. *Journal of Analytical Psychology*, *43*(2), 225–38. doi: 10.1111/1465-5922.00022.

Solomon, H. (2004). Self-creation and the limitless void of dissociation: The as if personality. *Journal of Analytical Psychology*, *49*(5), 635–56. doi: 10.1111/j.0021-8774.2004.00493.x.

Sontag, S. (1978). *Illness as metaphor*. Farrar, Straus and Giroux.

Stein, M. (1996). *Transformation*. Texas A&M University Press.

Waldron, S. (2013). Black holes: Escaping the void. *Journal of Analytical Psychology*, *58*(1), 99–117. doi: 10.1111/j.1468-5922.2013.02019.x.

Wilkinson, M. (2003). Undoing trauma: Contemporary neuroscience. A Jungian clinical perspective. *Journal of Analytical Psychology*, *48*(2), 235–53.

Winnicott, D.W. (1971). *Creativity and its origins. Playing and reality*. Routledge.

Winnicott, D.W. (1990). *The maturational project and the facilitating environment*. Karnac Books.

Woolf, V. (1985). *Moments of being: A collection of autobiographical essays*. Harvest Books.

Chapter 7

Envy as a disturbed search for self

In the German fairy tale 'The Three Little Men in the Wood', a young maiden is persecuted by her stepmother and stepsister and is ordered by her wicked step-mother to seek strawberries in the woods. While in the woods, the maiden meets three little men (dwarves, or sometimes referred to as 'gnomes') and kindly shares her food with them and cleans for them. Because of her kindness, the three little men reward her each with a wish: one declares that she should grow more beautiful every day, the other declares that a gold piece should fall from her mouth whenever she speaks, and the third declares that a king will marry her ...

The maiden returns home and, upon seeing the magical gifts she was given, her stepsister demands the same gifts for herself. The stepsister enters the woods and finds the three little men but refuses to share her food with them or clean for them. The little men want to punish her for her haughtiness, so one declares that she will grow uglier every day, the other declares that a toad will fall from her mouth when-ever she speaks, and the third declares that she will die a miserable death.

In this tale the envy and greed of the stepsister is egged on by the stepmother. Both represent the negative aspects of envy, but they also demonstrate lack and grabbing to get from the other. They reveal the turn against the feminine, internal-ised in self-destructive ways.

Envy through time

> Then if you reflect within yourself and ask yourself from what quarter the accident has come, you will remember that it comes from the region of things outside our will, which are not ours.
>
> Epictetus's Discourses III (pp. 105–6)

Throughout history there have been numerous definitions of *envy*. It has been viewed as a powerful force and a difficult emotion, often vilified for its destruc-tive associations in relationships. The following are a smattering of definitions; of course, there are many more.

Phthonus, an ancient Greek god, was the personification of envy in Greek mythology and the other half of the goddess of retribution called Nemesis. He was

DOI: 10.4324/9781003315254-8

particularly concerned with the jealous passions of love. In an ancient Greek vase painting he appears as an *Erote*, or the winged godling of love who accompanied Aphrodite. He was the son of Nyx (night) and Dionysus, although some sources cite him as the son of Aphrodite, the goddess of love. Phthonus killed several of his wives whom he suspected were unfaithful. He also told Hera about the adulterous affairs of her husband, Zeus.

In another Greek myth, which I explored in Chapter 5, Narcissus was oblivious to the envy of others. They desired him yet he ignored their appeals, remaining unobtainable and unreachable, as if his qualities were for him alone. A curse uttered by one of Narcissus's spurned lovers and granted by the goddess Nemesis doomed him: 'May he himself love and not gain the thing he loves'.

The word *envy* derives from the Latin *invidia*, meaning 'non-sight'. The 'Inferno', the first part of the *Divine Comedy*, the 14th-century epic poem by the Italian writer Dante Alighieri, describes the journey through the circles of Hell guided by Virgil. In it, Dante refers to the 'realm of those who have rejected spiritual values by yielding to bestial appetites or violence, or by perverting their human intellect to fraud or malice against their fellowmen' (Ciardi, 2005, p. 14). The envious, defined as those who derived pleasure from seeing others brought low, are deprived of sight. They labour under cloaks of lead, and their eyes are sewn shut with leaden wire. The etymology of the word and this reference suggest envy both arises from and results in a form of blindness or lack of perspective. It also implies a turn towards inward sight.

Guillaume de Deguileville's 14th-century story called *The Pilgrimage of Human Life* personifies the Vice of Envy with spears coming out of her eyes. As a female figure she is accompanied by the additional vices of Pride, Treachery, Slander and Anger.

Buddhist texts classify envy as part of hostility, a disturbing emotion aroused by focusing on other peoples' accomplishments. For the envious, who are excessively attached to their own gain above all else, this signals the inability to bear anyone else's achievements or excellence. The envious person is preoccupied with themselves and with what is lacking, while also being strongly taken with the desire for and hostility towards the imagined advantage of the other.

Envy was featured as one of the seven deadly sins dating back to the 6th century, when they were first grouped together by St. Gregory the Great, Pope from 590–604 CE. The sins of pride, covetousness, lust, envy, gluttony (including drunkenness), anger and sloth were the transgressions assumed to cause the death not of the body but of the soul.

Geoffrey Chaucer in 'The Parson's Tale', the last of *The Canterbury Tales* composed between 1387 and 1400, wrote, 'Certainly, then, envy is the worst sin there is. For truly, all other sins are sometime against only one special virtue; but truly, envy is against all virtues and against all goodnesses' (2000). The seven deadly sins are pride, envy, wrath, sloth, greed, gluttony and lust; they are healed by the virtues of humility, contentment, patience, fortitude, mercy, moderation and chastity.

Shakespeare also wrote about envy:

When Envy breeds unkind division:
There comes the ruin, there begins confusion.

1 Henry VI, 4.1.195–6, Exeter

Envy and the 'as-if' personality

Envy is a hallmark of the 'as-if' personality. The 'as-if' person is haunted by feelings of inadequacy, the need to shine, yet they anticipate defeat. Others are better, and the 'as-if' person is not good enough. All this is fuelled by the tremendous push to be the best. However, the envy of the 'as-if' person indicates their low self-esteem, sense of worthlessness and lack. It is a reaction to early emotional misconnections, but it can also inspire excellence. Envy can lead a person to underachieve due to the weight of anticipated failure or rise to the stars because of the need to answer the ache and want inside. The envious cannot rest.

Various forms of psychological and cultural wounding and exclusion create the reaction and emotion of envy, which derives from the lack of sufficient connection and support from family, partner, social group or self. In this emotion resides despair, hopelessness, longing and mourning for what was and was not. The 'as-if' person learns to become an image, maybe even a caricature, with no confidence in what's real. While psychological defences may serve an adaptive function to buffer anxiety and fear in the instance in which envy arises, if rigidly overgeneralised into other contexts and relationships, perceptions of oneself become inaccurate. These reactions contribute to the passion that could be there but is, instead, replaced by depression, anxiety and acting 'as-if'. In the search for understanding the disruptive inner and outer emotions aroused by envy, several factors, such as the personal and cultural complexes, affect the course of psychological treatment. In Jungian psychology the process of individuation or becoming oneself involves comprehending the layers of the unconscious leading to personality development as revealed in the analytical treatment.

The psychological and popular literature on envy is extensive and muddled with various models taking different pathways. However delineated, envy is usually noted to be distancing and uncomfortable to feel and to receive. Often associated with shame, envy constricts, restricts, hardens and turns the heart into an arid yet flaming patch. Envy is a perception of inferiority in which one feels diminished and others are imagined as having more. This emotion is made more difficult as the envious person anticipates disappointment. Whether true or not, the tragedy of this attitude is it develops into a renunciation of the self. Included in envy is emptiness, isolation, alienation and rootlessness, feelings seemingly impossible to negotiate. Envious people feel they have suffered terribly, and they want, expect and need special privileges. The resulting grandiosity is in proportion to attempts to overshadow feelings of internal deprivation.

The disquiet of envy lodges within the 'as-if' person. It never occurs to this person that what is assumed to be in others, also resides within themselves. Envy can 'lead us to what needs repair in our identities... pointing us to what we thirst for... and close the gap its wounds have opened' (Ulanov & Ulanov, 1983, p. 10). It can begin early from parental insecurity and jealousy of children who often have abilities the parents lack, or the child is otherwise equipped than what the parent wants, expects or can handle. The discomfort with the child's uniqueness and differences conveys misunderstanding and confusion to the child. Resources for solidity and confidence are stuck in a frustrated early history in which the child worked to gain love and attention, but this went unheeded. Fulfilled parents know how to hold up the mirror that says, 'I like and appreciate who you are'. This allows a person to recognise and honour envy rather than honing it to be destructive. After all, envy is natural, and health is not the absence of envy but how we use it.

When loving and safe parental figures are instead absent, neglectful or disconnected, envy enters the psyche of the child, affecting future relationships. No one should be better than the envious person and yet everyone is assumed to be so. Relationships are insecure; they lack balance. Others are assumed to have the advantage. Envy of others becomes a way to avoid oneself. This emotion promotes the pull to dissolve, withdraw into fantasy images and magnifies romantic illusions and disillusions. It also takes the form of creating insecurity in the world or in the ability to bear life's burdens.

Envy wears many masks. It also reaches into the dreaded anticipation of abandonment followed by catastrophic collapse. The composite clinical examples here illustrate the distress of envy causing wreckage to the personality with its unending lack of fulfilment. These people demonstrate the difficulty in therapy to get under the surface and access the roots of pain and suffering. Understanding the nuances and meaning of envy requires the turn inward and onto the path of individuation and facing this avoided and often dreaded emotion.

Caught in envy, the person is unable to trust due to a breakdown in intersubjectivity, leading to blocks in recognising the other as well as oneself (Bonovitz, 2010, p. 427). Its complexity arises at the moments one is envied for doing well, as then the envier becomes envied. Some resort to apologising or diminishing themselves to avoid the stinging envy from others. In this scenario, they are lessened, erased, and envy wins. Envy leads to the feeling of deprivation and comparison to others turns into lack rather than mere difference. Envy is easily projected on to others, so blame is placed on others, envy's pernicious effects substituting for self-examination (Ulanov & Ulanov, 1983, p. 18). When the envier looks outside for validation rather than inside, they find only insufficiency and defeat.

Some people do not admit to envy, although those of the 'as-if' personality type feel its excruciating pangs. Envy is a natural emotion, yet it creates much distress when subsuming the personality. The power and attributes of envy can lead us to examine its effects and recognise it within ourselves. This releases its energy from the unconscious for psychological transformation, increased consciousness and personality strength.

Jung did not directly address envy except in his foreword to the I Ching where he wrote, 'Since a share in something great always arouses envy, the chorus of the envious is part of the picture' (Jung, 1979, p. xxvii). Envy involves comparison and competition, as people envy what they lack or think they do. American Jungian analyst Nathan Schwartz-Salant (1982, p. 105) described envy as the ego's rejection of the self, hatefully projected onto the world. Envy of others is accompanied by secrets, self-condemnation, shame and the wish to be the object of envy. Selfishness, greed, anger and rage appear alongside envy. It serves as a safety net against intimacy and as a remedy against the underlying chaos and void (Britton, 1998, p. 181). Therefore, envy is not owned. An envious attack is vicious in that 'I so want what the person has, and for that person to not have it, I will destroy what the person has'.

'The distressing ravages of envy and jealousy foster unconscious projective identifications and its corrosive nature denudes the inner world' (Stein, 2017, p. 94). When unconscious, envy can tarnish hopes and dreams because nothing is ever enough. One is too old, too fat, without sufficient education, opportunity or money. The comparisons go on and on. Facing vulnerability and incompleteness seems impossible. Painful beliefs lead the envious to flee from themselves. The hostility aroused by envy can turn against the envier in disappointment and fears of failure so paralysing they do nothing. It can manifest as inner voices ridiculing desires; dreams aren't worth pursuing.

There is a fragility that finds ways to close the discussion down. Destructive envy has the effect of undermining a person's own goodness and capacities as they become tainted with contempt. They are frustrated in effecting desired change. Because the person cannot connect to the self, they cannot connect to the other. There can be no rejoicing over anyone's accomplishments, and this destroys their own goodness. They stand on the edge of a painful abyss, renouncing their own self, a defence limiting rather than opening the envious person to their own life. Envy shuts down the possibility of addressing emotional wounds by foreclosing on the promise of anything better.

The hole inside the envier aches. At the heart of envy are neediness and an emptiness going so deep they can hardly admit it. Envy brings out what we care about, deeply and longingly. It arouses the relational as we want what the other has. There is within envy the desire for response, presence, to feel. However, this also means feeling the empty, intense desire and need to be filled by the other. Envy is connected to feeling out of control. How can the envier figure out how to live when they are bewildered and feel helpless. Envy involves wild feelings and emotions. Desires seem too big. They present as defensive and defenceless combined with the need to self-protect from vulnerability.

Envy has an element of self-punishment around not having done more, achieved or obtained what the other seems to have. Anger at the other is anger at oneself. Love is withheld. The 'as-if' person assumes they did not get it right, and they envy the one who they think did.

The envied person becomes a blank, erased, no longer even human. Envy generalises and projects. The cause of pain and misery is located outside. To be envied is threatening in its intent to destroy and be invalidated, co-opted into another person's schema (Ulanov & Ulanov, 1983, p. 18). Both envied and envier are rendered helpless in an endless chain, disconnected from each other. The world is perceived through this distorted, convoluted and emotionally fraught lens. In such a scenario no one can exist, much less thrive.

Fairy tales replicate life characters and the conscious and unconscious situations and emotions we all experience in some form. As in the fairy tale of Cinderella and many others such as 'The Three Little Men in the Wood', envy appears in the form of the good opposed to the bad, the young to the old, the lovely to the ugly. The latter wants to not only have what the other has but also to destroy it. This can be likened to the phenomena of psychological splitting, idealisation, projection and denial of owning collective and personal shadows.

The topic of envy is hard to touch as it is uncomfortable and usually feels unsafe. Many people are reluctant to admit to envy because the emotion is perceived as so socially unacceptable. Therefore, it often is hidden, yet it exists in plain sight. Envy involves longing, including a sense of self-betrayal and bitterness, and it contains the uncomfortable desire for vengeance. It is the fear and denial of one's own vulnerability that causes hate and exploitation of the vulnerability of others (Kristeva, 1992, p. 55).

There is also a kind of envy without this pernicious quality. Jung said, 'In the intensity of the emotional disturbance itself lies the value, the energy which he should have at his disposal in order to remedy the state of reduced adaptation' (1969, CW 8, para. 167). This use of envy may lead the person to find and emulate good role models. For example, the child envies the good object in the parent, and this provides structure and support to the personality. Rather than resorting to spoiling and destructiveness, envy then recognises good qualities, skills and beauty. In this envy can activate desire and goals.

Yet, most often envy hurts. It has a voracious hunger that cannot be filled. Nor does stealing the goods from others satisfy. Warren Colman perceives envy as following primarily from feelings of lack based on interpersonal comparison (2007, p. 99). Envy is an emotion denoting pain, sorrow and anger resulting from perceiving adverse differences or gaps between oneself and others. Others' qualities are attacked, often leading not to satisfaction but to self-destruction and wretchedness. British Jungian analyst Barry Proner put forth the idea envy was destruction of the inner good object, resulting in envy of oneself and making the self the ultimate object of envy (2017, p. 470). This represents an attack on life itself, rendering the envier unable to acquire what they desire. All goes up in smoke and the personality disintegrates into ruins.

The envious are often those who cannot go along with life, those who remain stiff, insecure, vulnerable and with little relation to the present as they always desire more or something other than what they have. Envy can shatter the personality, dividing good from bad, creating loneliness and separateness, depleting energy. The envious cannot take in good and are left starving and confused. The wounds reside on many levels, internal and external, acute and cumulative, personal and cultural. Envy can be debilitating and destroys relationships, obliterating trust and confidence.

The pain of envy

Although this composite example takes place in therapeutic treatment, similar issues occur in all relationships. Francesca, in her late forties, in a long-term relationship and getting an advanced degree, expresses negative, demeaning and angry comments about feeling unseen and unacknowledged in various ways. She presents with a nonplussed and distant demeanour from the first session. It soon becomes apparent this attitude masks dependency needs, apprehension to be understood and the taking of few emotional risks. Whatever she feels is withheld. She wants to be understood yet assumes this will not occur. She trusts only her partner. At issue is the feeling of inner lack, distorted and masked by envy and rage. As the Buddha said, 'Do not overrate what you have received, nor envy others. He who envies others does not obtain peace of mind'.

Francesca is always right. As if the rest of the world is attacking her, something is always wrong. The therapeutic transference becomes predominately negative, and the envious elements create emotional distance, solidifying her aloneness. Her dissociated and disavowed parts are easily projected onto others, and onto me as the analyst who is inadequate, does not understand and holds the power position.

Francesca began life with longer than usual hospital stays, alone, her parents unable to be present. She early on faced what Michael Fordham described as the primitive defences of the self. This concept refers to the barriers between the baby self and the environment set up to ward off what feels inimical to survival (Colman, 1991, p. 365). This early emotional deprivation and trauma from aloneness left Francesca with the underlying apprehension of descending into pits of grief and never emerging. Therefore, she could neither get too deeply saddened nor find enough joy. In childhood, her parents were overwhelmed and undemonstrative. She needed more than they could give, and she was left alone with a terror she could not process. She could not make sense of why things were the way they were, why she was getting less than others, especially as she was good.

The defensive denial of the self arises from these formative experiences of helplessness (Meredith-Owen, 2008, p. 468). From the time she was a toddler, Francesca was pressured to perform but she could not. Later she was bullied in school for physical awkwardness and felt ashamed. Mother was not available for enough emotional care or attention as there were other children to attend to. Father was a frustrated man, a tyrant with daily critiques and diatribes levelled at the children. He was brutal, controlling with his violent words, and the mother provided no protection against him.

Francesca is hypervigilant, expecting anger and rejection from me in the analytical relationship. I supposedly have the power and she has none, repeating the terror induced from the father. There is no way to provide support when her needs are exposed as she reports only feeling worse and more helpless. The natural dependency goes unmet and fills with envy. It covers the emptiness caused by lack of emotional connection, causing hatred and anger towards the other and the self. Here I perceive envy as relational, even a social emotion as it is tied to others.

Francesca expresses existential isolation, helplessness and threat of disintegration (Colman, 1991, p. 366). The effects of feeling this when so young and without the love she needed at home have manifested as anxiety about her appearance and being interesting. Francesca feels ugly, unappealing. Each day weight is a battle, hounding her obsessively. She is embarrassed and ashamed to discuss these issues thoroughly. She mentions them briefly but will not persist as she considers this a sign of weakness and vulnerability.

Francesca had long ago erected a metaphorical barrier beyond which no one entered. This protects her firm belief that no matter what, others will get more and she less. She expresses loneliness and the feeling no one really knows her distress or cares. This is the psychic suffering derived from what is called in the analytic literature *narcissistic wounding*. In the transference she says I am not as able as she is, not humorous, and do not give support or trust. She needs more outer approval to gain herself, she says. And she does not get this in the therapeutic relationship from me as I do not compliment her enough or list her good traits. This reflects her early unmet needs as her own inner resources seem stunted and cannot come forward. Especially when she is upset, I cannot reach her, and my words are experienced as attacks, fuelling her anger and defensiveness. For a time, this aggression and contempt makes me irritable and frustrated. It creates a feeling of helplessness, failure, mistrust. While I recognise these projections, I try to assess whether there are truths in them. Yet, I know we are engaged in an enactment of her inner pain and need for attention to the vulnerable and fragile parts of herself behind the hard outer protective shell.

'Envy attacks in the analytic relationship reveal a person trapped by the paradoxes of despair and entitlement. Envy can block the ability to internally unite' (Meredith-Owen, 2008, p. 478). The ego in people like Francesca is fragile and frequently threatened with what feels like disintegration. The sense of self is often fragmented or split, and the person feels without a centre. The transference is often negative, characterised by subtly hidden nests of mistrust that are difficult to confront. The negativity, although challenging and emotionally trying, brings forwards the anguish, pressures, anxieties and depression. These are areas often filled with shame and tucked far within the personality.

The expectation of getting less is projected onto the psychological treatment. The negative transference seems so intractable, and my countertransference reactions are increasingly hopeless and frustrated at this created impasse. We both feel the failed encounters in the analysis, the piling up of one dissatisfaction after another. Francesca has a history of stopping partway through anything, overtaken by the inevitability of defeat. Sometimes she thinks it through to the end, decides she cannot have what she wants and stops. She expresses sadness, envy and anger at those with success. She says it is due to ethnicity, social class, privilege. She feels deprived. I, on the other hand, seem to have it all and do not share or give sufficiently, according to Francesca's rather tortured view of life.

The past failed encounters repeated in analysis emerge as expressions of non-satisfaction, defeat, feeling powerless and empty. Many of these reactions are shared yet many remain unshared. I cannot tell whether anything of significance besides the disconnection is happening between us. Can she take in anything other than me having power over her and she being powerless, helpless and misunderstood? The vociferousness of her attacks against any connection verifies she feels there is no place for her. Upon reflection, her expressed rage is an attempt to keep herself together because she feels on the brink of falling apart. Here is envy also tearing apart relationships and the psyche is left alone in sad ruins.

I surmise Francesca's explosiveness means there is something she needs to communicate and does not know how. These are the veiled needs and longings that indicate a difficult internal struggle behind all the pushback. The anger seems connected to her lack of being valued in herself, family and culture; nowhere can she find places of acceptance or security. The obstacles set up by envy leave little space for self-reflection or a secure relationship. As Jung said,

> It wants the human connection. That is the core of the whole transference phenomenon, and it is impossible to argue it away, because relationship to the self is at once relationship to our fellow man, and no one can be related to the latter until he is related to himself.
>
> (Jung, 1966, CW 16, para. 445)

Warren Colman contends envy results in a loss of self-esteem as it is 'bound up with a lack of differentiation' and a lack of 'the capacity to value one's own uniqueness as a separate person, different from, albeit intimately connected with others' (1991, p. 356). It can cause an inability to separate from the envied; the envier is tied to the person they envy through this strong emotion. Envy may cause increased depression and is often associated with shame. The envier feels inferior and insecure, internalising self-blame and then replacing it with blaming others. The result is distance from personal connections; life is everywhere bitter and despairing.

Jung did not address many specific emotions, but he did comment:

> On the one hand, emotion is the alchemical fire whose warmth brings everything into existence and whose heat burns all superfluities to ashes (*omnes superfluitates comburit*). But on the other hand, emotion is the moment when steel meets flint and a spark is struck forth, for emotion is the chief source of consciousness. There is no change from darkness to light or from inertia to movement without emotion.
>
> (1968c, CW 9i, para. 179)

Like all emotions, envy is a natural and human experience, but the key is how conscious one is of this difficult emotion and what can be done to handle and use it.

Melanie Klein and envy

Melanie Klein, British psychoanalyst in the mid-20th century, was famous for positing the centrality of envy and its origins in aggression early in personality development. In a rather reduced version of her concepts, she located envy experienced by the infant feeding at the breast when gratification is either withheld or delayed too much and for too long. This naturally happens at times but depends on many factors if it turns negatively against the child. Klein considered envy innate and oral, born out of a drive for food and intimacy in the healthy response of want.

In the Kleinian schema, envy is destructive and arises in the face of deprivation, yet it is unconsciously coupled with the hope of comfort, closeness and satiation. Even when gratified the infant also learns comfort can be taken away at any moment and then the infant is no longer connected to the supply of goodness. According to Klein, these experiences of goodness and badness, in the mind of a new-born child, seem inherently irreconcilable. This refers to the psychological reaction of splitting, bringing internal divisiveness and painful separation from the expected source of nurturance.

Melanie Klein surmised the first object of envy is the breast, and if the losses and gains are tolerated and worked through, the process leads to normal or unencumbered development. However, when the experience of envy is excessive and associated with too much failure in responsive parenting, the ego can become weakened, resulting in the lessening of resilient inner resources. These experiences multiply and the ease and comfort of being continues to remain unsatisfied and undernourished. In essence, envy originates when the loving and safe parental objects are absent, neglectful or unconnected. In reaction the fantasy of self-reference and omnipotence means the child learns they can only trust themselves and others will disappoint. This transfers to the disappointments in life itself.

When repeatedly unaddressed, early deficits in love and attention cannot be countered, creating internal defeat. Anger and the need to spoil any goodness are reactions seeking to remove the source of envious feelings. Melanie Klein ascribed this in therapy to the patient's 'unhappiness, pain and conflicts contrasted with what are presumed as the analyst's peace of mind – actually her sanity – and this is a particular cause for envy' (1975, p. 222). The therapist is turned into an unfulfilling object through projecting all good and all bad onto her. Envy is then accompanied by self-pity and destructiveness, and this becomes a self-perpetuating cycle, creating impasse in the therapeutic process. Envy remains hidden in the shadows and the analytic experience becomes filtered through the green eyes of envy.

Envy is an emotion – quiet, hidden, nagging and insidious (Abraham, 1927, p. 397). When too frustrated, the person cannot take things in from others or manifest pleasure. Whether the envier or envied, the experience surrounding envy is usually unpleasant, angry and spiteful, stimulating the inadequacy and injury experienced from the earlier emotional wounds. Yet, envy can indicate the tender emotional areas accompanied by aggressive responses, erasing understanding while seeking relief from the suffering.

Although we all need the other in a rather heavily dependent way to fill the emotional and relational gaps and lack (Colman, 1991, p. 356), Francesca says I am envious of her. I make no response but am shocked inside. Where did she get this? Is it a defence? Is it an example of how envy interrupts the analytic/relational process, making it lopsided and even colouring it with a cruel tinge? Her comment shows any otherness cannot be tolerated. It indicates the lack of sufficient connection and that 'envy is a disturbance in one's primary value' (p. 357). Francesca attacks, devalues or destroys anything given, any interpretation, thought or feeling, and cannot take in any good. All becomes bad and intrusive. She is 'left with feelings of invalidation and alienation that can ultimately lead to doubts about her own existence. [Her] reactions certainly indicated that she felt her survival was under threat, as if it was me or her' (p. 577). Envy confronts a person, with the anti-individuation forces gathered around the wish, whether conscious or not, to take revenge and destroy. A variety of compensations and adaptations attempt to avoid, manage and defend against this powerful wish. Envy includes ambivalence as the envier wants to both enact and not enact ruthless destruction.

Envy is difficult, associated with the forbidden and unspeakable, and is oppressive, leaving the emergence of the self distorted and stuck. A person can resort to what is called a *psychic retreat*. This is a system of defence into which a person withdraws from relationships to avoid contact both with the analyst in therapeutic treatment as well as from people in other situations (Steiner, 1993). The fragmentation of the personality and lost parts of the self are kept isolated within these psychic retreats whereas the point of individuation is to integrate them. Failures to expose the retreats, like those instigated with envy, obstruct getting through the impasses and, until understood, impede the analysis.

> What is so difficult for the layman to grasp is the fact that in most cases the patients themselves have no suspicion whatever of the internecine war raging in their unconscious. If we remember that there are many people who understand nothing at all about themselves, we shall be less surprised at the realization that there are also people who are utterly unaware of their actual conflicts.
> (Jung, 1960/1969, CW 7, para. 425)

The transference and countertransference, through fostering a third space in analysis, is central to the analytic process. The evolving union in the analytical relationship allows for the affective re-experiencing of the repressed. This creates the possibility of a different outcome and an exit point from the previous envious and destructive internal and external relationships. Analytical treatment fosters the individuation process and, through the relationship between patient and analyst, makes space for the transformation of self. As Jung said, 'Human nature has an invincible dread of becoming more conscious of itself. What nevertheless drives us to it is the self which demands sacrifice by sacrificing itself to us' (Jung, 1958/1969, CW 11, para. 400). Individuation can be understood as the drive towards consciousness, eventually expanding constriction in the personality through the analytical relationship.

Assuming she will be maltreated, however, Francesca retreats to a distant place – hateful, angry and superior to others in her mind. Many of my comments are rejected and experienced by her as cruel and attacking. She feels put down, misunderstood; she says I do not ask the right questions, analyse her dreams enough or correctly, and her interpretations are better. She is upset I do not know or read her mind sufficiently. A flood of vituperative commentary is followed by her energy abruptly stopping and the emotional wind dissipating. And, at these times, tears flow without words.

Francesca expresses biting defensive anger, railing against the cost of psychological treatment and accuses therapists of being rich. She comments on the Eurocentrism and social class in the field of psychology. Although Eurocentrism and social class have been factors in psychological perspectives, these are interpreted as personal attacks and fuel her feelings of being demeaned. These grievances, even though well-founded, have the effect of displacing attention from her personal wounds, as she argues over and over about inequities and prejudices.

After many months, she brings up the emptiness inside and questions whether she can be fully herself. She wonders why the process needs a relationship. At the end of this session, she admits her hatred of almost everything. In this, there seems a felt connection, a vulnerability and openness, but this is rapidly followed by anger. She expects to be dumped and treated as less than. Her arguing and rage seem to deflect from her inner confusion, uncertainty, envy. She insists on being right but will inevitably lose, as in her view, I am in control and do not allow her to be.

Francesca guards her psyche, suspicious she will be wronged, overlooked and misunderstood. Or, perhaps she would feel more pain and dependency and she does not know or trust it can bring healing. 'The early and primitive defences reveal the fears of authentic relating' (Solomon, 2007, p. 241). This occurs when there is too little experience of solid and supportive relatedness with others. As it is, her world is held distant and separate from others by the wall of envy with its barricade against anyone seeing what she considers personal weakness and anxiety.

'Envy occurs with the belief no one will care… leading to the negative transference' (Schwartz-Salant, 1982, p. 87). Envy, anger and defences operate so nothing kind or giving gets through, leaving little cognition or allowance for relationship. Resonance is rendered impossible. All attention is narrowed to a focus on anger and envy. 'The perverse relationship to reality leads to misrepresentation and distortion of the truth… and these misrepresentations are an obstacle to progress in analysis' (Steiner, 1993, p. 94). Each time a connection seems possible in therapy, it is broken with renewed anger and a litany of the past disappointments and infractions occurring in the therapy, which she cannot forget. Suddenly her indignant defiance turns to impotence, and Francesca collapses within, assuming she cannot get what she wants, and her dreams will not be answered.

She says she does not like people. As mentioned earlier, in the Kleinian theory this can be interpreted as 'the phantasy of being excluded from the receptive goodness of the breast leaves embittered impotent feelings' (Meredith-Owen, 2008, p. 470). Although she retreats by keeping to herself, she does not diligently attend to herself. She says with sadness and frustration she is easily distracted by the next task around the house and then loses focus. Francesca has yet to realise the extent of her envy and how its ruinous ramifications have turned against and affected her.

> Only then will she realize that the conflict is in her, that the discord and tribula-tion are her riches, which should not be squandered by attacking others; and that, if fate should exact a debt from her in the form of guilt, it is a debt to herself. Then she will recognize the worth of her psyche.
>
> (Jung, 1970, CW 14, para. 511)

Envious responses are a defence against dependency needs, but they also reflect experiences of intolerable separateness and aloneness. Francesca's omnipotent arrogance indicates the 'as-if' personality as a 'terrified young self, vacillating between omnipotence and powerlessness enacted in the therapeutic transference' (Meredith-Owen, 2008, p. 466). Francesca is defensive, disdaining the psycho-logical treatment and saying she does not know how to use the sessions. Her 'life force and creativity were stymied, obstructed by the preoccupying space of envy in her psyche' (Meredith-Owen, 2008, p. 478). Within herself the envy undermines her capacity for relationships, solid attachments, life, interests or enjoyment. Any empathy is ignored and magnified into her being disregarded.

Yet, although resisted, through the therapeutic transference Francesca comes in touch with her emotional yearnings. Several dreams show Francesca wanting to be in the analyst's house yet feeling crowded out by others who are already there. She feels unnoticed, insufficient and questions her importance and impact. Her words and reactions describe envy and desire, but she does not say so. That would be too vulnerable, and she needs to appear strong. She anticipates there is no way to be safely seen, owing to disillusionments, dominated by impotency and fear along with unaddressed envy. She cuts herself off, becomes secretly depressed and gives up, despairing of connection by assuming it is denied.

She frequently speaks of meaninglessness in the therapeutic work as no one cares and it makes no difference. She does not recognise the 'self-inflicted nihil-ism trapped within the rage and envy' (Meredith-Owen, 2008, p. 467). Rage is automatically turned both outward to the analytical relationship as well as to others and simultaneously against herself. The crudity and harshness of the rage from the early wounds are re-enacted in therapy. This could bring awareness about using the energy rather than continuing to lobe against herself and others. It does not in this instance. She remains where she began – frustrated in a lifelong search to express her genuine and spontaneous self and find a place with others.

Shadow of envy

Jungian psychology is founded on the recognition of the splits in the psyche that, when healed, can lead to relationship between self and other.

A man who is unconscious of himself acts in a blind, instinctive way and is in addition fooled by all the illusions that arise when he sees everything that he is not conscious of in himself coming to meet him from outside as projections upon his neighbor.

(Jung, 1968b, CW 13, para. 335)

Envy and its painful, ungrieved aspects live in the shadows, hidden in the secret thoughts, feelings, intentions, motivations, emotions, instincts, desires and beliefs. As a result, the development of the self suffers. Here is the 'as-if' person struggling but alone and lonely, trying to appear as if needing nothing.

If you imagine someone who is brave enough to withdraw all his projections, then you get an individual who is conscious of a pretty thick shadow. Such a man has saddled himself with new problems and conflicts. He has become a serious problem to himself, as he is now unable to say that they do this or that, they are wrong, and they must be fought against ... Such a man knows that whatever is wrong in the world is in himself.

(Jung, 1958/1969, CW 11, para. 140)

As individuation unfolds, so does confrontation with the shadow, erupting through the melancholy and the repressed grief and loss. Jung believes

the shadow is a moral problem that challenges the whole ego-personality, for no one can become conscious of the shadow without considerable moral effort. To become conscious of it involves recognizing the dark aspects of the personality as present and real. This act is the essential condition for any kind of self-knowledge.

(1968a, CW 9ii, para. 14)

Exposing the dilemmas can lead to integration through addressing the self and other, the shadow. The shadow includes the repressed contents in the personal unconscious as well as the material from the collective unconscious. Often the pain from the ill-functioning self pushes a person into therapeutic work to access the ability to survive and find meaning. Yet, psychic space closes when envy takes over, leaving the envier with the anticipation of failure and emptiness from emotional betrayals and disillusionments, reflecting the dejected assumption that hurts cannot be staunched.

The root of envy is a dissatisfied and insufficiently met heart. Painfully, envy is linked with the images of being exploited, belittled and forced into a submissive position. Envy, according to Bion, is described as 'a kind of psychological and auto-immunological disorder, an attack by the mind on itself' (Mitchell & Black, 1995, p. 103). If the analysand hides from the envy to present an acceptable but false personality, the psychological treatment becomes lifeless. The 'as-if' personality, unable to reveal confusion, wishes, fears, is susceptible to this.

Dream world

Over time it becomes clear Francesca entered psychological treatment because of a tenuous hold on life. In a brief one-line dream *an ocean woman took a mother standing on the shore under the waters.* Francesca says she tries to not go there, as it is deep and maybe she will drown. Depressed, she forgets the ocean contains food, the depth of the unconscious and the mysteries of life. In relation to this Julia Kristeva acknowledged 'an abyss of sorrow, a noncommunicable grief that at times... lays claims upon us to the extent of having us lose all interest in words, action and even life itself' (1992, p. 3).

Francesca's inner life remains buried under several archetypal dreams, calling her to go deeper, but she gets intrigued with the fact of the archetypes, rather than their symbolic meanings and how they apply to her personally. After this dream Francesca says she is not a good mother to herself. She forgets to eat. Her period was awful last month due to stress. 'We are enabled to examine our lives so as to avoid pretense and half-measure, all those small acts of weakness... where we give in to the easy exception to any rule, without really wishing to' (Perry, 2010, p. 187). Francesca is burdened by an internalised defeat from the cumulative succession of social and personal disappointments. The depth of the sadness looms large, and she backs away from experiencing the weight of the sorrow. 'The self wounded, incomplete, empty, is felt to have a fundamental flaw, a congenital deficiency. Such logic presupposes a severe super-ego and a complex dialectic of idealization and devalorization, both of self and other' (Kristeva, 1992, p. 6). There is a crushing loneliness, coloured with the anticipation she will sink into depression, rendered emotionally paralysed and helpless. There is the thought no one could or would help.

Envy is part of the raw psychological material bringing about the process of dissolution in which thesis and antithesis play integral parts (Hiles, 2012, p. 11). Although the process leads to re-construction of the personality, it is dissolution Francesca fears. Therefore, before therapy sessions, she prepares to answer what might come up. My interpretations or any comments stop her thoughts, and she gets lost, stuck. She is tormented with lack of accomplishment and registers a painful sense of difference unfavourable to the self (Colman, 1991, p. 364). These issues of difference revolve around money, class disparity, lack of privilege and worries about the future. She cannot risk, needing to know the outcome before she begins. The 'unbearable envy too often means the inner landscape remains sterile' (Meredith-Owen, 2008, p. 474).

Negative transference and emotional impasse express frustration while hiding shame and grief. The person does not feel enriched by the analytic relationship (Meredith-Owen, 2008, p. 461), and any support is only dimly imagined. The underlying dreaded exclusion feels like annihilation to the personality (p. 463). The therapeutic impasse arising from envy impedes feeling met or correctly read, compounded by Francesca's desire for engagement as well as the despair of ever getting it.

Francesca does not communicate the envy in therapy, pushes away any attempts to address what she considers disparities of power between us, hides sensitive feelings and reactions, anticipating being seen as needy, then abandoned. This scenario replays over and over. There seems no way for her to resolve the sorrow from what others got and she did not, no way to alter her need to pretend 'as-if' she is alright. To relax and feel safe enough to emote is interceded by Francesca's embarrassment to admit what she considers deficits. She is anxious, fearing mistakes, lamenting how many of life's basics she was never told.

In another dream *she and I are in an old magical forest. I give her something. She expresses trepidation about taking it and does not.* She feels flat and numb without emotion in the dream. She associates this dream to the hero Neo in the movie *The Matrix* who could take one pill and continue in the dull office job or take the other pill and the unknown will unfold. After the dream she has no feeling about what to do. This represents being at an impasse, a threshold time of transition and possible change. She does not know how to decide and here is the issue: vacillating between what she wants and what she fears, Francesca takes the safe and known route.

Therapy helps re-negotiate the wounded places, dismantles envious and defensive strategies while also revealing psychic panic. Francesca is offered something special in the dream, but she does not trust it, the unconscious or the relationship with me, the therapist. The therapeutic process and its self-exploration dredge up elements of envy, desire, passion and suffering. All are ingredients for renewal of the psyche. The process of increasing awareness means uncovering the denials guarding against her truths, the fantasies and bonds maintaining old inhibiting roles and reactions. Here is enacted the 'real existential anguish, doubt, not knowing and the risk it takes for her to reveal emotions and real feelings' (Solomon, 2004, p. 643). She wants assurance of being special, her character acknowledged, but this will not fill the lack of self-regard within. The work requires becoming conscious of the envy, grieving the losses, finding her voice and reigniting desires and passions.

Francesca has a difficult time symbolising so many of the dreams are interpreted literally. She needs to be seen in control, to be heroic, recognised, saving others and always alone. Envy interferes with her natural responses as she tends to alter them to fit what she thinks is expected. She becomes emotionally paralysed, trying to be a good patient, but this turns against her by deadening her inner conversation and affecting the spontaneity of relationship in therapy. She must be watchful for any surprises.

'It is the ego's envy of the alienated self, that creates its profound despair and deadly malevolence' (Stein, 1990, p. 161). Francesca says she is too shattered, disappointed and anxious. At night the demons emerge, and she cannot sleep, wracked with envy, worry, insecure and alone with the devastation she feels inside. She worries about the demise of the therapeutic relationship, perhaps she did or said something wrong. There is an experience of confusion, a sense of dread, and not having time to compose herself to be understood. She cannot reveal anything further. She returns to self-doubt and shame about where and how she was raised, yet continually defends the family who 'did their best'. Francesca feels trapped and ashamed to ask and often says she does not know the questions. She put on a brave girl persona as a child and now remains apprehensive of authority and follows rules, anticipating being wrong to the point of being scrupulous.

The psychological abyss and desire to withdraw conflicts with wanting acceptance. She relates *an image of being alone on a beach looking out at the ocean and in tears. Someone comes up to touch her shoulder, sits down, and they are both silent.* In the next session she feels shame over this expression of vulnerability and desire but cannot explain further. Then she expresses irritation and does not want any of my thoughts or interpretations, assessing they will be from the intellect but not the heart.

For a long time, she is unable or resistant to get in touch with 'the reality of these interior places distinguished by their lack of structure or organization' (Green, 1983, p. 37). However, the process continues as layer after layer of the emotional neglect is unwrapped, revealing the pull to be alone mixed with insecurity about engaging with others. This tender place is behind the envy and occasionally emerges. Too often she feels estranged from her affective core, and then life becomes meaningless and empty amid the self-loathing with its accompanying envy.

The ability to symbolise links the conscious and unconscious realms, activating the capacity to imagine and play with images and metaphors. Francesca dreams *I give her a piece of white frosted cake.* She expresses no reaction in the dream. I say it was sweet. To her, my comment makes the positive negative. In fact, she is quite upset by the next session. She would not choose cake, did not like the colour and so on. Yet, she went along as she became lost in the session and felt awful after. She could not find her words until later and then she became angry and defensive. The dream is symbolic, but she does not recognise this and puts it down as mere fantasy. She feels invisible, tired and worries the stress will take her out. The traumatic interactions early in life are replicated in the equally traumatic internalised object relationships, leaving in their wake the true self waiting to be found (Modell, 1996, p. 86). Again, the refusal of the cake metaphorically represents that what could be sweet is not and it has too many calories. I should know this, and it represents she feels unheard as I have given her the wrong food.

The person who is envious and spoiling, especially to herself, experiences the world mirrored similarly. Envy can work against affection and creativity, sabotage the desire to learn, and poorly affect relationships. Jungian analyst Murray Stein wrote, 'While everyone experiences envy, there are people who are chronically envious... continuously vulnerable to envy reactions, and it becomes their "central psychological task" to resolve issues related to envy' (1990, p. 169). The associated shame, embarrassment and self-consciousness diminish the sense of self-agency, as the person feels helpless, without control. The world is experienced as disillusioning. Awareness of envy means not only looking under the surface to find the blocks, but also discovering the resources for self-awareness and acceptance.

Keeping the treatment relationship at bay means Francesca is held at a distance also. It is a familiar position for this lonely person, desiring connection but assuming it is unattainable. Not surprisingly the impasse remains, as all she wants is an apology for my purposeful use of power over her. André Green surmised it is 'because of the lack of the object... [there is] a destruction of the psychic activity of representation which creates holes in the mind, or feelings of void, emptiness etc. a failure of symbolization' (Kohon, 1999, p. 290).

Francesca does spend some time in the analytic process. Some things improve for her while we proceed into the core of distrust and disappointment in the analytical relationship. However, envy contributes to the tenacity of the complex, creating much impasse in the analytical work. Envy has been a teacher but not an easy one.

Admitting envy

Envy can adversely affect the lifelong process of self-development. In such instances the person remains fixed in the wished for but always unattained. 'Envy at least has the almost saving grace of being an expression of our pain. The way out is to transcend oneself, to enlarge one's heart' (Russell, 2013, p. 76). The discomfort from realising such feelings also represents the wounds opening the path of self-discovery, providing movement out of old entrenched positions, both psychologically and culturally. The patient begins to recognise the desires lost in the painful effects of envy. Opening the memories allows the submerged and rejected material into conscious awareness.

When taken out of silence, envy and its powerlessness along with its power plays can shift and find spaces for the self to grow. Working with and through envy, gradually and with delicate attention, tells a story of movement out of the shadows by addressing the wounds with healing attention. Sometimes the envy is too tenacious, the splitting too strong, and a person can only get as far as possible given limitations. Other times, the envy can be fully explored, understood and integrated into the knowledgebase of the personality. The work is not just to repair what was lost or unavailable to begin with but also to answer current needs. Envy indicates where one is saying no unconsciously to oneself. The aim of the Jungian individuation process is a synthesis of the partial, incompletely formed aspects of our conscious and unconscious minds. Recognising and claiming these aspects can develop aliveness and plant new seeds, overcoming envy and living into creativity. The 'as-if' person can strip off the envy to experience being real.

> I envy not in any moods
> The captive void of noble rage,
> The linnet born within the cage,
> That never knew the summer woods: ...
>
> I hold it true, whate're befall;
> I feel it, when I sorrow most:
> 'Tis better to have loved and lost
> Than never to have loved at all.

Alfred Lord Tennyson, *Memoriam 16*
(https://poets.org/poem/memoriam-h-h)

References

Abraham, K. (1927). *Selected papers on psycho-analysis*. The Hogarth Press and The Institute of Psycho-Analysis.

Bonovitz, C. (2010). Comparative perspectives on envy: A reconsideration of its developmental origins. *Contemporary Psychoanalysis*, *46*(3), 423–38. doi: 10.1080/00107530.2010.10746070.

Britton, R. (1998). *Belief and imagination*. Routledge.

Chaucer, G. (2000). The parson's tale. In *The Canterbury tales and other poems*. Project Gutenberg ebook: Vol.2383. www.gutenberg.org/cache/epub/2383/pg2383-images.html.

Ciardi, J. (Trans.) (2005). The divine comedy by D. Alighieri. Introduction by A. McAllister. Pocket Books.

Colman, W. (1991). Envy, self-esteem and the fear of separateness. *British Journal of Psychotherapy*, *7*(4), 356–67. doi: 10.1111/j.1752-0118.1991.tb01141.x.

Colman, W. (2007). Symbolic conceptions: The idea of the third. *Journal of Analytical Psychology*, *52*(5), 565–83. doi: 10.1111/j.1468-5922.2007.00686.x.

Green, A. (1983). *On private madness*. The Hogarth Press.

Hiles, D. (2012, October). *Envy, jealousy, greed: A Kleinian approach* [Paper presentation]. Centre for Counselling & Psychotherapy Education (CCPE), London, England.

Jung, C.G. (1958/1969). *The collected works of C.G. Jung: Vol. 11. Psychology and religion*. Princeton University Press.

Jung, C.G. (1960/1969). *The collected works of C.G. Jung: Vol. 7. Two essays on analytical psychology*. Princeton: Princeton University Press.

Jung, C.G. (1966). *The collected works of C.G. Jung: Vol. 16. The practice of psychotherapy*. Princeton University Press.

Jung, C.G. (1968a). *The collected works of C.G. Jung: Vol. 9ii. Aion*. Princeton University Press.

Jung, C.G. (1968b). *The collected works of C.G. Jung: Vol. 13. Alchemical studies*. Princeton: Princeton University Press.

Jung, C.G. (1968c). *The collected works of C.G. Jung: Vol. 9i. The archetypes and the collective unconscious*. Princeton University Press.

Jung, C.G. (1969). *The collected works of C.G. Jung: Vol. 8. The structure and dynamics of the psyche*. Princeton: Princeton University Press.

Jung, C.G. (1970). *The collected works of C.G. Jung: Vol. 14. Mysterium conjunctionius*. Princeton University Press.

Jung, C.G. (1979). *Foreword to the I ching*. Princeton University Press.

Klein, M. (1975). *Envy and gratitude and other works 1946–1963*. The Hogarth Press and The Institute of Psycho-Analysis.

Kohon, G. (ed.) (1999). *The dead mother: The work of André Green*. London: Routledge.

Kristeva, J. (1992). *Black sun: Depression and melancholia*. (Trans. Leon Roudiez). New York: Columbia University Press.

Meredith-Owen, W. (2008). 'Go! Sterilize the fertile with thy rage': Envy as embittered desire. *Journal of Analytical Psychology*, *53*(4), 459–80. doi: 10.1111/j.1468-5922.2008.00741.x.

Mitchell, S. & Black, M. (1995). *Freud and beyond: A history of modern psychoanalytic thought*. Basic Books.

Modell, A. (1996). *The private self*. Harvard University Press.

Perry, L. (2010). *Brief history of thought*. (Trans. Leo Cuffe). Harper Collins.

Proner, B.D. (2017). The latency complex: The dead hand of anti-development. *Journal of Analytical Psychology*, *62*(4), 567–84. doi: 10.1111/1468-5922.12337.

Russell, B. (2013). *Conquest of happiness*. Routledge.

Schwartz-Salant, N. (1982). *On narcissism*. Inner City Books.

Solomon, H. (2004). Self creation and the limitless void of dissociation: The as if personality. *Journal of Analytical Psychology*, *49*, 635–56. doi: 10.1111/j.0021-8774.2004.00493.x.

Solomon, H. (2007). *The self in transformation*. London: Karnac.

Stein, M. (1990). *Sibling rivalry and the problem of envy. Journal of Analytical Psychology*, *35*(2), 161–74. doi: 10.1111/j.1465-5922.1990.00161.x.

Stein, M. (2017). Where East meets West in the house of individuation. *Journal of Analytical Psychology*, *62*(1), 67–87. doi: 10.1111/1468-5922.12280.

Steiner, J. (1993). *Psychic retreats: Pathological organizations in psychotic, neurotic and borderline patients*. London: Routledge.

Ulanov, A. & Ulanov, B. (1983). *Cinderella and her sisters: The envied and the envying*. Westminster Press.

Chapter 8

The encounter of transferences

Athena plays a prominent part in Homer's great epic *The Odyssey*. The story captures the return of its protagonist Odysseus, the king of Ithaca, to his homeland. This journey takes him ten long years, and he is eventually able to reunite with his family and take back his land from the horrible suitors who filled his palace. Athena, the mighty goddess of wisdom and strategy, takes the role of both protection and wisdom in the epic as she guides the titular character as well as his son, Telemachus.

Initially, Athena uses the tactics of disguise to influence the prince to find his father by shapeshifting into Odysseus's old friend Mentes and predicting Odysseus is still alive. She uses her great skills of strategy and wisdom to instil confidence and strength into Telemachus to help him become a man by stepping forth on his journey to find his father. Moreover, it is with her help that Odysseus can become a stronger, nobler Homeric hero. Beginning with her first act of assistance to her final peace-making, Athena is largely responsible for the creation and conclusion of the plot of *The Odyssey*.

'Psychologically, Athene brings illuminating perception... applied consciousness... facilitates reflection which attends upon effective realization of the self' (Shorter, 1986, p. 174). In analytical psychology reflecting on images, dreams and symbolic messages from the unconscious helps restore the personality. Jung described 'a process by which a new content forces itself upon consciousness either from without (through the senses) or from within (from the unconscious) and, as it were, compels attention and enforces apprehension' (1971, CW 6, para. 683). Creativity and imagination arise in analysis to bring forth images, their meaningful content and thoughtful reflection upon it.

Jung called this the transcendent function arising within the analytic discourse and facilitating personality expansion.

> The suitably trained analyst mediates the transcendent function for the patient, i.e., helps bring conscious and unconscious together and arrive at a new attitude. In this function of the analyst lies one of the many important meanings of the transference ... The understanding of the transference is to be sought not in its historical antecedents but in its purpose.
>
> (Jung, 1960/1969, CW 8, para. 146)

DOI: 10.4324/9781003315254-9

Writing about this personality type frames it, makes it coherent, recognises through the clinical work in the consulting room the unconscious thoughts made conscious, exchanged and put into words. The process honours and recognises the existence of the patient as analysis is a container in which we grow.

The therapeutic space includes an encounter with vulnerability, fantasies and tragedies. Within this is the tender and fragile, shy parts of the self. With affective emotional engagement in therapy, emotional learning occurs that may bring profound changes in the inner patterning that determines the way the patient is able to relate (Wilkinson, 2017, p. 539). The need to understand the gap between the true and the 'as-if' brings people into psychotherapy, yet it is difficult for them. They might begin saying, 'Something I am interested in learning is to help guide myself into the future I want. I struggle with anxiety and depression, and I often feel like I hold myself back from becoming the best version of myself'.

In therapy the 'as-if' person seeks reassurance that they are liked, that they fit in, that they aren't upsetting the therapist for fear of expected retaliation and rejection or anger. The analytical sessions become layered with unconsciousness and sleepiness. When these elements are addressed 'in the transference-countertransference the traumatic complex can be detoxified and the individual freed to fully embrace and constructively express and develop themselves and their relationships' (West, 2013, p. 74).

By entering the problems in a real way and accepting and untangling projections common to all relationships, analysis helps a person feel safe. Analysis and therapy are containers in which a person can grow beyond the known and create new possibilities from the relationship. Hope can be activated in analytical space as a bridge to connect and transition between what was not existent previously into what can now emerge. These experiences increase the capacity to manage as analyst and patient stand together in the space between what seemed unimaginable and now becomes possible – to be one's real self.

The journey is a revisiting of fragmented psychological places, old unfinished business, a retracing of memories. There might be all kinds of panic, torpor, disorientation and lingering, unresolved issues revealing the afflicted consciousness. The patient's mental distress is apparent as is their devotion to the real, which resides among the acuity of the details. Naming and visualising illustrate the obstacles, the joys and the tragedies and the way into the unconscious to enrich conscious life. Therapy is a photograph of time, but not stuck in time. The point is to move the energy through to new combinations. It is a retrospective, prospective and intimate relationship symbolically providing the gold paint.

In the transference and countertransference both participants together recognise the emotional distress, mourning the losses and searching for recovery of the personality. To address such situations, analysis revolves around the conflicts and tensions needed to uncover the resolution and reconciliation of the opposing forces in the individual (Seligman, 1986, p. 83). The alliance between therapist and client secures trust and evolves through the relationship as it depends on separation and connection between both participants. This process requires the capacity to recognise and gather the multiple personal and collective threads. The transferences are put to creative use to find a thoughtful and sensitive way to think and feel about what is true.

The 'as-if' person often hides their emotional injuries, so there will be no surprises or threats to their system. The perspective of Jungian analytical psychology, with its focus on both the conscious and unconscious, symbolism and union of disparate personality parts, uniquely provides a comprehensive encounter for treatment. The analyst's fluidity of thought and reverie can move the process towards wider perspectives.

> Using their own symbolic attitude, the analyst offers a form of meaning to the patient that enables them to take a 'third position' to their own proto-symbolic productions. In other words, the analyst's interpretative activity promotes the patient's imaginal capacity, enabling a conscious attitude to the spontaneous fantasy productions emerging from the unconscious and to find new meaning in them. In this way, the analytic process involves the development of co-constructed meanings.
>
> (Colman, 2007, p. 575)

In this chapter the composite clinical examples illustrate the 'as-if' person challenged to symbolise, reflect and find meaning.

> The Jungian symbol tends towards the dimension of the not-yet. It anticipates that which the culture will explicate only in the course of time and in times and in ways that are impossible to determine a priori. Thus, the Jungian symbol has a dimension that is not only individual and subjective but collective and cultural.
>
> (Connolly, 2003, p. 365)

The ability to symbolise and find the metaphorical in life is affected by the patient's difficulty managing anything that seems unfamiliar. For the 'as-if' person this is followed by the strong impulse to retreat in the face of the awkward and unknown. The ego is easily threatened. To hide the anticipation of being seen as loathsome and not preferred, the 'as-if' person distances through self-absorption.

Kintsugi

The psyche becomes visible through metaphors, images and symbols. 'When people begin to symbolize their difficulties, the work itself becomes deepening and they are on the road to recovery' (Astor, 2005, p. 419). This can be illustrated through the Japanese art called *Kintsugi*, or the repairing of cracked pottery with gold paint.

Kintsugi is a centuries-old Japanese art of repairing broken pottery and transforming it into a new work of art with gold, the traditional metal used in Kintsugi.

The name of the technique is derived from the words *Kin* (golden) and *tsugi* (joinery), which translates to 'golden repair'. The scars and cracks of the broken ceramic become the focus, turning the object into something unique and exquisite. The whole pursuit pertains to the Zen ideal of *wabi sabi*, the concept of embracing imperfection. It means finding pleasure in aged and worn objects and valuing the blemishes accruing through time as beautiful. Kintsugi treats breakage and repair as part of the history of an object, rather than a reason to disguise or discard. The art denotes a respect for that history, like the history of one's psyche, personal and collective, each affecting the other, not to just be erased, but acknowledged and worked with.

In Jungian analytical psychology symbols are a language of images conveying, by means of concrete reality, something hidden or unknown with a numinous quality dimly perceived by the conscious mind. Here it is used as an apt analogy to the analytical processes to transform and repair the split and broken pieces of the personality. The cracks in ceramic pottery as well as the psychological cracks in the personality represent the breakage needing repair; pieced together they become a work of art. The breakage happens over time and not only on new pottery. The pieces or dissociated parts are rearranged into something new but made from the old ingredients. This creates beauty from accentuating, not hiding, the cracks. And the pottery piece, like the personality, is forever changed in the process.

Kintsugi demonstrates the beauty emerging through the work as it progresses from damage to repair. Likewise, by examining emotional problems, the 'as-if' personality works with and transforms the feelings and attitudes arising from assumed imperfections. They learn to use the issues with conscious awareness and to grow from rather than limit. Jung said, 'The symbol becomes in me such that it has its substance, and I mine' (2009, p. 249). Like the use of the gold paint, both Kintsugi and analysis are delicate, painstaking processes with the purpose of bringing about change. Nothing looks or is as it was before. However, both processes lead to strengthening the container – be it the pottery or the personality – while addressing the need for attention. They each contain and embody the conscientious significance of the work in the process.

We live in an era offering a plethora of treatments, and long-term therapy provides depth exploration and has many potential rewards. As with Kintsugi, inner work supports the idea of self-knowledge and character change requiring more than just a short, narrow, linear path. To aim higher and not rest content with mere symptom relief, we must persevere in the labyrinthine search for wellbeing. It is an energetic configuration to break the deadlock and restore energy.

A woman dreams *she has a necklace of strands and twists and twists them and as she does this, and as expected, they separate, and all the baubles spread out on the floor. She begins to pick them up but decides she will only pick the ones she likes.* Similar to the process of Kintsugi, the broken necklace will come together but now more to her liking. The process of growth is like the dream, separating and coming together, choosing what fits now, as in the medieval science of alchemy with its stages of *separatio*, or 'separation', and *conjunctio*, or 'bringing together'.

The 'as-if' person finds the imperfect repugnant. The cracks in the personality seem glaring and the faults unrepairable. There is despair under the presentation of outer confidence. This Japanese art originating from an Eastern culture meets with the Western, like the process of conscious meeting unconscious and the participants meeting in the analytical process. It all is a meeting, an encounter with the unexpected and not linear or logical. Perspectives are expanded just as the psyche benefits from unifying the different and often unknown parts. Jung conjectured

> there are and always have been those who cannot help but see the nature of the world and its experiences are in the nature of a symbol, and that it reflects something that lies hidden in the subject himself, in his own transsubjective reality.
>
> (Jung, 1968, CW 11, para. 859)

The unification process is never finished, and the cracks are reminders of how we repair the vulnerable and weaker areas by focusing on them, uniting them with the glue, or a third element, to hold them together.

Kintsugi is a tradition and method of thought for valuing the whole piece rather than one part. All pieces are needed to reconstruct the pottery, and the repaired crack is a way to preserve, accentuate and strengthen the whole. This means incorporating the problem areas rather than trying to get rid of them. The process is lengthy, like analytical work and, at times, quite painstaking. Both the pottery work and the analytical process are transmutative on many levels. The processes are transformative, and the participants are changed. Both involve attachment but in conscious intentional form. Kintsugi is a person with an object and the object is transformed and added to. The result is other than what appeared at the beginning. The process evolves in time. All that is known is that it will not be as it was and all this parallels the analytical process of self-recovery.

'Every psychological expression is a symbol if we assume that it states or signifies something more and other than itself which eludes our present knowledge' (Jung, 1971, CW 6, para. 817). The analytical process involves two people and the object between is what will evolve, and it also is unknown. What was is no longer. Both processes emerge from the space between and require a valued investment of time and effort.

The analytical process and Kintsugi itself develop the capacity for integration of the four functions of thinking and feeling, intuition and sensation. The analytic pair, or potter, uses the least accessed, the awkward pieces, and finds how they fit together with those that seem stronger and more developed. Boundaries and connections between self and other require a similar sort of emotional fluidity for growth. This involves the ability to sustain the tension of paradox, essential to healthy development, making space for difference and variety. The analytical process fills in the spaces, leading to trust, creativity and increased self-awareness.

Peeling layers from the self in a safe space is an exploration that takes time and effort and reaches into the core of a person's system. Like Kintsugi, it is a serious work of art based on repair to change and become other than what one was.

Self-knowledge and character change follow a longer, wider, winding path in the search for wellbeing. It is a substantive aim beyond mere symptom relief. Through the relationship with the therapist, the 'as-if' person can break the unconscious deadlock and restore energy.

Do you know my name?

For all life rests on appearance, art, illusion, optics, necessity of perspective and error.

Friedrich Nietzsche, *The Birth of Tragedy* (1910)

According to American relational analyst Jessica Benjamin:

the need for mutual recognition, the necessity of recognizing as well as being recognized by the other – this is what so many theories of the self missed. The idea of mutual recognition is crucial to the intersubjective view; it implies that we have a need to recognize the other as a separate person who is like us yet distinct.

(1988, p. 23)

Analytical inquiry and treatment can be defined as a 'dialectic of consciousness and unconsciousness, of presence and absence, of affirmation and negation upon which the analytic enterprise rests' (Ogden, 1977, p. 22). The interaction of the patient and analyst occur on the intersubjective and intrapsychic levels with a dynamic tension between these. Much is changed in the process of creating oneself as the personality pieces are transformed by the reflective, conscious and unconscious interactions.

Facing the psyche or soul to bring body and body phenomena out of the shadows and to situate them more consciously is at the heart of psychotherapy or analysis. In the room there are not only two souls but also two breathing bodies in a constant, reciprocal interaction and exchange.

The process incorporates recognition and repair of those past emotional gaps. The intersubjectivity is necessary to escape the solipsism of the 'as-if' person's separated and often isolated existence, developed from past pain and suffering. It is a gradual process of bringing out the damaged pieces, examining and feeling them, being confused. The inter-subjectiveness of analysis finds ways to open the formerly futile and often deceptive wanderings in the 'as-if' person's internal world. In the process, the participants experience together what cannot be done alone.

The therapist and 'as-if'

The emptiness, longing and needs of the 'as-if' person are re-enacted through the therapeutic relationship. Jungian analytical treatment creates a space where the analytical pair can dissolve the reliance on falsity and persona and support the gradual emergence of the more complete personality.

> The facets of their experience, behaviour and ways of relating, include aggressive and self-destructive elements. Only when these elements are addressed as they manifest, inevitably, in the transference-countertransference can the traumatic complex be detoxified and the individual freed to fully embrace and constructively express and develop themselves and their relationships.
>
> (West, 2013, p. 74)

This will affect the course of the psychological work. It also means the analyst's presence will facilitate pondering what lies behind and within the patient's dreams, offering guidance in and through the 'as-if' personality with its protective mechanisms.

In my work as a Jungian analyst, I have witnessed many 'as-if' people struggling with various and disparate personality parts. Known for a slickly contrived persona or ego image the 'as-if' person withdraws into fantasy and illusionary worlds, making up continual narratives based on lack, emotional deprivation and disappointments.

> I wandered lonely as a cloud
> That floats on high o'er vales and hills,
> When all at once I saw a crowd,
> A host, of golden daffodils.
>
> William Wordsworth, 'I wandered lonely as a cloud' (1802)

These issues affect intimacy with self and others owing to how difficult they are to acknowledge, and they keep the person from being fully present. Human beings are naturally passionate, according to Jung, but the 'blocking of libido', as he called it, can lead to feeling life has lost its zest and enjoyment and one becomes stuck and lost. 'Libido is appetite in its natural state. From the genetic point of view, it is bodily needs like hunger, thirst, sleep, and sex, and emotional states or affects, which constitute the essence of libido' (Jung, 1967, CW 5, para. 194).

Kennedy came to analysis for the first time in her fifties. She described herself as intelligent, quick, in a high-ranking position with a large salary, surrounded by many friends and well-liked. She went to the best schools and was the top of her class. She repeated this fact often. Over time I realised the repetition evidenced 'display of a grandiose self, affording magical protection and an independent or omnipotent self, needing no others as compensation for the absence of safety' (Modell, 1996, p. 88). There was an appeal to Kennedy, yet she was emotionally removed. I dreamt of her and wondered if this signalled the presence of an emotional distance. Is this the allure of the never related 'as-if' personality? I pondered what was behind the dreams and how the therapy could continue without disturbance, all cracks hidden,

Kennedy compliant, and us getting nowhere. I surmised the dreams were alerting me to the smoke and mirrors aspect of this possible 'as-if' person, but I did not know what that meant at the beginning. I just knew there was discomfort.

With people like Kennedy, partial selves act as integral selves, reinforcing the 'as-if' position. With her mental mechanisms framed to eliminate all opposition, she tried to maintain psychological certainty. She could not be moved by desire, as the world needed to be smooth and undisturbed, so nothing could be taken into the self. To question the framework within the reconceived acceptable and familiar presentation meant rethinking and feeling assumptions, all of which she avoided. She was sufficiently protected by the relied upon but pathological organisation that allowed her to avoid the chaos inside herself.

There is often a reluctance to allow either the analyst or patient to escape from the familiar interactions. Through the analytical work there are moments when the 'as-if' person emerges from the psychic narcissistic retreat and is then faced with terrible anxieties and the damage done. But Kennedy was not able to show her soul; she felt others would not understand or realise she lived behind a wall. The chaos was too much – all must be ordered, static, unmoving, her life one of work but inner isolation, stagnant and without the instability of growth and change.

Kennedy tried to please yet hid anything authentic about herself. She seemed almost dehumanised. This must have arisen from past emotionally undernourished experiences. She expressed no trust in anyone, and she had little idea what being alive meant. Her loneliness was unknown to most people she encountered. However, it was evidenced in her too slick presentation and frantic manner, verbally filling the therapeutic time and space, letting there be no pause. These perceptions indicated how little Kennedy could reveal to herself as well. There was a defence against anything unknown squeezing through. She seemed unable to be honest or intimate with anyone, even herself, adopting the current style of thought, dress and calculated manoeuvrings with mimicry of others so she would fit in. It was like she pasted these behaviours on but did not examine anything deeply as she only wanted approval, along with status and adulation. Beyond her initial charm something was stifled, avoidant, while she seemed social and open. Who she really was remained the mystery.

She talked of being teary and even depressed. She said she had not previously acknowledged this and was apprehensive now due to some anticipated change. But what does she want to change? She said her partner did not notice her, yet she also described not being present, secretly resentful, angry for years and purposely emotionally separate. Although she said she wanted change, her words sounded hollow, vacuous. Status, wealth and career position had kept Kennedy busy and away from feelings and reactions she dared not or maybe could not unfold.

Her talk filled the therapeutic space while she seemed nervous and off balance. Each therapy session was a flood of material, the same themes and stories over and over, yet she could not admit she was shaken. Her presentation was rapid, and she did not take in and defended against any commentary on her story. She felt it as an intrusion. In this manic defence she had no room for the interactive, no pause to reflect or allow any different reactions. There was also no separation or space between us. She felt both connected, but in a superficial way, and distanced to the point of being unapproachable, indicating the fragility of the personality.

Kennedy had trouble giving genuinely and emotionally or responding flexibly and adaptively to any other's behaviour. Her internal and external worlds were poised between what she feared in her mind as demise and what she externalised to the world as her being in control. Unconscious of this and needing safety, she attached through demands for sameness with fusion allowing for no differences. This set up sensations of being trapped, rigid defence systems, fear of intimacy with any other who might be different. She anticipated being taken over, found wanting or ignored.

She is an example of those with reluctance to allow either the analyst or themselves to escape from the familiar interactions and stories they have repeatedly told, hence the defences, and the walls erected against being seen or known. She did not do well with the unknown. However, through the analytic work, I could see moments when the person emerged from this psychic narcissistic retreat of singularity. Kennedy was then faced with what seemed like terrible anxieties around recognising the damage done. Repair becomes possible through developing the dialogical analytical relationship, and this is difficult for the 'as-if' person as it means being seen and open.

The tension between ego and self, surface and shadow, are part of forming an identity in which the various selves can co-exist. Conscious awareness of the emotional wounds arouses past disillusionment, profound disappointments and the means of coping. Facing these illusions is restorative but requires both participants to be actively involved in the interplay of the unconscious processes in the consulting room. Hopelessness and impasse then have a possibility of shifting. The psychological process takes patience because the unmasking of reality connotes a threat to the ego or persona front relied upon when facing the world. Behind the well-calculated front portraying an innocence and appeal lay the tender vulnerability and feelings Kennedy found necessary to repress. The 'as-if' person is trapped by the need for unconditional love, anxiety about hostility and the expectation of being refused.

Needing continual approval from others and so involved in her own strivings, Kennedy usually did not see anyone else as wanting or deprived. Her superficial cover avoided and denied her own depth. This is because she was one of those who had been deprived of recognition and thus suffered and were condemned to harbour grave feelings of invalidation of their personhood and live in virtual aloneness (Mills, 2019, p. 6). The process begins with self-reproach and with reflection, time and inner examination, a circling in which she could find herself. The desired transformation means the 'as-if' person must hold the weight of the conflict between rebirth and annihilation. This frightening tension of opposites meant Kennedy was alone and she worried she could not do it.

Like many with the 'as-if' personality, Kennedy, not trusting herself, hired a coach for everything – what to eat, how to meditate, exercise, business, etc. The coach is a metaphorical and less threatening role. The answer lay elsewhere, outside herself;

Kennedy did not know how to access or trust her own wisdom and depth. She was under the realm of the culture that taught her she was passive, that she did not know how to access her own guidance and had to follow what someone else said or knew.

The world was made secure by others, and she did not trust herself in it. She was beginning to realise she had done a lot to make sure she was safe but had not been living in emotional resonance or closeness. She was shocked to realise how numb she had been and how fearful of change. This was not the story she told herself.

Yet the other story might be the adopted defence to not move into the unknown. The unconscious still carries the original experience because when the events occurred there was no way to process what happened or to integrate them. The subjective relation to and relationship with the interior informed the capacity to create meaning, connect to others and engage in life with fulfilment. This relation to the interior evolves over time and persistently demands we analyse ourselves in authentically honest and confessional ways. This includes facing how we find ourselves in the past, present and future. There is an innate restlessness to the psyche searching for more than complacency, naturally wanting and desiring to redefine and grow. This is part of accessing our spirit and life force in psyche and soma for reflection and self-conscious awareness.

However, in my dreams Kennedy appeared naïve, fragile and innocent. From our sessions I gathered this was a signal to me that the outer and inner were dissonant, the self unavailable, ensconced behind thick layers of ego and persona. I wanted to be alert and sensitive to the disguise and barrier she raised to avoid internal challenges so nothing could shake her world. This 'as-if' person remains impenetrable for many reasons. Kennedy's fragility and lack of trust were exposed by the way she tried to control the analytical process. She desperately needed to keep at bay any contact with overwhelming or unfamiliar experiences of relationship, memories or anything that would shake her carefully modulated world.

Being real seemed impossible and it was unclear she knew what real meant. Her concrete thinking excluded the unthinkable. Kennedy mistreated her body by not registering instinctual physical needs such as hunger or tiredness. She believed her survival hung on a fragile thread in danger of being severed. She was convinced she would be left in poverty and lost without any resources and, as she said, one step from the dumpster. The level of deprivation and fear this short phrase conveyed was astounding given her outer presentation and financial situation. It was a psychological statement indicating the reasons for my dream image of her innocence and fragility. Aspects of her self had never been known and 'their only image is a radical absence' (Colman, 2006, p. 362). She presented like a doll, a plastic mannequin set for display, and this façade was what she put forth in psychotherapy. She wanted something but had to remain in control, and this prevented psychological movement. There could be no penetration, union or joining. The cracks were solidly eliminated.

Control was exerted over food, body, exercise, physical shape and other people. She was frantic to keep the image that all was in perfect order. She needed the profession where she was valued and most of all noticed, substituting for the absence of emotional rewards at home. Kennedy admitted there were many things she did not say and kept inside. Her personality was parcelled out in various relationships but never entirely seen. Not knowing other ways or even what was lacking, she filled an image but now could not locate the real.

Freudian psychoanalyst Helene Deutsch referred to the 'as-if' persona as one with:

> a completely passive attitude to the environment, with a highly plastic readiness to pick up signals from the outer world and to model herself and her behavior accordingly. The identification with what other people are thinking and feeling is the expression of this passive plasticity and renders the person capable of the greatest fidelity and the basest perfidity [*sic*]. Such a person can rapidly exchange one love object for another, just in case she is abandoned. The authentic self is concealed from others and there is alienation from feelings.
>
> (Deutsch, 1943, p. 265)

Kennedy *dreamt a tiger, panther or puma was at the bottom of the stairs and she was frozen and wondered what to do.* The resources of control and attempts at security were not possible in the face of a wild cat. Rather, she must be aware, embodied and acknowledge the instinct of fear and not run away. This would be natural, but she had cut off these responses to the detriment of her personality and now she was without ballast. To counter how much was controlled in her life she must surrender to the wildness of these various forms of the cat, a symbol of the feminine looming before her as she descended the stairs and came down from her lofty distance, above it all.

Why did I dream of her? I felt the analytic relationship was precarious and my dreams compensated for the emotional distance and lack of connection. Was this signalling I could not reach her while she remained impervious? She looked together yet I could tell this was a defence – a cover to the habitual, duplicitous, deceptive behaviour that served to keep the self in division and far from others.

Was I picking up her avoidance? This might reflect my own countertransference in an unconscious need for similarity as some way of finding connection. The distance also meant I could not unite or separate. Kennedy repeatedly aligned us, assuming similarity in home, style, body size, any difference negated. 'When there is no third position, negation of any kind seems intolerable because it is literally unthinkable' (Colman, 2007, p. 576). The search for acceptance became collapsed into the insistence on a false sameness as a way of bridging the space between us. It seemed she was doing this to connect, but was this connection real? The fusion meant she could see her real self. Lack in the capacity for self-observation only reinforced her deep-seated belief there was nothing within or nothing of value. This created the fearful attitude against opening into the unconscious.

The fragility of her psychological constellation could accept no challenge or difference and no change. Unconscious of this and needing safety, she could only attach through an imagined fusion allowing for no differences. This defence indicated fear of intimacy as acknowledging difference is part of union. However, Kennedy anticipated being taken over, found wanting or being ignored. She might not be the person she was thought to be. The way she portrayed herself to herself would then begin to crack. This became the fissure through which self-knowledge might have a chance to seep.

However, it seemed the unconsciousness continued in the therapy. I knew it lay between us – so prevalent it could not be acknowledged. I dreamt *a session lasted twice as long and I did not realise it until later. In the dream she gave me jewellery and I wondered why.* I pondered upon awaking, why I was unconscious of the time. Was the jewellery her seemingly giving? Was it envy of her position, status, power, even? Or, perhaps the dream was trying to tell me I wanted the jewels from her as in the sharing of her psyche for a real relationship and connection, not only in the therapy but significantly with herself.

Relatedness and real connection means letting down the façade and being real and open in the therapeutic relationship. With Kennedy, the outer presentation continued, glazing over the gaping abyss of inner lack and denying other means for connection. She avoided the process of deeper relating. In situations like this the reaction to change or the opening of the psyche may become so frightening, the 'as-if' person leaves the analytical work abruptly. Although I felt the work was undone, in pieces and filled with possibility for deeper change, Kennedy left the therapy after a period, giving little reason but insisting she had gained a better inner balance and increasing calm.

Last notes

In the transference, the 'as-if' person often begins treatment as polite, careful, adept at the socialised self. Conformity and outer acquiescence to the process can also hide the acuity of secret self-condemnation, loss of vitality and meaning. The private self is unavailable as it feels too precarious. This person might have spent a lifetime feeling helpless, powerless and dependent, their needs unmet. They are strongly susceptible to outer influences and feel they must hide the intensity and reality of who they are. The process is difficult as this person struggles to be in touch with real feelings buried within the hole of needs and desires unmet in the personality. The process is one of uncovering and feeling into the issues, so the previous aloneness and separation is filled with attentive presence. 'What is greatest about our existence and renders it precious and ineffable also makes careful use of our painful experiences to enter into our soul' (Rilke, 2018, p. 54, 4 Jan. 1923).

Attachments to others and intersubjective communal matrices form the psychological edifice of our natural dependency needs. The analyst is a participant in co-creating the analytic interplay. This occurs through the conscious and unconscious processes of analyst and analysand as they present themselves in the consulting room. The analyst uses her countertransference creatively to find thoughtful and sensitive ways to connect and listen to the unconscious messages. The analysand also comes to think and feel into what is true for them. The pottery cracks of the self can be filled with gold, and the 'as-if' person can attempt the process without seeking perfection as the result.

The ability to imagine, symbolise and play is necessary for all successful analytic work. This is a way through and into the 'as-if' personality. This ability is ascribed to the transcendent function or the emergence of the symbolic and the imagination. This arises from the psychological and physical conflicts spurring on the process of alignment between the conscious and unconscious. The psyche looks to complete itself, to manifest modes of consciousness, to fill the lack and the gaps. To unify psychological opposites and elevate itself, the psyche is on a quest for truth and fulfilment in this natural and organic developmental process of repair and reshaping the pieces together.

References

Astor, J. (2005). The self invented personality? Reflections on authenticity and writing analytic papers. *Journal of Analytical Psychology*, *50*(4), 415–30. doi: 10.1111/j.0021-8774.2005.00546.x.

Benjamin, J. (1988). *Bonds of love*. London: Routledge.

Colman, W. (2006). Imagination and the Imaginary. *Journal of Analytical Psychology*. *51*(1). pp.21–41.

Colman, W. (2007). Symbolic conceptions: The idea of the third. *Journal of Analytical Psychology*, *52*(5), 565–83. doi: 10.1111/j.1468-5922.2007.00686.x.

Colman, W. (2008). On being, knowing and having a self. *Journal of Analytical Psychology*, *53*(3), 351–66. doi: 10.1111/j.1468-5922.2008.00731.x.

Connolly, A. (2003). To speak in tongues: Language, diversity and psychoanalysis. *Journal of Analytical Psychology*, *47*(3), 359–82. doi: 10.1111/1465-5922.00325.

Deutsch, H. (1943). *The psychology of women: Vol. 1. Girlhood*. Allyn & Bacon.

Jung, C.G. (1960/1969). *The collected works of C.G. Jung: Vol. 8. The structure and dynamics of the psyche*. Princeton University Press.

Jung, C.G. (1967). *The collected works of C.G. Jung: Vol. 5. The symbols of transformation*. Pantheon Books.

Jung, C.G. (1968). *The collected works of C.G. Jung: Vol. 11. Civilization in transition*. Princeton University Press.

Jung, C.G. (1971). *The collected works of C.G. Jung: Vol. 6. Psychological types*. Princeton University Press.

Jung, C.G. (2009). *The red book: Liber novus* (S. Shamdasani, ed.). W.W. Norton & Co.

Mills, J. (2019). Recognition and pathos. *International Journal of Jungian Studies*, *11*(1), 1–22. doi: 10.1163/19409060-01101001.

Modell, A. (1996). *The private self*. Harvard University Press.

Nietzsche, F. (1910). The birth of tragedy (W.A. Haussmann Trans.). Project Gutenberg (Ebook #51356). www.gutenberg.org/files/51356/51356-h/51356-h.htm.

Ogden, T. (1977). *Subjects of analysis*. Jason Aronson.

Rilke, R. M. (2018). The Dark Interval: Letters on Loss, Grief, and Transformation. *Modern Library Classics*.

Seligman, E. (1986). The half-alive ones. In: A. Samuels (ed.), *The father: Contemporary Jungian Perspectives* (pp. 69–94). New York University Press.

Shorter, B. (1986). The concealed body language of anorexia. In: A. Samuels (ed.), *The father: Contemporary Jungian Perspectives* (pp. 171–86). New York University Press.

West, M. (2013). Trauma and the transference-countertransference: Working with the bad object and the wounded self. *Journal of Analytical Psychology*, *58*(1), 73–98. doi: 10.1111/j.1468-5922.2013.02018.x.

Wilkinson, M. (2017). Mind, brain and body. Healing trauma: The way forward. *Journal of Analytical Psychology*, *62*(4), 526–43. doi: 10.1111/1468-5922.12335.

Chapter 9

Ageing, image and illusion

The first hexagram of the *I Ching, The Chinese Book of Changes*, reads:

> The hexagram is consistently strong in character, and since it is without weakness, its essence is power or energy. Its image is heaven. Its energy is represented as unrestricted by any fixed conditions in space and is therefore conceived of as motion. Time is regarded as the basis of this motion. Thus the hexagram includes also the power of time and the power of persisting in time, that is, duration. The power represented by the hexagram is to be interpreted in a dual sense in terms of its action on the universe and of its action on the world of men. In relation to the universe, the hexagram expresses the strong, creative action of the Deity. In relation to the human world, it denotes the creative action of the holy man or sage, of the ruler or leader of men, who through his power awakens and develops their higher nature.
>
> (Baynes, 1950/1979)

As Jung commented, 'The east teaches us another, broader, more profound, and higher understanding – understanding through life' (1967, CW 13, para. 2). Ancient Chinese Taoism and traditional Chinese culture view longevity as an accomplishment, a symbol of pride that includes qualities of endurance, perseverance, flexibility and harmony. Taoism recognises a relationship to the living spirit in nature, the divine within all creation. The Tao is the source of everything and the ultimate principle underlying reality for self-cultivation. This is evident in a quote from the Tao Te Ching, a Chinese classic text written around 400 BCE and traditionally credited to the sage Lao Tzu:

> To know harmony is to endure.
> To endure is to be enlightened.
>
> (1995, Verse 55)

This chapter explores the challenges ageing presents in the West with its youth culture and, especially, to the 'as-if' personality, using dreams, a poem from 20th-century American poet Sylvia Plath and composite examples. I contrast the concepts

DOI: 10.4324/9781003315254-10

of the old man or senex and old woman or crone with their youthful counterparts, the puer and puella. All these personality aspects parallel development and dovetail into one another throughout life. However, for the 'as-if' person, life's changes, joys, losses, regrets and delights pose threats as they age. I also apply the concept of precarity from American philosopher Judith Butler to ageing. The question within all this is how to open the many boxes older people are much too frequently put into and the cultural belief systems and labels holding them back from themselves. Jung contended:

> We are confronted, at every new stage in the differentiation of consciousness to which civilization attains, with the task of finding a new interpretation appropriate to this stage, in order to connect the life of the past that still exists in us with the life of the present, which threatens to slip away from it.
>
> (Jung, 1959, CW 9, para. 267)

A growing number of older people want to explore, expand and find purpose and meaning through entering and returning to depth psychological work. The 'as-if' person, although often lonely, has an intensity and creative edge but remains burdened within a morass of unexplored past and present sorrows and disillusionments. This can signify the return of the repressed, the no longer avoidable, personal and collective, conscious and unconscious material. With age, however, the urge for its expression and re-evaluation becomes more insistent.

Woman in the mirror – youth and age

A woman of age 55 dreams: *A woman emerges from a clawfoot tub in a red flowing dress. She gives the dreamer the shard of a mirror. The dreamer looks in the shard of mirror and sees an eye. It is not hers and she does not know whose it is.* This dream brings up many questions. She comes to analysis wondering where she is at this stage of life and whether she can realise more of her potential. Or is it too late? Career, relationships, physical health all seem timelier and more precarious now. Who does she see in the mirror's shard and who is the woman who gives it to her? They no doubt represent both sides of herself and perhaps both equally unknown. Why is the mirror a shard? Is she in pieces or does she only see pieces of herself? As with so many dreams, the layers unfold as the psyche unwraps itself from past constraints and gains receptivity to the total self.

The image in the outer and inner mirror is a visual echo of the self. Sometimes we do not recognise who we see in this mirror. Am I this age? Am I able? Should I try, still? The image becomes distorted as the idealised and illusionary preoccupy the 'as-if' person and clash with the images of the ageing self. Jung defined the image as

> a condensed expression of the psychic situation as a whole ... an expression of the unconscious as well as the conscious situation of the moment.

> The interpretation of its meaning, therefore, can start neither from the conscious alone nor from the unconscious alone but only from their reciprocal relationship.
>
> (Jung, 1971, CW 6, para. 743)

This quote implores us to expand beyond the narrow image into its wealth of potentiality.

The mirror image is explored in 'The Mirror', a poem by Sylvia Plath in which she describes a woman in the mirror and how the woman evaluates the reflected image that reveals her ageing process. This is an example of a person struggling with the restrictive definitions of beauty and being older, an image she abhors. The poem can be seen as exemplifying many of the contradictions and dilemmas faced by the 'as-if' personality. It is also applicable to anyone struggling for self-realisation while endeavouring to conform to superficial and social expectations. In the poem the image in the mirror becomes a doorway into another reality. It is set up as a paradoxical situation because the mirror image is and is not herself as the woman in it sees herself as both the observer and the observed.

Sylvia Plath was an American poet who killed herself at age 30 and thus only anticipated the horrors of age as revealed in this poem. At the time, she was married to British poet Ted Hughes, but this poem does not portray relationship or love in the gaze of the other or oneself. In fact, Ted Hughes came to represent male denigration of the feminine with his affairs, betrayals and even alterations of her writing for publication. For years Sylvia Plath struggled with the expected image of how she should be while trying to find out who she really was. Her writings show the ageless search of intense self-exploration. The dramas and conflicts were made more poignant as she aligned her intimate personal struggles with the collective human experience.

Jung stated about poetry: 'The unsatisfied yearning of the artist reaches back to the primordial image in the unconscious which is best fitted to compensate the inadequacy and one-sidedness of the present' (1966, CW 15, para. 130). Sylvia Plath represents the 'as-if' personality type who experienced early emotional misattunements. Ambivalence, mourning and the loss of parental attachments continued through her lifetime, leading to a loss of self. The disappointments piled up, as she felt misaligned with herself, others and the collective culture. She wore masks and façades, hiding her real self. Her poems describe this in the distance between who she was and who she wanted to be. In much of her work, she sought renewal and rebirth into ever younger forms. In her journal she noted looking in a mirror and being appalled at the wrinkles of age in the used-up person she saw looking back (Plath, 1963, p. 17).

A mirror needs a receptor, and in 'The Mirror', it is the woman striving to find herself in this external object noted to be male, nonplussed but critical. An idea of who she is emerges from the act of looking into the mirror, possibly paralleling the connection between the conscious and unconscious. However, if, like Narcissus, she is spell-bound by the image and the surface, she becomes trapped in a solipsistic self, searching for reassurance and confirmation from the mirror. The poem, however, describes the disharmony between the woman and the mirror image. Although the woman seems to seek stasis, the poem evolves and in doing so illustrates that the woman cannot remain frozen in time.

Sylvia Plath's use of the image of the mirror is a metaphor of the struggle within the 'as-if' person, between her mother, the image of herself as older and the images men hold of women. All represent narrow definitions of beauty that are only possible in youth and only in certain forms. The woman in this mirror is objectified even as she objectifies herself. For example, in the poem, the mirror both hides and reflects the self.

Plath portrays an internalised counterpart of the watching consciousness, possibly narrating her lifetime of interactions with a nameless, faceless woman, or herself, who imagines ageing as disfigurement. This woman could also symbolise the cultural view of the feminine, her mother's view of her own ageing and Sylvia Plath's despair about all of it. Although the speaker of the poem is a mirror, the true protagonist is the woman who sees herself both in and as a mirror, perhaps even as a non-person among a duality of images. She reminds me of the queen in *Snow White*. That queen needs reassurance of her beauty from a mirror. Neither beauty nor self-assurance comes from herself, nor does she look for it within. Like the 'as-if' personality, the queen looks outside of herself for validation. When it is not there, when she's not the best or the loveliest, she rages, and envy takes over. She lives on being the most beautiful and outstanding beyond all others. Everything and everyone else, within or without, has no value.

In the poem and in the fairy tale, the mirror speaks. A woman is assessed as attractive by some standard outside of herself. This is reminiscent of body dysmorphic disorder in which the body is never right or good enough nor is it seen in the light of reality. There is only misalignment and distress. The mirror only shows the problems and critiques. This becomes more pronounced with ageing, especially for the 'as-if' person, and especially for women who are still more harshly judged by their outer appearance than men.

The poem emanates ambivalence about the mirror, showing it is not easy or pleasant to be confronted by this mirror described as male, squared off, metallic, hard, even cold. Yet the mirror reveals the truth 'unmisted by love or dislike'. A flat wall behind the woman in the poem reveals a dull, almost lifeless corporeality reflected in the mirror. Moreover, this situation has gone on for so long the woman is now a non-entity, unimportant, merely part of the darkness in the background. In this, Sylvia Plath depicts how the woman recoils from the materiality and reality of her body. The expressed self-disdain is not allayed but accentuated by the mirror, and sadly, this is the plight of many of the 'as-if' type. The wall reflects the blankness, the lack of response replicated in society, in the woman's profession, marriage and all the social strictures against which Sylvia Plath struggled. Like the 'as-if' personality, even if she is in the right costume and attains the look she wants, she is still held back. Here is the disappointment predicated on the feeling that all is fleeting, and outer beauty, which is what counts, will not last.

To add another perspective, 20th-century French psychoanalyst Jacques Lacan was famous for what he called the *mirror stage of development*. This references the time of identity beginning when the small infant starts to differentiate themselves from their mother and see themselves as an individual. Prior to the formation of the ego, infants are unable to distinguish between themselves and the outside world. The mirror stage means the infant looks in the mirror and sees their image and that their body has form. They begin to perceive their physical features in relation to their physical movements and awaken to their being in relation to the world around them. Identity begins to cohere. In the mirror the infant sees themselves.

However, as true with many of the 'as-if' personality type who seek outer reassurance and approval, the woman in the poem is drawn to the mirror with its messages, even though it repulses and frightens her. What is it she sees in this mirror that keeps her coming back, obsessed, day after day, even though she is upset by the image? It might be age, inevitably and inescapably taking over.

The mirror shows the image of woman as reflector, and this is like the dual image Sylvia Plath presented to the world. She was woman and poet, a strict and tightly disciplined achiever who glitteringly fulfilled all social and cultural expectations. Underneath was the tremendous struggle to be her real self. Yet, she portrayed a perfect mirror, the persona, mimicking the expected parental and social standards of elegance, beauty and achievement. This was the outer cast of her personality, frozen in a Cover Girl smile. A woman who adopts this type of reflecting role exhibits a self-aggression that wins out over feelings of tenderness, and she becomes cruel, primarily to herself. Sylvia Plath strove to be known for her work, yet acutely felt the pressure of her gender as a woman and its limits in her world.

In the second section of the poem the mirror changes to a lake with a woman bending over and searching for herself. Both mirror and lake reflect images from the surface. Each can also reach into the depths where the shadow resides, and the woman searches for herself. The poem ends, 'In me she has drowned a young girl, and in me an old woman / Rises toward her day after day, like a terrible fish' (Plath, 1981, p. 173). In searching for identity, the lake also can illustrate the impact and inevitability of time, age and the woman's reactions of horror to it all. She embodies a deep sadness, a sense of alienation, the struggle to carve out space for herself. The demands of the history and culture of her era echo, in this portrayal, the agonies and strife of many in current times.

The image suggests the lake contains a monster in its depths. This is called a terrible fish and represents the *personal demons*, the negative feminine images lurking beneath the surface. The monster in the depths is also the monster on the surface, or the monstrosity of mere surface when there is lack of depth, or a lack of acceptance of what is in the depths. The horror is to be trapped in one-sidedness. Or perhaps this woman has accepted depersonalisation and passivity while still longing for other possibilities in the depths. Symbolically, the fish inhabits these areas and represents spirit, and this might be what draws the woman. After all, she can find answers by searching within herself. The monstrosity might also represent the psychological process of ageing mixed with layers of oppression and desire for release from societal and personal constraints. Sylvia Plath's words and portrayal of the woman's struggle in the poem put a visage on the process of self-examination, as this is an increasing imperative as we age and for gaining consciousness.

Sylvia Plath conveyed her personal experiences through her creative work, aligned with social and cultural history. The descriptive yet malign thing within her is within all of us as well, reflecting the courage it takes to articulate and attempt renewal and release. In describing the plight of the woman and ageing, she reveals being opened to unwanted truths shaped by patriarchal, societal and personal beliefs. Meanwhile, she demonstrated her discontent, disequilibrium and inner tension in breaking with tradition and defiantly striving to be herself, continually seeking transformation and renewal.

From the perspective of the 'as-if' personality, the ageing process can be difficult as they face the avoided material accrued from a lifetime of façade. The 'as-if' person is unprepared for the reality of life through ageing because they lack the resources to nourish the self (Solomon, 2007, p. 197). The 'as-if' and imposter personality tends towards self-absorption, narrowness and singularity of vision. Life conflicts as well as stagnation and depression can overwhelm and become problematic. By peeling the psychological layers, the instinctual and natural self is revealed, as in the following quote from the *Tao Te Ching* by Lao Tsu (1995): 'to never leave whatever you are is to abide, / and to die without getting lost'.

Precarity

The narratives and dreams in this section illustrate how people grapple with the vulnerability and precariousness of ageing, propelling a search for rebalancing body, mind and soul. Judith Butler, American philosopher, defined *precarity* in reference to disenfranchised others throughout history who have been rendered helpless due to economic and political lack and peril. 'Precarity designates that politically induced condition in which certain populations suffer from failing social and economic networks of support more than others, and become differentially exposed to injury, violence, and death' (Butler, 2015, p. 33). Precarity can be interpreted as a condition of displacement and insecurity, an existential state encompassing and leading to stark realisations of mortality and vulnerability – socially, physically and psychologically. The philosophical frame of precarity mirrors the psychological attitudes towards ageing manifested by anxiety, disenfranchisement and loss of hope. 'Past loves shadow present attachments and take up residence within them' (Nussbaum, 2001). Without sufficient predictability, recognition or security, a person can experience a sense of powerlessness and neglect.

Individuals often enter analysis when their inner chaos has reached a critical point. This chaos can accompany many events over which they have little control, such as physical illness, the breakup of a relationship, loss of a loved one, a change in career or the general frustration and confusion around ageing. Each person brings their story of love and loss, joy and pain. They come suffering in the present, but their pain is often woven with threads from the past and the many generations layered behind them.

Ageing is a struggle, a shift in image, a despair for many, especially those 'as-if' personalities. Life goals seem pointless, and they feel lost. Often the chaos expresses itself as a symptom like depression, anxiety, fear or simply the feeling that nothing makes sense anymore. The old order has lost its meaning as a person revisits the past and evaluates what has changed and what has not.

Society crushes ageing bodies through ageism discrimination. And yet, age has the potential to bring us closer to authenticity than at any other stage of life. This means becoming creators of our continuing vibrant selves, shaped through making conscious choices. However, older people face a myriad of challenges warping or shaping choices and deterring or enhancing authenticity. At issue is that an ageing person might be different while remaining themselves. In other words, they are becoming.

Yet, precarity is an uneasy situation. The ageing person's status is undetermined or negated. They feel deprived and without import, subsumed with generally unacknowledged loss and grief. The 'as-if' personality is trapped by impersonating and performing as a means of gaining acceptance and standing out. If beset by anxiety, too often outer conformity sacrifices the naturalness and originality of living outside the restrictive box. The personality can shrink when searching for what turns out to be the illusionary safety of tradition and what has been rather than what can be.

Judith Butler commented, 'Accepting loss means we are changed, undergoing a transformation from the loss' (2004, p. 21). In ageing loss can occur in almost all aspects of life, accompanied often by societal and individual reactions of invisibility and lack of worth and energy depletion from despair and depression. This is influenced by how people face each other and demonstrate restrictive conceptions of older people, excluding or erasing them, as if no longer important. The 'as-if' person acutely experiences this exclusion. They consider ageing cruel, subsumed by limits. They want to deny it. They find no benefit to this part of life.

However, by refusing the fixities of societal norms and conventions around ideas of ageing, they make room for the shifting and provisional and support actions oriented to acceptance, authenticity and self-authority. This leads to questions of how to enact the truth of oneself, how the self is constructed, including attitudes to the body.

To move on and live, we must mourn what was not. Life cannot be realistically mourned when people are already lost or never existed sufficiently, and they seem to live on in a continued state of deadness (Butler, 2004, p. 33). The healthy reaction of mourning life passing and making room for growth does not occur. The 'as-if' person retains an enchantment with youth, leaving them emotionally bereft, refuting natural change, growth or creation.

Analysis is a dialogue, emergence and exploration of the range of the other and yet to be developed parts within identity. Julia Kristeva noted the strangeness in our evolving identities as a metaphor through which we accept what seems like the strangers within (1992, p. 290). We are meant to encounter these others within us and open to the timelessness and changing aspects of our psychological and social selves. About the analytical process Jung commented:

> Psychotherapy is at bottom a dialectical relationship between doctor and patient. It is an encounter, a discussion between two psychic wholes, in which ego knowledge is a tool assisting the goal of transformation. This is not one that is predetermined, but rather an indeterminable change, the only criterion of which is the disappearance of egohood. No efforts on the part of the doctor can compel this experience. The most he can do is to smooth the path for the patient and help him to attain an attitude which offers the least resistance to the decisive experience.
>
> (Jung, 1970, CW 11, para. 904)

The unconscious keeps on presenting various characters and situations, demonstrating every person is full of differences and constant encounters with those who are other than themselves. The challenge, especially for the 'as-if' person trapped by singularity of image and idea, is the struggle to welcome these differences and become acquainted with and use them.

Ageing spurs the need for personality integration as what has been ignored previously catches up. We come into ourselves by going off balance, being challenged with new ways of being. If ageing remains unaddressed, the person stagnates, limiting growth, and life itself becomes meaningless, empty and futile, without zest or enjoyment. This person is stuck within, overtaken with fear, apprehensive of the body and the psyche, becoming as rigid as a stone. This is the melancholic reaction to ageing when regarded only as decline, inundated with precarity, unease, insecure and unstable. Invaded by saturnine moods, the melancholy psyche is faced with its finitude. Age brings an increased awareness of time passing and eventually death. Time weighs even as it is fleeting. The need to come to terms with our human physical vulnerabilities and impending mortality naturally intensifies as the margin between life and death narrows. While each person's ageing is personal, it is a developmental, collective and cultural stage with the potential for deepened states of consciousness, not just a period of catastrophic loss and depletion.

The benefits of ageing heighten the meaning of the moment and the value of time. When stuck in the present, like the 'as-if' person fearing the future, life itself cannot be acknowledged or felt. This lack negates the ability to amass the curiosity needed for finding value. Depth gets missed.

The meaning of life, purpose and reasons to care all coalesce. For some this means lack, and for others it means development and creativity. Some people come up with nothing but despair, and some with hope and energy. Accepting ageing, loss and change can initiate a radical psychological transformation. An interior and physical turnaround offers the psyche the opportunity to be freed from the tyrannical demand to be unconditionally happy or attain the false aim of perpetual youth or more achievements but with internal emptiness.

The basic developmental phases we go through physically and psychologically will always leave some needs unmet, creating tension to be resolved at the later stages of life. These are parts of ourselves yet to develop as they were neither ready nor previously addressed, yet they remain part of our personality. Psychic changes happen anyway, perhaps in an unconscious or destructive manner, when we resist authentic psychological change and natural biological development and knowledge of eventual death. Analysis provides a dynamic, relational vehicle for using this natural change, for going through the transitional periods in life and making the most of its entire arc. For example, a man in his sixties said after his cancer operation he thought no one would ever want to be with him. He imagined being alone the rest of his life. But then he began to ponder this, and a ray of hope came through. He entered Jungian treatment to find out what had gotten in the way previously in relationships. He wanted intimacy and wondered what about him could welcome the love he so desired.

From the perspective of Jungian psychology, the transcendent function is how the personality parts come together to be recognised and reconciled. This process ignites the imaginal and creative. In one of many definitions Jung described this:

> The tendencies of the conscious and the unconscious are the two factors that together make up the transcendent function. It is called 'transcendent' because it makes the transition from one attitude to another organically possible, without loss of the unconscious.

> (Jung, 1957/1969, CW 8, para. 145)

Conscious and unconscious opposites can be bridged by the emergence of symbols from the phantasy-producing activity of the psyche as expressed in dreams, images and metaphors. It is in the activation of the transcendent function that maturity resides (Humbert, 1988, p. 125). The transcendent function imbues life with emergent new attitudes, and the personality unfolds through the process of symbolisation. As evident in dreams and the therapeutic relationship, it requires fortitude to summon other and often unused personality resources.

Another man looked at his hand and it looked old for the first time, wrinkled. A woman said she was afraid and alone, older, less strong. She had let herself go and now she faced weakness, worry, what will happen? Can she walk down the street and be safe? Another woman, older than 90, said on her birthday,

> A new chapter, indeed. I feel there is always more to explore. Thank goodness we can contribute to the world in our small ways. I feel fortunate to get to have more time, given that I feel well and enjoy my life.

Another woman wondered whether, after many years of partnership, things could change, could she and her partner grow closer? She *dreamt of her boyfriend from college, the wrong kind of guy she said, a player.* And this dream had repeated on and off for 40 years. Why, she wondered, and what was it trying to tell her? The dream brought up the questions of whether she wanted intimacy, what kind, and how close could she get emotionally. This male dream figure was neither someone for the long term nor was he stable or capable of love. She knew that but was a bit shocked to think he was an aspect of her personality who had gotten in the way of deeper love all these years.

She and her partner were used to an emotional and psychological distance of sorts. Was it worth going for more at this stage of life? The old boyfriend could be called a *puer* in Jungian terminology – youthful, flighty and uncommitted. After some period of analytical work, she recalled the last dream with him *when she got dressed up to be with him and then saw he was with another woman. She became angry, told him off and left, slamming the door.* She finally ended the psychological connection with the male who disregarded her, had chosen someone else and was unavailable anyhow. Her reaction was relief he was no longer active in her psyche, evidenced by her leaving and him finally disappearing from her dreams.

Now in her sixties she realised she had been so occupied with her career she forgot her need for care and attention – not receiving much from her partner but also not asking for much. There lingered an absence of passion, and she described feeling unreal, a step removed, a life lived on the surface. Many truths remained hidden, such as her inner aloneness, unmet emotional desires, those unknown and repressed, a restlessness, depersonalisation and an inability to inhabit the present. She was scared and wanted to stay married, but she did not yet know how to obtain the intimacy she wanted. It would mean re-imagining with her partner what they each desired now after many years together.

She felt insufficient and wondered about her value and impact, especially as she was realising her age. It takes patience to unmask and become real after years of repression, denial and distraction. Age means she can no longer continue in the same vein. She has caught up with herself. It has become dissatisfying to live 'as-if', an observer, her emotional needs on hold. Illusions, disappointments and irritations must be faced, not only with herself but also with her partner. After the dream she took action to establish what she wanted and needed. Her psyche became more energetic, and she gained the impetus to reveal more emotionally to her partner, to share and ask for intimacy. Finally, she broke through her shield of isolation instead of using it to hide behind. Although generous in giving to others, she became able to give to herself and accept others giving to her. There was a flow to her emotional connections, rather than a sense of unsatisfying and unsettling compromise.

And yet another woman took a different tack and said she had no desire and did not want much from life. She watched television and that was it, no energy, too many losses – partner, friends and people gone. She no longer cared about her art and just did what she needed to do for that day. Although she sounded defeated, she was engaged in psychological work and questioned her despair, lack of energy and loss of desire. She did not know where this exploration would lead but felt an impetus to find out.

Each of these people is grappling with finding new ways of being. They question why ageing is associated with visceral aversion, repugnance and rejection.

In the flight from ageing, we spend time distancing from the old and resisting ourselves. The old become associated with sadness, put outside, useless in a world moving on and having nothing to do with them. Indifference to ageing reigns as does a conspiracy of silence surrounding the older person, their voices suppressed and unheard. If heard, the fears and pleasures, possibilities and defeats of ageing would have to be recognised. Recognised or not, these abound.

For example, gender pressure haunts women more than men in a culture devoted to youth. In a youth-oriented society, it is assumed with age you will lose your looks, brains and body because you are considered less appealing than others. From this limited perspective, age does not include beauty, strength, mind or wisdom. Rather, age represents despair, fear and invisibility. The older person is ugly and worn out, no longer appreciated by others or seen as sexual. Ideas of beauty are narrowed and can produce anguish, self-alienation, eating problems, body distortion, body hatred, defeat, illness and distress. Caught in a narrow myth that reduces all to a sameness of beauty, image and ultimate frustration, the older person is invisible, anxious about their body. Sexuality is dulled and limited beauty standards lead to loss of cultural self-expression and creativity. In all this, the culture of youth harms.

Most people prefer to shut their eyes to reality and their quality of life in an attempt to flee from the unwanted impact of their own ageing and mortality. The old are treated as inferior, judged as a haunted version of their former selves, and there is only pity. The stereotypes around ageism are ingrained, undetected and unconsciously and repeatedly enacted. Demeaning characteristics of the old and the associated false generalisations put much of the life cycle into the shadows of negation, especially as people are living longer.

Jung stressed the development of the individual throughout life to access the potential still to be developed. Jungian psychology purports the ability to range backwards and forwards in time to explore these unknown landscapes, to expand the unconscious and unused parts of the personality as a way of coming to terms with continued meaning and purpose. In addition, Jung referred to the valuable role of older people as the carriers of the society's heritage, the wisdom keepers helping to preserve the collective inheritance of the past (1953/1966, CW 12, para. 114).

As an example, Ryhanna was propelled by an unacknowledged ache in her soul and finally answered this call by beginning Jungian psychotherapy in her early eighties. Now widowed and without the naysayers, she was able to listen to what she had desired for years, an exploration into the vicissitudes of her life. She faced the intricacies of her mind, previously tied up in early internal conflicts and unhappy relationships that manifested in an autoimmune disease several years earlier. Due to this, her vulnerability and fragility were no longer deniable. She described the desperation and chaos arising from her emotional states, some depression and loneliness after the death of her latest husband. She was beginning to link it back to the abandoning and frightening childhood experiences she had forgotten as she had to survive and not feel, react or think then. She said she needed to make sense of what had happened those many years ago as, at the time, she just tried to save herself.

'The chaos can accompany life events over which we have little control, such as physical illness, the breakup of a relationship or the loss of a loved one, a change of career, or a conflict with the surrounding world' (Skar, 2004, p. 252).

Rhyanna had waited years to begin analysis. Now she said she must tell her story, to have a witness, to put the pieces together. Drawing the lines from then to now, she examined past relationships of turmoil, agreeing with partners although she was unheard and negated by them, internalising the sorrow of disappointments and now the attitudes of her adult children who tended to patronise her. She continued the creativity expressed in her art and gained strength and comfort with aloneness and a quiet life, her garden and her choices. Prior to analysis she never told anyone how she felt, not the family, husbands, children or friends. And no one asked. She learned early on to hide the poverty and family hardships, to study hard, comply and be as perfect as could be. She put up with many lonely situations, a lack of resources, and experienced little love through her life. She had an impatient need to explain it all, reveal and face the real.

The old are expected to look and act a certain way, dress to be invisible and meanwhile are banished from being active in society. Haunted by pervasive views on ageing as a problem, an ageing person cannot be themselves. Older means to be vulnerable, yet this vulnerability is common to all, no matter what age. Ageing is something we cannot control, and we all live with it. How we do this is the question. The denial of older people's humanness and inclusion is felt acutely by the 'as-if' person. Already this person experiences life without sufficient import or meaning; much is for naught, accentuating their despair about their value. This is registered psychologically, physically and reinforced culturally, especially around ageing.

Rhyanna felt all this strongly and wished for sex, touch, closeness with a desire thus far unmet. The physical is also part of the discourse on ageing so essential in analytical work. This allows for feelings of loss, grief and worry, and perhaps the discovery of a physical celebration associated with age.

For example, Rhyanna dreamt *of herself in a gorgeous gold dress.* She dreamt this the night before beginning analysis. She said the dress represented her, now in the gold light, with the ability to look and feel other than she had previously. The gold dress fashioned in her style is appealing to her and its close fit was flattering. She took the dream to mean uncovering and defining the inner parts she was not used to expressing and had suppressed long ago. She had held the unhappiness with family, deaths, divorces and depressions isolated within. She interpreted the dream to show a different attitude was on the horizon, shining like the dress, stylish and daring, more open. Yet, she was somewhat afraid as she did not know what this would mean or how she would change. Her dream is an example of the persona image of hope, transformation and emergence. The persona here can be considered as an essential part of the rich and complex tapestry of the whole person. It brings an opening to the self, as demonstrated by the dream. In fact, the dream became a central symbol for her, embodying light, body, psyche – all glowing and filled with hope.

According to Judith Butler, the meaning of gender depends on the cultural framework within which it is performed. In her book, *Gender Trouble* (1990) she formulated a postmodernist notion of gender with an ethos of the concept of deconstruction. At the time, she presented ideas contradictory to the traditional notions about gender as fixed categories and universalities. Butler defined *gender* as a social role performed and enacted by individuals and validated as acceptable by society.

Applying these concepts to age, we can ask how much we unconsciously comply with cultural limitations and circumscribed roles. In this way, age fixities and social frameworks become restrictive and devaluing of older people. Butler emphasises the 'performance of gender identity is not a conscious choice, but rather the result of the sedimentation of the ways in which we are gazed upon, handled and assumed to be from the moment of birth' (1997, p. 405). By linking this to older age, I can perceive the traps. When believed, they work against a person evolving throughout life, busting barriers and creating as they desire. How much wasted potential exists in this trap that insists on the defeat and invisibility of age.

Age, like gender, is also a continuous unconscious and consciously evolving performance of being, acquiring new meaning through time. Through age we encounter the others within, including those who are both different and known. The complex layering of identity is acquired as we age, displacing convention and out-of-date attitudes that formerly stifled creativity and general well-being. Breaking with traditional ways of understanding identity as something fixed and stable is key. Coercive forms presented to us during socialisation allow us to cling defensively to a specific identity. Through what mechanisms do we end up clinging to those identities, and how is this a way of keeping ourselves safe? In what ways do we not rock the status quo and go along with exclusion, rejection and marginalisation?

Judith Butler described gender as provisional, shifting, contingent and performed. Cannot age also be flexible and fluid, without limit and driven by being oneself? This view rejects static identities and meanings, promotes authenticity, authority, universality and subjectivity. It regards the value of an entire life and fits with Jungian psychology recognising the meaning in ageing: a time of significant change and development, building on one's wisdom.

Ryhanna later dreamt *she was sitting across from a man her age; both were intense, spiritual, and in love with each other. It was a love involving them in a non-traditional marriage as they were each with a religious order in the dream. Their bond was deep and full,* and Ryhanna knew the dream was an image of her inner strength. It could provide support as she faced some illness and physical decline, yet her desires and mind were sharp, curious and inquisitive. Ryhanna gained strength and confidence from the dream as it supported her within and reinforced her ageing accompanied with love.

Invisibility

The collective resistance to aging betrays our refusal to accept death as part of the life cycle. 'This resistance always leads to tragedy … just as the quest for eternal youth distorts our humanity' (Sawin et al., 2014, pp. 158, 159). As has been noted, many negative images of the old are thrust upon us in Western culture. The vibrancy of being older is denied by the 'as-if' personality who tends to follow the cultural persona focused on recognising only youth as significant and attractive. When this perspective prevails, older people in Western cultures are treated as dull, sad, dimmed non-entities. Many attempt to push older people and ageing as far away as possible, denying it will ever happen to them, even though it already dwells within the daily life cycle. The process of ageing becomes one of 'othering, both the othering that takes place without – in society and its institutions – and the othering that takes place within. Aging thus constitutes a form of double alienation' (Gilleard, 2022, p. 290). Ageing denied becomes a sinking into a supposedly better and more glorious time that rests on past laurels. This means many people assume being less and therefore striving for less – if they strive for anything at all.

This view portrays a psychic state of living without feeling alive, a sense of being eliminated, invisible. The body as well becomes invisible to the world – unseen, ignored, overlooked, turned from by oneself and others. Many just go along with this prejudice and accept its depotentiations. Some become fallen, exhausted, unable to fully fathom the loss or find what can be gained. Some are so immersed in grief and loss they can only look back and see no path forward. Sadly, the ageing person is made invisible by others personally and culturally. This is difficult for the 'as-if' person who has spent a lifetime dependent on notice and physiological appeal. Typically, 'as-if' people try to persuade themselves time has not touched them. They attempt to erase the face and body of age. Such attitudes deprive people of the beauties of change. As Simone de Beauvoir wrote in *The Second Sex*, 'She denies her finitude; to the poverty of her existence ... she tries to see the possibilities she has not exhausted' (2011, p. 620). I was, therefore, surprised when she was referred to as one who 'saw little to appreciate in old age, viewing aging as a process of increasing alienation from one's self and from the wider society: in short as generalized othering' (Gilleard, 2022, p. 286).

The attitudes regarding ageing as unacceptable often portray the ego as narrow, shallow and lacking vibrancy, energy diminished. Surrounded with the cloak of invisibility, many accept being unnoticed. Excluded from the life of society, many are condemned to conditions where their sadness merges with boredom, and for some this validates their bitter and humiliating belief in being useless in a world indifferent to them. 'de Beauvoir sought to go further, to understand what it was about aging that led to the "double" alienation that she felt aging encapsulated, of becoming both other to oneself and being othered by society' (Gilleard, 2022, p. 287). But this did not lead her to appreciate her beauty, denigrating the older woman as unattractive. Surprisingly this intelligent, beautiful and influential woman sounded saddened and ignored as she aged. In her seminal book on ageing, *The Coming of Age* (1972), de Beauvoir described looking at older age as arousing a visceral aversion, often a biological repugnance, banishment experienced as an alienating degradation. No one wants to be old.

Wallowing in the past at the expense of the present and future is an attempt to ossify our being into something it was, instead of acknowledging ourselves as stretching and dynamically becoming into the future. Older people also need goals to live and keep open-minded. Jung commented, 'Savor the Now; be as fully present in the immediate moment as possible' ('Letter to the Earl of Sandwich', 10 August 1960; in Jung, 1975, para. 580). Have the courage to meet age and its challenges with curiosity. Judith Butler posits that 'asking for recognition … is to solicit a becoming' (2004, p. 44). Her words poignantly and succinctly describe the process of individuating and becoming oneself throughout the life cycle.

Isolated and empty with age

Henry, age 71, enters Jungian therapy after many years of previous therapeutic work he described as allowing him to survive life and remain safe, but not connect with anyone. His presenting issue now is the need for relationship. However, he has never been close to anyone or anything. Not even the desert when he was hiking. No one ever approached him, nor did he approach them. He views others as robots, just as he seems to be. 'One wastes so much time, one is so prodigal of life, at twenty! Our days of winter count for double. That is the compensation of the old' (Letter to Joseph Dessauer, 5 July 1868, Sand, 1883). Daily habits and a job filled time but neither his spirit nor his soul was in harmony or connected with anything. Now retired, the sense of dread is encroaching. He had been so inward, preoccupied and alone.

Henry is seeking something as he enters therapy. He could remain as he has been but something within is pushing him to let the world closer, discover why he could barely survive but not feel passion or love. Although he could not do much previously beyond performing daily tasks amid a life of isolation and separateness, he now wants more. Henry's soul seemed to die early, but he is drawn to recover it. Now, depressed, he despairs and is unsettled.

Ageing offers him a chance to become more himself and dreams bring clues about the psyche's recuperative powers. Dream products from the unconscious can bring vitality, direction and meaning to one's conscious life. The following dream of Henry's tells him about the influence of his father on his psychological state and how he has been inhabited with an empty father. Deadened many years, both psychologically and emotionally, he could not face this previously or acknowledge the loss, hurt and emptiness. Now the dream presents the task of facing the reality of feelings long suppressed and now made apparent to him.

I am in a room that is empty. I open the door to another room I did not know was there. It is grey, filled with grey things and people. It is a pretty grey, but grey. The first room was my father's store and the second is mine and although grey there are some things in it. Henry discusses the dream and talks about feeling empty, the fear of falling apart and on the verge of emotional collapse. He is surprised, not by the grey, but that it is pretty. His father also lived a flat life, never showing any passion or emotion to Henry. Few possessions or things are in the father's room, but Henry's has some and this represents potential. He is sad as never before, realising the sparsity of his life, where it has taken him and what he wishes for. He is surprised to be mourning, and tears of grief frequently come as his emotional responses, formerly absent, emerge. 'In the last analysis every life is a realization of a whole, that is, of a self … every carrier is charged with an individual destiny and destination, and the realization of these alone makes sense of life' (Jung, 1953/1968, CW 12, para. 330).

At this point in life, Henry is examining the lack of relationship with his father, a dry and austere man, and how this impacted his world. It is a factor in his isolation and distance from others. He has nothing he considers pretty, secluded in a small world both physically and psychologically, and is easily wounded by others. As we talk, the amount of compensation Henry adopted to keep the world grey and at bay becomes apparent, and although the realisation is distressing it also brings internal release. The empty, bland and unrelated father creates a tenacious complex, like being stuck with glue, unable to separate and with no room to connect to others. The emptiness is so pervasive, Henry does not realise what has happened. Slowly, he begins to open the doors of his psyche and become less afraid. He even puts himself on internet dating sites and joins some senior groups. This represents an initiation towards others reflecting the initiation towards himself. There is value to changing the perception of life as holding a future, even if time is shorter.

Henry had been repressed, avoiding all feelings, conscious and unconscious, but he has a desire to find them now. He no longer resists psychological change and has opened to the room in the dream and is attempting to expand beyond the bland, empty father figure so unconsciously influential in how he lived for many years. Analysis provided a dynamic, relational vehicle for change through this transitional period brought forward by retirement and no longer being busy. Henry faces walking the bridge between what was and what will be. Although it is not clear that Henry can completely overcome the lengthy past of such isolation, he has amassed the energy to attempt the process.

The body

Jung recognised the shadow as part of the individuation process, and this involved coming to terms with the body (1975, p. 338).

'It doesn't happen all at once', said the Skin Horse. 'You become. It takes a long time. That's why it doesn't happen often to people who break easily, or have sharp edges, or who have to be carefully kept. Generally, by the time you are Real, most of your hair has been loved off, and your eyes drop out and you get loose in the joints and very shabby. But these things don't matter at all, because once you are Real you can't be ugly, except to people who don't understand'.

(Williams, 1922)

The somatic aspect is suddenly more apparent with ageing as the body changes, with weight gain or loss, illness, trying to remain strong. With few positive role models of elder people, men and women, preoccupied with ageing and their body shapes, perpetuate formerly unexamined ideas and ideals. Whether self-absorbed or ignoring, these attitudes indicate ego fragility and provide no answers, only a disappearance from self. When the body is perceived as a thing to change and associated with feelings of shame, some people desperately resort to various forms of altering their appearance. Too easily this can take the form of superficial face and body alterations solely influenced by collective pressures to be ever younger. By denying the inevitable physical change, these people attempt to remain static, not only hiding their age but also possibly signifying no growth.

An unrealistic self-reflection leaves a person without joy or pleasurable physical relationships. With age, inner dilemmas heighten in intensity. There is a longing for escape from constriction and engulfment, and the need to cast away an outgrown self. Ageing requires the ego give up the shallow narcissism, turn inward and engage in the psychic process of mourning for realistic and continual development (Solomon, 1998, p. 29).

'The body implies mortality, vulnerability, agency: exposes us to the gaze of others, also to touch ... The body has also a public dimension' (Butler, 2004, p. 26). In Western cultures the pervasive loathing for the ageing body means the old no longer feel desired. But more acutely there is implied denigration. Natural faces, and indeed natural bodies, need not be objects of shame, disregarded, or let go and given up. Chasing after cosmetics, body re-shaping and other thoughts and behaviours to remake the body can turn into a search for the unrealistic, a false perfectionism rather than an enhancement of what is. The 'as-if' person is especially vulnerable to a certain look, perpetuating the psyche out of joint, separated from the real. The call to age with awareness and consciousness and pride is, for the 'as-if' person, a burden as they have mostly lived without access to their foundations. Now might be the time.

Precarity devalues ageing in a society that denies death. The fear of death accentuates youth-oriented culture. Rather death becomes something to avoid, and the obvious solution is to turn from ageing. The 'as-if' person is especially susceptible. The future is not growth and opportunity but bleak and limited; the feeling is one of being trapped in the present. They are stuck in what never was, an imagined world based on illusion, so the present can only be disappointing and depressing.

The main defence is the external, the world based on superficial appearance, approval from others, feeding on the outer not the inner. The 'as-if' person avoids looking in the mirror as the reflection of the body is not what it was. When a person depends on others to give them value, they cannot access the value within.

Senex/crone consciousness

Old Destiny is slowly forming her mute expressionless face.
Wrinkles are moving onto it.

(Rilke, 1995, p. 121)

The archetype of ageing has many symbols and images. It can represent bitter truth, cold reality, melancholy, structure, intellect, foundations, law and order. I must include in this wisdom, strength of character and even of body. There are numerous other descriptions, giving an idea of the breadth of the archetype of age. James Hillman, Jungian archetypal psychologist, addressed the tension between senex, the old man, and puer, the young boy (2013, p. 242). These aspects of life are inextricably linked, conjuring each other unconsciously as they evolve together. One might vie for dominance and expression, calling forward and chasing away the other. However, they both can reveal, conceal, exhibit, cloak and grow in tandem. Each reaches to the other and adds to life's surprises and expansion. At any stage of life, we must make a place for both puer and senex. The *I Ching, Chinese Book of Wisdom*, in hexagram 60, Limitation, says:

> Unlimited possibilities are not suited to man; if they existed, his life would only dissolve in the boundless. To become strong, a man's life needs the limitations ordained by duty and voluntarily accepted. The individual attains significance as a free spirit only by surrounding himself with these limitations and by determining for himself what his duty is.
>
> (Baynes, 1950/1979, pp. 231–4)

In fact, whoever lives one pattern exclusively risks constellating the opposite. Enantiodromia is the emergence of the unconscious as an opposite position from consciousness, seeking to recover balance from an extreme. Enantiodromia waiting in the wings means the more one-sided we are, the more likely the opposite will break through to spin life around.

Defined in the classical Greek culture, 'senex essence is where time verges on endlessness without alteration, where becoming has been crowded to the edge' (Hillman, 2013, p. 272). Endurance is key to remaining aware of the senex as it is expressed in culture and the human psyche. James Hillman (1989, p. 25) described the senex, or the ageing masculine, with qualities of limit, discipline, containing and rules and order. The puella/puer needs the crone/senex energy as this type often has been unable to find belonging, and the puella/puer feels precarious and lacks internal solidity, all exacerbated as one ages. Ageing includes the energy of youth, the puer/puella, inspiration, excitement, activity. This can also be ignored in the rigid assumptions about ageing, limiting and separating these metaphors and symbols for an entire life when they belong in tandem with each other.

Following the etymology of the word, the *crone* denotes positions of power, midwifery, respect, divination. The word *crone* comes from *crown*, indicating wisdom emanating from the head. Her form as *hag* comes from *hagio*, meaning 'holy' and, in another aspect, as the *witch*, which comes from *wit* meaning 'wise'. Crones, hags and witches associated together were the leaders, midwives and healers in their communities. Over time, however, the age and sex of women became demonised, and their power and respect diminished. As an inner and outer figure, the crone represents the value and wisdom acquired from living consciously. Further, the crone is connected to the feminine forms of mother and maiden as the triple goddess images existing within us all.

The 'as-if' personality faces challenges integrating the senex/crone, or male and female qualities disparaged and undervalued because these symbolise older age. This crisis can promote individuation, a call to understand more deeply the creative, developmental processes keeping alive the psychic structures throughout life. After all, curiosity of the psyche and its potential has no time limit. Yet, many people stop their forward movement, stuck in the fear and apprehension of living and dying. Lauding the young over the old sadly means not accessing the wisdom, creativity and life force available as long as we are alive.

Later age brings the necessity of acquiring patience – to move methodically, to listen to the world quietly, to engage with reverie, to contemplate the silence and the self. All these are qualities that the 'as-if' person, the imposter, and the psychological and archetypal constellation of the puer/puella or eternal youth, cannot bear. The response of the 'as-if' person to ageing is often based on denial and attempts to defend youth, limit the imagination and remain with one-sided images. Jung was known for purporting that especially in the second half of life we are faced with the tasks and responsibility to acquire deeper and more refined attitudes towards ourselves and others.

Growth of the personality means both the puella/puer and crone/senex remain in contact. In many mythologies or fairy tales the crone/senex does not just hold back, remaining in a decrepit position, but creates plural, open, diverse yet conjoined complexity in the continual flowering and encouragement of the psyche, without avoiding the necessary trials in the process.

The following is a Baba Yaga fairy tale, famous as the old woman helps the younger. It demonstrates, like many of these tales, the value of her wisdom and knowledge about how to handle life.

In a distant kingdom, a woman named Baba Yaga, bony-legged, has an only son of virtuous character. He marries a human girl. Baba Yaga begins to despise her daughter-in-law and plots to kill her someway or other. While her son is away, Baba Yaga begs with false kindness for the young woman to go to the woods and milk her cows. She walks towards the cow pen, but her husband intercepts her in time and reveals that the 'cows' are, in fact, bears that will kill her. Baba Yaga's son then suggests she milks some mares and give it to Baba Yaga.

The next day, Baba Yaga asks her daughter-in-law to shear her sheep in the woods. Her husband appears again and tells her that the 'sheep' are wolves that will tear her to pieces, so he teaches her a magic command. She climbs up a tree, chants the magical command and the wolves shear themselves.

Seeing the young woman's newfound success, Baba Yaga then sends her to her sister with a request for a reed for weaving. The young woman meets her husband, who gives her oil, lard, needles and pins as well as a comb, a tablecloth, a brush and a ring. She begins her journey: she oils the hinges of a door, gives pieces of ham to two dogs, gives lard to a cat and needles and pins to a group of girls. The young woman asks Baba Yaga's sister for the reed. Baba Yaga's sister lets her have the reed, while she goes to prepare the bathhouse.

The group of girls warn the young woman that the witch is planning to devour her, so she must take the reed and escape, so she flees from the house. When Baba Yaga's sister enters the house and notices her absence, she complains that the female servants, the cat, the dogs and door have not stopped the young woman, so the witch flies away on her mortar. Realising that she is being pursued by the witch, the human girl throws behind the comb, the tablecloth, the brush and the ring to create magic obstacles to hinder the witch's pursuit. The young woman delivers the reed to Baba Yaga, who warms up to her daughter-in-law.

This tale addresses the range of an archetype, containing the tension, ambivalence and the recognition of the spectrum of life with its opposites. The puella/puer (youth) and crone/senex (older person) are together. The poles of tradition, stasis, structure and authority of the crone/senex combine with the qualities of immediacy, wandering, creation and idealism of the puella/puer. Symbolically the older consolidates, grounds and disciplines whereas the younger flashes with insight and thrives on fantasy and inventiveness, the unusual or edgy. These diverging, sometimes conflicting qualities are interdependent, forming two faces of one flexible configuration. They function similarly in the psyche if we are open to all aspects. As Jung famously commented, 'The afternoon of life is just as full of meaning as the morning; only, its meaning and purpose are different' (1953/1966, CW 7, para. 114). In fact, later life can be a period of profound creativity and vibrancy, a chance to review and integrate while coming to terms with reality, loss, limits and the body's changes.

The personal and cultural pressures to worship the unrealistic and youthful as the ideal contribute to the lack of mature and visible societal and cultural models. Jungian analytical psychology has much to say about how we can manifest new channels in the psyche, to be creatively engaged and involved in our lives. 'Learning to digest experiences through both wisdom and folly – which admits both mystery and irrationality – allows us to come to know ourselves' (Sawin, Corbett & Carbine, 2014, p. 53). Ageing can be a time to become curious about what needs further attention and development. Age brings increased perspective on the totality of life, in all its rhythms of grief and gladness, beauty and ugliness. It brings forth the work of attending to the internal and external, personal and collective, conscious and unconscious.

We go through basic developmental phases physically and psychologically. Unmet needs create tension that can lead us to reassess, rework and develop at this later stage in life. From a Jungian standpoint, archetypal forces work unconsciously on us, in the sense that they are parts of ourselves that have not been able to develop or become part of our conscious personalities (Skar, 2004, p. 253). As we move through life, different archetypal energies are constellated, demanding recognition into consciousness. This naturally creates periods of uncertainty and the unknown as a part of the larger process moving us on to further developments.

'In the last analysis every life is a realization of a whole, that is, of a self ... every carrier is charged with an individual destiny and destination, and the realization of these alone makes sense of life' (Jung, 1953/1968, CW 12, para. 330). The life still unlived insists on expression, recognising the creative is not dead or gone. However, the 'as-if' personality can become lost in melancholy and regret due to the empty self, impotent, frustrated in a world where they feel unacknowledged. When feeling flawed, as is the tendency and belief of the 'as-if' personality, the changes that occur with ageing are sad, frightening, even overwhelming. Fear and anxiety take hold; there is not enough time. What to choose, and is it too late? Unrealistic self-reflection makes the body an even more worrisome place and anxiety builds as the 'as-if' person waits for the inevitable and expected decline. In denial and without desire, libido is diminished, dreams dashed, energy languished, defeated. The spirit is cut off from its roots as they engage in an unending war of interior upheaval, exacerbated when they are separated from the self.

Ananke was the ancient Greek goddess of necessity, compulsion and inevitability. She was an incorporeal, serpentine being whose outstretched arms encompassed the breadth of the cosmos, symbolising the generative. She permits no resistance. Likewise, there is little escape in later life from losses, loneliness, separations and illness. The changes bring one face to face with the transitory nature of life.

And this leads to death. Avoiding death leads to the avoidance of life. The meaning and value of each venture, thought or feeling becomes lost in death anxiety. The 'as-if' personality, distracted by the reality of each day and the passing of time, misses the value of ageing. The need to be seen only from the outside deprives this person of exploring the inside, a need that becomes more insistent with age. Western culture, with its lack of attention to this huge time of life, makes it seem meaningless, especially for the 'as-if' person who struggles to find within the beauty and value in ageing.

This time calls for wholeness, for addressing the depths of the psyche, its complexity and the wealth of the self. The shedding of the past with some of its attachments transforms perspectives on life and is part of the ageing process. Jungian thought emphasises the creativity and vitality of this time as they are part of psychological and physical well-being. This means establishing individual differences, realness and expansion through inner reflection towards outer expression. The word *old* derives from Indo-European/Latin roots meaning to grow, to get well, to feed, nourish, increase. With ageing, the world widens even as it narrows: 'age gradually pushes one out of time ... and forward into futures yet unborn' (Jung, 1975, p. 10, Letter to Adolf L. Vischer, 21 March 1951). It presents the ordeal to be oneself, without pretending. If not now, when?

References

Baynes, W. (1950/1979). *The I Ching*. Princeton University Press.

Butler, J. (1990). *Gender trouble*. Routledge.

Butler, J. (1997). Performative acts and gender constitution. In: K. Conboy, N. Medina & S. Stanbury (eds.). *Writing on the body: Female embodiment and feminist theory*. Columbia University Press.

Butler, J. (2004). *Precarious life*. Verso.
Butler, J. (2015). *Notes toward a performative theory of assembly*. Harvard University Press.
de Beauvoir, S. (1972). *The Coming of age*. G.P. Putnam.
de Beauvoir, S. (2011). *Second sex*. (C. Borde, Trans.). Vintage.
Gilleard, C. (2022). Aging as otherness: Revisiting Simone de Beauvoir's old age. *Gerontologist, 62*(2), 286–92. doi: 10.1093/geront/gnab034.
Hillman, J. (1989). *Puer papers*. Spring Publications.
Hillman, J. (2013). *Senex & puer. Connecticut*. Spring.
Humbert, E. (1988). *C.G Jung: The fundamentals of theory and practice*. Chiron.
Jung, C.G. (1953/1966). The collected works of C.G. Jung: *Vol. 7. Two essays in analytical psychology*. Princeton University Press.
Jung, C.G. (1953/1968). *The collected works of C.G. Jung: Vol. 12. Psychology and alchemy*. Pantheon Books.
Jung, C.G. (1957/1969). *The collected works of C.G. Jung: Vol. 8. The structure and dynamics of the psyche*. Princeton University Press.
Jung, C.G. (1959). *The collected works of C.G. Jung: Vol. 9i. The archetypes and the collective unconscious*. Pantheon Books.
Jung, C.G. (1966). *The collected works of C.G. Jung: Vol. 15. The spirit in man, art, and literature*. Princeton University Press.
Jung, C.G. (1967). *The collected works of C.G. Jung: Vol. 13. Alchemical studies*. Princeton University Press.
Jung, C.G. (1970). *The collected works of C.G. Jung: Vol. 11. Psychology and religion: West and East*. Princeton University Press.
Jung, C.G. (1971). *The collected works of C.G. Jung: Vol. 6. Psychological types*. Princeton.
Jung, C.G. (1975). *Letters*: 2, 1951–61. (G. Adler, ed.). Princeton University Press.
Kristeva, J. (1992). *The black sun*. Columbia University Press.
Tsu, L. (1995). *Tao te Ching*. (S. Mitchell, Trans.). Harper.
Nussbaum, M. (2001). *Capabilities as fundamental entitlements*. Routledge.
Plath, S. (1963). *The bell jar*. Heinemann.
Plath, S. (1981). *Collected poems*. HarperCollins.
Rilke, R.M. (1995). *Ahead of all parting: The selected poetry and prose of Rainer Maria Rilke*. (S. Mitchell, Trans.). Modern Library.
Sand, G. (1883). *Correspondence, 1912–1876. Project Gutenberg. Ebook # 13839*. www.gutenberg.org/cache/epub/13839/pg13839.html.
Sawin, L., Corbett, L. & Carbine, M. (eds.) (2014). Jung and aging: Possibilities and potentials for the second half of life. *Spring Journal Books*.
Skar, P. (2004). Chaos and organization: Emergent patterns at critical life transitions. *Journal of Analytical Psychology, 49*(2), 243–62. doi: 10.1111/j.1465-5922.2004.00456.x.
Solomon, H.F. (1998). The self in transformation: The passage from a two- to a three-dimensional internal world. *Journal of Analytical Psychology, 43*(2), 225–38.
Solomon, H. (2007). *The self in transformation*. Karnac Books.
Williams, M. (1922). *The velveteen rabbit*. George H. Doran Company.

Chapter 10

Body fragility

Jacques Derrida described his philosopher friend Sarah Kofman as having the 'irresistible joy of uncontrollable laughter on the verge of tears' (2007, p. 7). A brilliant scholar of Freud and Nietzsche, a French Jewish woman raised during the Holocaust in Paris, Sarah Kofman at age 60 committed suicide on the 150th anniversary of Nietzsche's birthday. This chapter references the psychodynamics of mental distress and its traumatic remembrances held in the body. 'By writing her self, woman will return to the body which has been more than confiscated from her, which has been turned into the uncanny stranger on display' (Cixous, 1976, p. 880).

Sarah Kofman's narrative from *Rue Ordener, Rue Labat*, her autobiography and last book, depicts her many childhood traumas. In this slim volume, she recounts her life, experiences of war when her father was taken to the concentration camps and killed, and the conflict between good and bad mothers and how these were all enacted in her body. Trauma is often unsayable and nonverbal. It takes time to express, and many do not want to revisit it or hear about it. Eventually, however, trauma needs to find a form beyond being held within. In this chapter, I use Sarah Kofman and her story to illustrate an example of the 'as-if' personality who finds adaptation necessary and compensatory to living in reality. Although perhaps an extreme example, the situations detailed in her book occur in many people's lives.

The autobiography contains 'not only pieces of Sarah Kofman's memories, but the imaginary and the unverifiable, inexorable effects of the structure of trauma- tized memory' (Rizzuto, 2006, p. 7). In contrast with all her other intellectual, professional writings on European philosophers, she wrote this book in a simplified and childlike style. The contrast is illustrative of the effects of trauma as it returned her to an earlier time in her life that she could only express years later. Her bare raw feelings were stripped of sophistication.

In this book the chaotic psychological and societal events Sarah Kofman lived through as a child became recodified during the last year of her life into the coher- ency and order of the written word. The unspeakable events she endured 'beg the question whether it is possible to fit the shock, psychical crisis, and acute suffer- ing into a narrative, when such experiences are in themselves profoundly anti- narrational in character' (Stone, 2004, p. 17). Moreover, the narration transforms

DOI: 10.4324/9781003315254-11

the trauma as trauma itself is without sense, reason or progression. The story told is always somewhat dissonant from the overwhelming distress of the events and their memories. This dissonance does not disappear but seeps into the reader's bones.

Although much of her story took place during World War II (WWII), her situation is pertinent to many today. How do people survive the traumas of war, family, separations and any catastrophic event? How do they restore body and soul? The answers to these questions have both individual and collective significance. Donald Winnicott (1960, p. 146) wrote in the mid-20th century about trauma arising in a situation in which the subject is deprived of the external environmental conditions necessary for good psychic functioning. The pressures to act 'as-if' become heightened by shock, destruction and emotional wounding, all typical of trauma situations and reactions, enacted in and on the body and psyche. Sarah Kofman's story, like all those in this book, provides one of the many perspectives on the 'as-if' personality and its formation.

Both Jung, in his essay on the 'Positive Aspects of the Mother Archetype', and Green, with his theory of the dead mother complex, describe difficult mother mis-attachment situations when the psyche becomes misaligned and fragmented. These affect experiences of self and other, connection and separation, body and psyche. They are the background theorists, and the foreground is filled with Sarah Kofman whose last writing can be seen as a way of reassembling the traumatic events held within her after a lifetime of silence.

Loss of the father

Sarah Kofman wrote close to 30 philosophical books, but these have been relatively unacknowledged, with few translated into the English language. In France, in the mid-20th century, she only became a full professor in the year prior to her death. She is one of many unacknowledged women who were shut out because she was female and, at the time, a Freudian scholar when Freud was not popular. As a Jew during WWII, she was also shut out, prevented from studying, and her family and world decimated while the reverberating effects had nowhere to go but to remain internalised in psyche and body.

Theorists of trauma suggest traumatic experiences are not only processed and assimilated into the mind but also simultaneously encoded in the body, recalled via bodily sensations and not only through words. The body is 'a container and signifier, a kind of stage upon which the unfelt psychic pain can be dramatized and eventually relieved' (Sidoli, 2000, p. 97). Psychological spaces and the mind's complexity of conscious and unconscious is perceived through the body as well. As Jung stated, 'The separation of psychology from the basic assumptions of biology is purely artificial, because the human psyche lives in indissoluble union with the body' (1969, CW 8, para. 232).

During WWII Sarah Kofman's father was deported and killed in Auschwitz. Her mother was left to care for the home and her children, and their lives were in peril. Jews needed to hide and alter their physical, cultural and societal identity to survive. At that time any neglect of disguised identity could be worth life itself. The security and safety of openly existing in space and time were cut off early on in Sarah's world as the war demanded she erase herself from being noticed.

French philosopher Gaston Bachelard described home and parent as inter-twined. The idea of a home surrounding and protecting its occupiers like a loving parent is conveyed by Bachelard's description of the home as the initial shell that shelters one's being (Bachelard, 1964, p. 7). He expressed the profound effect of place having a solid and safe foundational effect on a person. These familiar things hold identity, stability and security yet all were eradicated for Sarah Kofman.

> The self is a mind integrated with its body but also with its material environment and a matrix of relationships, which are all sources of rootedness, a sense of continuity and reference points for variability and discontinuity, the texture of our existence.
>
> (Luci, 2020, p. 267)

Sarah's matrix and foundation were fractured, and she had to be 'as-if' other than she was. At age eight the multiple losses of father, home, security and mother were inseparable from the collective trauma of war, loss, mourning, brutality and inexplicable pervasive horror. Many years later, she wrote, 'How to speak "the unimaginable?"' (1998, p. 43). In such situations, words fail while the body and psyche store the need both to remember and to forget.

> Under the most severe traumatic conditions, this can be understood as a dis-placement of the central axis of Self, in which the ego complex yields its position to other complexes, with a deep change in the organization and func-tioning of self.
>
> (Luci, 2020, p. 260)

The work of memory is to open the inner sanctum storing the repressed memories, as Kofman finally did through her autobiographical writing. Ann Smock, translator of her autobiography, noted, 'It seemed that rather suddenly she was able to turn toward a sort of knot in her past, into which her heart was tied' (Kofman, 1996, p. xi). The book begins with her taking her father's pen from her mother's purse:

> I used it all through school. It 'failed' me before I could bring myself to give it up. I still have it, patched up with Scotch tape; it is right in front of me on my desk and makes me write, write. Maybe all my books have been the detours required to bring me to write about 'that'.
>
> (Kofman, 1996, p. 3)

This last writing was also an exercise in mourning and reparation, attempting to regain her father who was forcibly taken and killed by the Nazis.

Because of the lack of resolution to trauma, no matter how big or small, it continues to linger.

> One part remains linked to the traumatic situation, while the other eventually adapts to the new reality like nothing happened. The dissociation between a true self that returns to an inner territory of innocence before the trauma, a rapidly growing personality component exhibiting traits of exaggerated autonomy.
>
> (Fleischer, 2022, p. 135)

Surviving the collective trauma requires representing and putting into words the unnamed reality of what was also personally experienced. Jean Knox explains this phenomenon. 'What another person is feeling, initially by direct neural resonance is not the result of a process of reflexive thought or inference. In other words, it is a form of embodied knowledge without conscious representation' (Knox, 2010, p. 31). Sarah was also experiencing the emotions of her parents, their losses and the ethos of war and horror in addition to her own personal atmosphere of reactions permeated with this plethora of traumas.

Split mothers

Sarah experienced mothering separated into the 'good' one in the Christian Parisian mother who saved them. However, the bad mother was her own. The fights between Sarah and her mother, going on since early childhood, represented resistance to this strict, emotionally undemonstrative, tomb-like mother. Over time one mother transformed into the other, the good merging into the bad and vice versa, with each representing conflicting forces. To both mothers Sarah as herself was insufficient. Pleasing one meant displeasing the other and she could not escape this conflict. In other words, 'the refusal to break with the desired attachment leads to withdrawal and sets off an internal split against the self like what would be levelled against the object or the ideal' (Butler, 2006, p. 179). Sarah was left with the question about where she could be real and have her wants and needs for emotional attachment satisfied. It remains unclear if this ever fully happened.

The 'as-if' person cannot find the mothering to self in situations when the connection between mother and child was disjointed and fraught. Yet the child is usually expected to comply and please the mother. This might be driven by the felt apprehension that mother will fall apart because she is fragile. Or mother might be intrusive and domineering and the child retreats. 'The child's instincts are disturbed, and this constellates archetypes, which, in their turn, produce fantasies that come between the child and its mother as an alien and often frightening element' (Jung, 1959/1968, CW 9i, para. 161).

If the mother is devouring, there is no room for the child. The attachment becomes confusing, and a needed, but also empty mother is one who cannot recognise the child as separate from herself. This creates developmental blocks and impasses taking many forms. To hide disappointments, the 'as-if' child learns to compensate intellectually, joke, withdraw or the child becomes angry, depressed or just numb. The possibility of identifying with mother repeatedly comes to naught.

The development of self derives in part from the quality of mirroring between the mothering parent and child. This means learning to negotiate the normal events occurring with both good and bad mothering. However, too severe a split between these parts can create tension in the child from the unresolved disenchantment in mother that then continues into adult life. Psychologically, when the mirroring between mother and child are off-balance, a negative mother archetype overtakes and becomes internalised, affecting the child's relationship to their body.

The process of personality transformation and growth evolve as the adult becomes aware of inner mother images and is a part of gaining consciousness of psyche and body. Jung commented on the mother saying,

> All those influences which the literature describes as being exerted on the children do not come from the mother herself, but rather from the archetype projected upon her, which gives her a mythological background and invests her with authority and numinosity.
>
> (Jung, 1959/1968, CW 9i, para. 158)

Symbolically, archetypal manifestations of mother appear in the forms of the witch, the dragon, large fish or serpent, the grave, the sarcophagus, deep water, death, nightmares and so on.

Andrew Samuels suggests archetypes 'carry a strong, potentially overpowering charge of energy which it is difficult to resist' because of their polarised nature (Samuels, Plaut & Shorter, 1986, p. 26). This applies to the mother archetype, often described symbolically as what is secret, hidden, dark; as the abyss, the world of the dead; as anything that devours, seduces, poisons and is terrifying and inescapable like fate. She presides over both the places of magic, transformation and rebirth as well as the underworld and its inhabitants. To continue this list, mother is also symbolically associated with solicitude, wisdom, spiritual exaltation, instincts and growth.

Sarah called the other mother, the one who saved Sarah and her mother, *Mémé* – a name meaning the same or grandmother depending on its accent. Described in the book as 'this Christian woman' she had Sarah eat non-kosher food for her health – horsemeat, in fact – told her she looked too Jewish and changed her name. In other words, Sarah had to be altered to be acceptable to *Mémé* and to her Parisian cultural standards. Her own mother was upset at Sarah's growing closeness to *Mémé* who provided food, love and the very culture that was oppressing the Jewish one. This all became an intense source of conflict for Sarah who expressed increasing resentment towards her emotionally unloving, angry and distressed mother.

Sarah's mother demanded that she follow of Jewish rituals and rules and was prone to beating her physically and emotionally. 'The unloving mother can destroy the foundations of a child's existence' (Neumann, 1990, p. 62). Sarah Kofman experienced her own mother as failing to comfort, shelter or nourish. She paradoxically wrote, 'The real danger: separation from my mother' (1996, p. 27). *Mémé* was also complex, however, as she embodied negativity and repulsion about being Jewish, which was synonymous with the social alienation of the era (Faulkner, 2008, p. 56). *Mémé* saved Sarah and her mother, taking risks herself for them, yet she seemed to both accept and not accept their Jewishness. The ambivalence in being Jewish and having to be concealed to avoid persecution and death was at the heart of Sarah Kofman's autobiography and identification (Faulkner, 2008, p. 42), and this was enacted between the two mothers. One mother represented fear and the other safety and reassurance.

Sarah Kofman's autobiography attests to the mother conflict between the life-saving and destructive, although both mothers were inhibiting and suppressing, each in different ways. 'Trauma breaks up an idealization of an object by the individual's hate, reactive to that object's failure to perform its function' (Winnicott, 1989, p. 145). These feelings were enacted towards the mother she could not leave at the beginning of the story and at the end did not acknowledge her death. She did not she attend *Mémé's* funeral either. Neither mother performed the function of encouraging Sarah to be who she was.

Food

Sarah Kofman's autobiographical writing reveals the tension between foods, mothers and cultures of significantly contrasting paradigms of thought. Steeped in the Jewish way of life, the teachings and rituals of her youth were saturated with her rabbi father and mother. This was countered by the Greek philosophy and Jewish intellectualism introduced by the Christian *Mémé* who encouraged Sarah's secular schooling. Equally *Mémé*'s anti-Semitic words were both poisonous and eradicating to Sarah's identity as *Mémé* critiqued the Jewishness of Sarah's looks and through food betrayed the Jewish law of her father and the bond with her mother. Gradually severed from her Jewish roots, Sarah leaned more and more towards *Mémé*. Yet, throughout her autobiography, Sarah Kofman recounted her refusal to eat pork as it was disallowed in Judaism. *Mémé* encouraged it, however, and Sarah, in conflict, ate it and vomited frequently.

Behaviours to satisfy the mothers fostered an internal fragmentation that interrupted the continuity of Sarah's being.

> Nothing forces us to know
> What we do not want to know
> Except pain
>> Aeschylus, *The Oresteia: Agamemnon, The Libation Bearers,*
>> *The Eumenides*

The psychological conflict also attested to the indigestibility of her father's death and the unpalatability of the fraught relationship with the mothers. The food paradoxically represented the push and pull of desire to return to mother and her roots. Eating the food mother disapproved of was, for Sarah, on the one hand delicious (Stanislawski, 2004, p. 143), whereas, on the other hand, it set up a double bind. Sarah both rejected and needed her mother as enacted through the vomiting that expressed her true feelings and protected her from ingesting what she could not. Eat, vomit, eat was the rhythm Sarah adopted as she swung emotionally between the two mothers. The vomiting began when she and her mother walked from their former home to live with *Mémé*. The conflict in love and affection was enacted through the food she wanted and could not take in, nor could she digest it or what was happening to her. Her vomiting highlights the difference between remembering and not forgetting (Hirvonen, 2012, p. 159), emphasising the unbearable internal conflict Sarah met at every turn.

Further, the food reflected the conflict laden, ambivalent relationship with mother and her body.

> The primal relationship was attended by pain, emptiness, cold, helplessness, utter loneliness, loss of all security and shelteredness: it is a headlong fall into the forsakenness and fear of the bottomless void … in the symbolism of the alimentary stage, hunger and pain are characterized as gnawing and devouring.
>
> (Neumann, 1990, p. 74)

According to British object relations psychoanalyst Melanie Klein, famous for her theories of the good and bad breast, the mother not only nurtures but also is the object of dread. Sarah Kofman wrote, 'One is expecting to see the good lady, sweet, smiling and there it is instead menacing and false. The bad breast in place of the good' (1986, p. 66). Insufficient mother nurturance along with guilt, sorrow or betrayal makes a daughter desolate as she attempts to repair the damage and tries to please. The negative, blank or dead mother leaves a daughter without love or self-authenticity. The type of complex denoted here becomes hardened as the psychic fragments become stronger and more split off due to the traumatic wounds to the psyche, body and world.

Body and collective trauma

'All consciousness begins with the experience of the body by way of the body image' (Colman, 2008, p. 357). However, in her world, Sarah's body, because Jewish, was subject to death and her very existence hung by a thread. 'The Future sometimes dwells in us without our knowing it, and the words thought to be untruthful describe an immanent reality' (Proust, 2021, p. 45).

Everything we know, everything we do, and everything we are, is mediated by the body. We learn about the world and ourselves through our bodies as the basis of subjectivity and self-expression. 'Situations occurring from early childhood unable to be consciously registered or verbalized, can appear, and be told through the body' (Deligiannis, 2018, p. 181). Trauma not only returns in stories and words, but also is expressed as bodily reactions and sensations. The pain of loss and trauma 'emerges not from the story itself, but from the recurring bodily imagery through which its story unfolds' (Robson, 2004, p. 608). Only much later could Sarah finally record what her body could not forget. The past was impossible to write about consciously until almost the end of her life. The tension and need to accept the loss and the impossibility of doing so all were configured through her body (Hirvonen, 2012, p. 159).

The speech of the body is a figure of memory as its cry bears witness to the traumas no matter how repressed and silenced. The body cannot hide its fragility, vulnerability and precarity as it acknowledges the trauma endured. Therefore,

> the analyst must pay a great deal of attention to the subliminal messages conveyed by the body and much less attention to the verbal, factual report. The unintegrated emotional fragments are located in the body … When the attachment sets in, the patient will slowly use me to make up for the mirroring experience he or she missed.
>
> (Sidoli, 2000, p. 102)

Mother as abject

Sarah Kofman attempted, in her last writings, to recover a lost part of herself, the part objected in the mother.

> There looms, within abjection, one of those violent, dark revolts of being, directed against a threat that seems to emanate from an exorbitant outside or inside, ejected beyond the scope of the possible, the tolerable, the thinkable. It lies there, quite close, but it cannot be assimilated. It beseeches, worries, and fascinates desire, which, nevertheless, does not let itself be seduced. Apprehensive, desire turns aside; sickened, it rejects.
>
> (Kristeva, 1982, p. 1)

French psychoanalyst Julia Kristeva describes the *abject* as the unprocessed, rejected elements, the traumas and the need to mourn them. Kristeva's concept of the abject includes the physical, despised and ignored elements. The abject means what is put outside and attributed to what disturbs convention, identity and existence. Kristeva expands this idea to include any 'entity that compromises the existence of the self and ascribes abjection as ambiguity towards what is felt to be dangerous' (p. 10). She described the potentially harmful entity that cannot or will not be assimilated and how this affects the body.

Kristeva identifies the maternal as the receptacle for what has been repressed or abjected. This parallels Sarah Kofman's description of her refusal of her mother, yet the impossibility of getting away. Kristeva emphasises the maternal function with its importance in the development of subjectivity and for accessing culture and language (1982, p. 10). The primal language of the mother is a bodily drive associated with basic life rhythms, tones and movement. Abjection is activated when a person is unable to incorporate the experiences or symbolise them as they seem too awful or too much. As Sarah Kofman portrayed, the loved sense of self was not mirrored by the original mother figure.

The abject is inherently liminal, meaning the space between is neither a discrete object nor a non-object. Its threshold status calls into awareness the borders between self and other, life and death, being and non-being, Sarah and her mother. The abject acts as a force of estrangement or an attempt to 'other' what or who is placed outside certain categories of identity and ways of being. Abjection enables identity by separating from what threatens or pollutes while bringing the subject and other into contact (Kristeva, 1982, p. 13). As such, it breaks apart the psychic processes creating boundaries and identities and yet they sustain contact. Sarah could neither take in her mother, nor affectionately connect with her, feel protected or separate. She was caught in the events of her world and her psyche but without the safety or security of mother or father. 'The psychic echo of violent physical separation from the mother is always within us. Thus, during the struggle of the child to become a subject, a third party, eventually the father… helps the future subject' (Kristeva, 1982, p. 13). As noted previously, Sarah Kofman lacked both parents, and the separation from and mourning for both was made more complex due to multiple traumas.

Rue Ordener, Rue Labat is 'a story of the body, body memory, opening the unbearable pressure of the presence of absence' (Hirvonen, 2012, p. 159). Sarah Kofman enacted the difficulty and concomitant necessity for recounting the traumatic losses so long silenced. 'At work in her writings is a performance of identity as fragile, incomplete, and transitory… that must equivocate between incompatible extremes' (Faulkner, 2008, p. 58). Sarah expressed the pain, conflict and loss of her entire world, a personal history aligned with cultural and collective memory. Yet, her suicide about a year after publishing her only book-length autobiographical text inspired speculation about the potential relation between writing trauma and how it might affect suicide.

Sarah Kofman's slim autobiography explored abandonment and deaths; shock as formerly unexpressed wounds and attendant grief were given words and release.

> The ego complex, displaced and eradicated from the self, keeps itself apart as an observer of the profound changes in the self, its organization and its self-perception, the perception of others, the perception of one's body, the creation of meaning.
>
> (Luci, 2020, p. 275)

Sarah Kofman demonstrated through her writing the need for integration of the body and mind, and the effects of both personal and collective traumas fuelling creation and destruction. Her narrative is not only her personal truth, but also reflects the human struggle for authenticity and the truth about trauma needing to be expressed psychologically and culturally.

In analysis

> the reality of the collective trauma with all its ... horror of the non-representable may gradually find – within the analytic dyad – a symbolic way to be retrieved, metabolized, and elaborated. When unknown and unconscious, complexes can cause psychological and physical symptoms of distress.
>
> (Fleischer, 2022, p. 130)

Until then the real self remains silent and isolated, vulnerable in a state of non-communication with the rest of the personality.

Trauma is experienced as a loss of language and cognition. Telling about the traumas turns them into narrative language and linear memory and is a means for opening to the psyche and the body. Although she denied for years the need for self-writing, in a previous autobiographical essay Sarah Kofman mused, 'Who she is as a person, a self. Is there one?' (Stanislawski, 2004, p. 141). A 1976 interview commented, 'We were asked to take her words in exchange for how self-recognition has come to her disguised in layers of her histories... a discourse of scarcity and impoverishment... in its materiality and fearsomeness' (Kofman, 1986, p. 6).

Sarah Kofman's intellectual writing is read as an attempt to work through the traumas. As an expert in the philosophies of Freud and Nietzsche, she exposed how these authors' desires and ideas are inextricably woven together into the fabric of their texts (Chanter & deArmitt, 2008, p. 29). Although death is inscribed in many of Sarah Kofman's volumes, it is not about getting over mourning but, instead, a recognition of the impossibility of doing so and how necessary it is to invent from it. It is also important to remember she was noted as a thinker, as affirmative, contrary, playful, profound, duplicitous, nuanced, fiery and determined.

Dream of the witch/mother

'When the primal relationship is disturbed the helplessness and defenselessness constellate the terrible, negative mother... she becomes a witch, the diabolical mother of suffering and pain... she rejects, and condemns to solitude and sickness' (Neumann, 1990, p. 74). Sarah Kofman described a feeling of crushing maternal self-annihilation and her mother's guilt-inducing refusal of her autonomy.

For Jung (1959/1968, CW 9i) the mother complex arises when a mother persists in the possession and will to power annihilating to the personality and life of her daughter. Mother cannot be countered, and the daughter obeys unquestioningly. Mother clings to daughter, imposing an unconscious tyranny under the guise of loyalty and devotion. This mother is emotionally distant and unable to handle the natural identification of the daughter onto her. The daughter can react by accentuating the feminine and the maternal instinct, or the maternal atrophies so she cannot mother herself or others. The daughter leads a shadow-existence, sucked dry by her mother in a sort of continuous blood transfusion (para. 169). She feels she must save the mother to obtain a semblance of mothering for herself. This described the conflict Sarah also carried, intensified by the cultural and collective instability and constant threat to the life of herself and her mother.

The mother complex is feeling-toned and shaped by experiences with the personal mother that influence the forms of the mother imago within. As Jung said:

> to have complexes ... only means that something discordant, unassimilated, and antagonistic exists, perhaps as an obstacle, but also as an incentive to greater effort, and so, perhaps, to new possibilities of achievement. In this sense, therefore, complexes are focal or nodal points of psychic life which we would not wish to do without; indeed, they should not be missing, for otherwise psychic activity would come to a fatal standstill.
>
> (Jung, 1971, CW 6, para. 925)

In addition to personal experiences, complexes are influenced by the culture and era in which we live. This refers to the variety of religious, social and cultural icons to which we are exposed, inhibiting or expanding our psyche.

Sarah Kofman wrote about the life and death struggles of her mother complex, which was composed of the connections and missed connections between both of her mothers. 'Mind/self and memory are implicitly interrelated with our total environment from the beginning. It is, therefore, the rupture of this organizing gestalt anywhere along the continuum that constitutes the specific trauma' (Dowd, 2019, p. 253). Sarah's mother complex was significantly disorganised early on, and she recorded hating her mother who beat her yet also saved her from being killed in WWII.

She recorded a childhood dream:

> I am in a room from my childhood, with my mother, my brothers and sisters, at night. A bird enters, a kind of bat with a human head, pronouncing in a loud voice: 'Woe unto you! Woe unto you!'

My mother and I, terrorized, run away. We are in tears in the Rue Marcadet: we know we are in great danger and fear death.

> I awaken very anxious.
>
> (Stanislawski, 2004, pp. 144–5)

Her nightmare functions as a referential space, both concealing and disclosing her childhood suffering. Sarah associated this dream with what she called the evil hour when the *Kommandantur*, whom she named the bird of misfortune, came to warn the family they were on the Jewish round-up list for the concentration camps. Her dream was personal, a statement of oppression and fear. It could also be taken as impersonal and relevant to the collective and cultural situation at the time. Trauma does not have a locale solely in the self as it is beyond the person yet, at the same time, it is the person created (Kohon, 1999, p. 100).

Sarah learned three months after remembering the nightmare and writing about it that the bat represents Lilith in Jewish folklore. She wrote the *Mardewitch*, an avatar of Lilith, haunted her whole childhood. The *Mardewitch* was pictured as an old woman coming to punish Sarah by carrying her far away from home. Lilith is a female figure in Mesopotamian and Judaic mythology, the first wife of Adam. The story goes after she was banished from the Garden of Eden for not obeying Adam sexually, Lilith was denoted as a powerful she-demon able to kill children unprotected by their parents.

Sarah recounted how her mother locked her in a closet as a child and said the *Mardewitch* would come for her as punishment. 'Nightmares are not proper dreams, but reproductions of traumatic experiences' (Luci, 2020, p. 174). The nightmare connotes the violence and disruption in Sarah's self-experience, originating at home and replicated later in society during the war with no safety or security in either. Sarah said the unconscious put together the two terrifying figures of her childhood – the *Kommandantur*, the bird of misfortune, and the sorceress, *Mardewitch* (Stanislawski, 2004, p. 145). Both symbols were associated with her mother who could not express love but rather conveyed fear, her own losses, and exhibited cruelty to her body and psyche. Sarah's security needs could not be met as her mother split from being a nurturer into the Terrible Mother or witch. This latter part of mother was a destroyer and progress-inhibiting, betraying Sarah in various ways.

In relation to dreams, it is perhaps not only the fright occurring in the dream that is traumatising, but also the waking from the dream that creates the real trauma in the experience of its recall. Traumas involve life-threatening experiences but also the ability to survive them. The psyche is in a battle to overcome the threat to life by grasping the fact of survival and returning over and over to the frightening events. The psyche reclaims the experience, ensuring survival and one's continued existence through retelling the trauma. This offers a way to comprehend the ways the narrator is not, in fact, debilitated by the trauma and it can become a point for moving forward.

Sarah Kofman commented:

> I might possibly write an autobiography one day. At the same time, I keep postponing the decision as though I would in this way postpone the date of my death. Really, I believe that all the work I have put into my writing (my 24 books) gives me the right and perhaps the duty to speak about what happened in my childhood. Sometimes I wonder whether the emphasis I have placed on achieving a certain level of fame may have been merely an attempt to gain the right to write this autobiographical account. Up until now, I have written only autobiographical fragments that have appeared scattered in diverse journals. I hope my (female) readers will encourage me to continue.
>
> (1995, p. 6)

In 1994, at the age of 59, Kofman published the autobiography, *Rue Ordener, Rue Labat* telling the story of her life from age eight to eighteen. The last book written by this prolific philosopher addressed the losses and ambivalence in the pull between diverse cultures and her physical enactments to the internal and external losses, separations and war traumas. The two streets in the title of the book represented the two mothers, the mother–daughter conflicts and the traumas in mind and body pervading the book.

Dead mother

Children depend on primary caregivers not only to meet their most basic needs for survival, but also for reliable, accurate and empathic emotional responses. However, Sarah experienced maternal disinvestment and conditional attachment and was caught in an unconscious identification with an emotionally deadened, grieving, lost mother. Sarah was described as someone with the impossibility of coherent self-representation (Hirvonen, 2012, p. 154), and her identity a pastiche lacking a central core (Faulkner, 2008, p. 43).

This references the effect of the dead mother complex as described by French psychoanalyst André Green. According to him, this mother is psychically dead, unable to manage her depressive moods, dissociated from her affects and has killed off her inner life (Kohon, 1999, p. 100). This mother withdraws attention from her child because she is bereaved by the extent of her losses. Surely, Sarah's mother was overcome with grief and '[could not] give up what is no longer there and the child's life and the mother's relationship with the living child have been negated' (Kohon, 1999, p. 184). Sarah's mother would not let her become who she wanted to be, wouldn't allow separation and was unable to convey warm motherly love. The traumatisation, loss and melancholic identification with the mother unable to provide love and care impacts the child's experience of life. This emotionally dead mother is omnipresent, seizing the child and making her captive in her own mourning and death. Any other love is not possible because it is already mortgaged to her and 'the place is occupied, in its centre, by the dead mother' (Green, 1986, pp. 153–4). 'A life of thought is perhaps a life that does not already live enough, or that lives too much, or again, quite simply, it is a life that attests itself, inscribing that it took place' (Jean-Luc Nancy, quoted in deArmitt, 2008, p. 1).

The mother is essentially and emotionally unavailable and this can cause depression and emotional wounding to the child as well as disconnection from the body. 'No life is possible beyond the boundary of the dead mother and certainly no peace of mind resides within her embrace' (Kohon, 1999, p. 118). Green described a psychic life founded on loss:

> the absent other marks a place of moving forward but also has become the graveyard where madness reigns. The absence is nuanced, complex and paradoxical ... as the creative emanates from the struggle with negativity and while the dead mother is never absent, the absence can mean potential presence.
>
> (Kohon, 1999, p. 114)

For many years Sarah Kofman filled this absence with her writings and philosophical explorations.

Comparing this with Jung's four psychological descriptions of the mother complex with its impact on a daughter (1959/1968, CW 9i), I find each contains enlivening and deadening features. Both mother and *Mémé* fit the devouring and controlling mother as each tried to mould Sarah to be what she wanted. This type of mother cannot recognise the child has a life distinct from hers. Especially threatening to this mother is the child's psychic aliveness and so she withholds permission for the daughter to exist as a separate being. Her word is law; she cannot be countered and under the mask of loyalty and devotion the daughter must obey. The more unconsciously destructive the mother is to herself, the less the daughter can bear to separate from her.

A daughter can develop rage at her mother and abhor the idea of being like her. 'Such a woman forms her feminine identity over and against her mother, in contrast to her mother's identity, sometimes even in spite of it' (Ulanov, 1981, p. 26). This attitude upsets mother who exerts on the daughter either crushing demands or emotionally laden inertia, creating low self-worth.

The mother's emotional distance and the vacuum of intimacy frustrate, agonise and absorb the daughter. Mother conveys mixed messages to not leave her as the mother's conscious and unconscious fears of loneliness seep into the daughter. From the maternal rejection and without healthy attachment, the daughter's development is arrested. Throughout life the recapitulations of abandonment and subsequent suffering lead to conscious and unconscious entrapment in suffering and loss.

Jung also referenced the negative mother complex in a daughter who excels in intellectual activities where her mother has no place (1959/1968, CW 9i, para. 186). Sarah Kofman fits all these areas to an extent but mostly in this latter category. Sarah, as an extreme, represents an example of the 'as-if' personality type who experienced losses, mourning, emotional parental absence and missed attachments. She coped as an adult by developing her intellect and love of words and her ability to mask her inner world from others. Jacques Derrida commented frequently on her laugh.

> Sarah Kofman seems to sense in this repression … a cunning affirmation of life, its irrepressible movement to survive, to live on, to get the better of itself in itself … to affirm this truth of life through the symptom of repression.
>
> (2017, p. 24)

Was this the façade covering the real self? Such behaviours are often indicative of the 'as-if' person who is veiled and internally shuttered.

Sarah Kofman's roots were decimated by war, the death of her father and the mother figures who pulled at Sarah emotionally in opposite directions. The grief and loss surrounding her mother was translated into Sarah Kofman's body and enacted in her vomiting and possibly in her suicide. Identifying with a mother she could neither understand nor get close to kept her attached yet emotionally distant and without sufficient love. For Sarah the benevolent and creative inner foundation for security, identity and attachment was unavailable with her own mother. The creation of self was inundated by maternal emotional absence and the environmental traumas of loss, death, fear and real identity being unsafe. Sarah faced the encroachment of both mother figures trying to take over her body, placing her identity into a double bind as she ambivalently struggled to release the mother hold.

Eventually the silenced self formerly barricaded in a place of non-communication brought forward the repressed information. Language with its agency and action has a vital quality, accentuated when the isolated interior monologue becomes shared and public. To re-experience the distress and disorder also brings relation to the self. Without memory there can be no mourning (Feldman, 2022, p. 108). Inner speech becomes an outer expression of awareness, consciousness and knowledge with transformative effect on the individual and culture. The 'reclamation of the "I" depends on the psychical fragmentation if the acute distress is to be transformed' (Stone, 2004, p. 28). The writer becomes a reader of her own shock, and this can build a bridge to transformation.

Sarah Kofman illustrated the situation when insufficient mother nurturance and the ambivalent mother complex leave guilt, sorrow or betrayal. There is absence and death in the mirror identification with what Green called the dead mother. A daughter flees her own body as it seems to have limited value. Paradoxically the internal conflict can also be what fuelled Sarah Kofman's extensive and thorough intellectual writings, providing the impetus for movement and exit out of the psychological and cultural entrapments. Her identity was rearticulated through her writings in the attempt to reconstitute it.

After the war Sarah returned to her mother on yet another street called Impasse Langlois. Grief has an insatiable appetite and does not let go. Mourning both gives up and preserves what was lost. 'The melancholic identification permits the loss... as it averts the loss as a complete loss... resisting the relinquishment of the lost love' (Butler, 1997, p. 134). Therefore, the work of mourning is not the end of mourning. 'Her writing was how she lived, attesting to existence and when it declined in the last year of her life, she could no longer live' (Hirvonen, 2012, p. 168).

References

Bachelard, G. (1964). *The poetics of space*. Orion Press.

Butler, J. (1997). *Gender trouble*. Routledge.

Butler, J. (2006). *Precarious life*. Verso.

Chanter, T & deArmitt, P. (eds) (2008). *Sarah Kofman's corpus*. State University of New York Press.

Cixous, H., Cohen, K. & Cohen, P. (1976). The laugh of the Medusa (K. Cohen, P. Cohen, Trans.). *Signs*, *1*(4), 875–93.

Colman, W. (2008). On Being, knowing and having a self. *Journal of Analytical Psychology*, *53*(3), 351–66. doi: 10.1111/j.1468-5922.2008.00731.x.

DeArmitt, P. (2008). Introduction: The lifework of Sarah Kofman. In: T. Chanter & P. deArmitt (eds.), *Sarah Kofman's corpus*. https://sunypress.edu/content/download/451868/5496653/version/1/file/9780791472675_imported2_excerpt.pdf.

Deligiannis, A. (2018). Imagining with the body in analytical psychology. Movement as active imagination: An interdisciplinary perspective from philosophy and neuroscience. *Journal of Analytical Psychology*, *63*(2), 166–85. doi: 10.1111/1468-5922.12392.

Derrida, J. (2007). *Introduction to selected writings by Sarah Kofman* (E. Rottenberg, G. Albert & T. Albrecht, eds.). Stanford University Press.

Derrida, J. (2017). *The work of mourning*. University of Chicago Press.

Dowd, A. (2019). Unrooted minds: Displacement, trauma and dissociation. *Journal of Analytical Psychology*, *64*(2), 244–69. doi: 10.1111/1468-5922.12481.

Faulkner, J. (2008). Keeping it in the family: Sarah Kofman reading Nietzsche as a Jewish woman. *Hypatia*, *23*(1), 41–64. doi: 10.1111/j.1527-2001.2008.tb01165.x.

Feldman, B. (2022). After the catastrophe: Working with intergenerational transmission of collective trauma in Jungian analysis. *Journal of Analytical Psychology*, *67*(1), 105–18. doi: 10.1111/1468-5922.12752.

Fleischer, K. (2022). At the train station: The self suspended in collective trauma. *Journal of Analytical Psychology*, *67*(1), 130–44. doi: 10.1111/1468-5922.12754.

Green, A. (1986). *On private madness*. Hogarth Press.

Hirvonen, A. (2012). The ethics of testimony: Trauma, body and justice in Sarah Kofman's autobiography. *NoFo. An interdisciplinary journal of law and justice*, *9*, 144–72. www.helsinki.fi/nofo/index.html.

Jung, C.G. (1959/1968). *The collected works of C.G. Jung: Vol. 9i. The archetypes and the collective unconscious*. Princeton University Press.

Jung, C.G. (1969). *The collected works of C.G. Jung: Vol. 8. The structure and dynamics of the psyche*. Princeton University Press.

Jung, C.G. (1971). *The collected works of C.G. Jung: Vol. 6. Psychological types*. Princeton University Press.

Kofman, S. (1986). Damned food. *SubStance*, *49*(8–9), 6–13.

Kofman, S. (1995). Writing without power: A conversation with Sarah Kofman. *Women's Philosophy Review*, *13*(13), 5–8. doi: 10.5840/wpr1995136.

Kofman, S. (1998). *Smothered words* (M. Dobie, Trans.). Northwestern University Press. (Original work published as *Paroles suffoquées* in 1987).

Kofman, S. (1996). *Rue Ordener, Rue Labat* (A. Smock, Trans.). University of Nebraska Press.

Kohon, G. (Ed.). *The dead mother: The work of André Green*. Routledge.

Knox, J. (2010). *Self-agency in psychotherapy*. W.W. Norton & Co.

Kristeva, J. (1982). *Powers of horror: An essay on abjection*. Columbia University Press.

Luci, M. (2020). Displacement as trauma and trauma as displacement in the experience of refugees. *Journal of Analytical Psychology*, *65*(2), 260–80. doi: 10.1111/1468-5922.12590.

Neumann, E. (1990). *The child*. Shambhala.

Proust, M. (2021). *Sodom and gomorrah*. Yale University Press.

Rizzuto, N. (2006). Reading Sarah Kofman's testimony to les annees noires in *Rue Ordener, Rue Labat*. *Contemporary French and Francophone Studies*, *10*(1), 5–14.

Robson, K. (2004). Bodily detours: Sarah Kofman's narratives of childhood trauma. *Modern Language Review*, *99*(3), 608–21.

Samuels, A., Plaut, F. & Shorter, B. (1986). *A critical dictionary of Jungian analysis*. Routledge & Kegan Paul.

Sidoli, M. (2000). *When the body speaks: Archetypes in the body*. Routledge.

Stanislawski, M. (2004). *Autobiographical Jews: Essays in Jewish self-fashioning*. University of Washington Press.

Stone, B. (2004). Towards a writing without power. *Auto/Biography Journal, 12*, 16–32.

Ulanov, A. (1981). *Receiving woman*. John Knox Press.

Winnicott, D.W. (1960). *The maturational processes and ego development*. Routledge.

Winnicott, D.W. (1989). *Psychoanalytic explorations*. Harvard University Press.

Chapter 11

Longing to belong
Culture, complex and analysis

The faithful dog

In this Mexican fable a man has a dog that he mistreats because of, among other things, the poverty he is experiencing. The spirit of the animals, Kakasbal, speaks with the battered dog, suggesting that he abandon his master since every day he receives many beatings. The animal refuses, saying that he will never escape because he is a faithful dog, even though his owner never thanks him. The spirit is so insistent that the dog makes him believe that he will accept his proposal. For this, he must sell his soul. The dog asks the spirit for one bone for each hair. The spirit begins to count the hairs until the dog remembers his master and moves on purpose so that the spirit loses count. The dog says he moved because of fleas. This process is repeated up to a hundred times until Kakasbal realises the dog does not want to sell his soul. He says to the dog, 'You have cheated me, but you have given me a lesson, because now I know that it costs much more to buy the soul of an animal than that of a human being'.

The question addressed here is how othering processes affect and undermine development and impede the formation of the 'as-if' identity with its personal, psychological and cultural effects. In this chapter, I explore transference, the shadow and healing through the transcendent function as it is activated in the therapeutic and analytical relationship. The process traces the social and psychological conditions under which people feel left out. Feeling left out leads the 'as-if' person to shape themselves into what is deemed acceptable to survive. Without the desire to understand – to be surprised, to listen and bear witness – we lose our humanity, impeding psychological growth and development.

The ancient Greeks called the act of being reached out to as *philoxenia*, or friendship with the strange. Nowadays those considered strangers too often evoke fears of the unknown and we register threat, not openness. When this happens, energy recedes into the unconscious, fostering a climate of separation and exclusion or us vs. them. The different and unfamiliar become even more so when beliefs and automatic exclusions are unexamined and remain unknown. The illusion that, within a group, we are all the same feeds the fantasy that the group can achieve its own completely secure and harmonious existence. This is a dangerous

DOI: 10.4324/9781003315254-12

fiction of purity predicated on the annihilation of difference and perpetuating 'as-if' and imposter responses. Regarding people as having lives of equal worth means recognising each person as unique with a common core of humanity to which we can relate.

> And you shall not mistreat a stranger, nor shall you oppress him.
>
> (Exodus 22:20)

His story

This is the story of a Hispanic man in his mid-thirties whom I will call Mike. Mike was born in the United States. The pressures of his desire to belong clashed with his desire to freely express himself in both the mainstream and his inherited culture.

> So far as I can judge, these experiences occur either when something so devastating happens to the individual that his whole previous attitude to life breaks down, or when for some reason the contents of the collective unconscious accumulate so much energy that they start influencing the conscious mind.
>
> (Jung, 1960/1969, CW 8, para. 594)

He came to therapy with depression from fear of his family being split apart due to his wife's possible deportation after she received a letter from US Immigration and Customs Enforcement. Their impersonal legalistic policies and the threat of destruction to his life replicated the childhood brutality with which he had been raised. His reactive depression weighted by the threat of societal repression brought him to Jungian analysis.

The identity and narrative of those born elsewhere, or outside what is considered the mainstream, ascribes to them the label of 'other' or 'the enemy'. What matters, however, is how we appear in our own stories as persons in relationship to other persons, occurrences and objects in our worlds. For Mike, identity and pride were a road littered with terror and trauma. Ancestral trauma, which had an ongoing impact, had been passed down through the generations. This comprised the unheeded dimensions of individual and collective trauma to identity, in particular shame and problems of self-expression in modern societies. Jung commented,

> But are we really free? We are weak and unimportant, and we try to be so; our style of life is narrow and our outlook hampered not only by ordinary hills but by veritable mountains of prejudice against anything and everybody that exceeds our size.
>
> (1964/1970, CW 18, para. 1338)

Along with the sense of estrangement, when people are excluded, depression, unconscious complexes and psychological splitting can dominate, and they might pretend to be other than who they are and thus feel shame.

In despair Mike heard glass breaking. Was it his heart? He felt like he was drained and without hope, trapped in deep loneliness. He had so much pain, mixed with a sense of not belonging and longing to be understood. As Mike explained, although a US citizen, he did not feel safe. Various forms of psychological and cultural wounding and exclusion can come from the lack of belonging to family, partner, social group or self. In this can reside despair, hopelessness, longing and mourning, contributing to the lack of passion that could be there but is, instead, replaced by depression and anxiety.

This scenario creates a longing based on emotional pain, psychological stress and trauma. In the search for understanding the disruptive inner and outer emotions that arise from a lack of belonging, several factors in the personal and cultural complexes influence the course of psychological treatment. In Jungian psychology the process of individuation, or becoming oneself, involves the unconscious as an emergence to wholeness. Belonging, or attachment, is a key element in living and its absence can lead to spiritual and personal crises.

The longing to belong is a shared archive of individual and collective tragedy. The loss can feel so intolerable we try to deny it, although the pain, paradoxically, takes us to the core of who we are. The verb *to lose* has its taproot sunk in sorrow; it is related to the *lorn* in *forlorn*. It originates from an Old English word meaning 'to perish', which comes from an even older word meaning 'to separate or cut apart'.

Mike's story illustrates not only the hurt but also how to cope with and heal from losses engendered by both personal and intergenerational trauma. In the process of healing, he discovered the light hidden in the darkness of what was disowned in the family and cultural lineage and the defences developed in response to generations of trauma. Through therapy, this process repatterned and opened him to increased consciousness and ease in being himself. The experiences of loss and separation also represent a desire to unite, indicating a move towards individuation and finding meaning. Whereas remaining unconscious truncates and throws a person into chaos, the ability to reflect and connect brings forwards the strength of the self.

As more people suffer migrations and war as well as being othered, rejected and abandoned, cultural complexes come into play. We are not isolated beings; rather we exist in multiple shifting relationships through conscious and unconscious interactions. Cultural identifications define the personality and hinge on emotional connection and attachment with others through religion, language, history, customs and so on.

Longing is a strong, persistent desire for something seemingly unattainable or distant. It is related to hunger, a yearning for family, a partner, a group or self. Psychologically, longing relates to a primal human desire – the need and impetus to overcome the ego alienated from the unconscious, to feel a sense of inclusion, not exclusion; acceptance, not rejection; and love, not hate. At the crux of longing is the desire to be who we are without having to act 'as-if' to be accepted. Exclusion stirs longing and the dominant social gaps and projections then become even more prominent.

Mike's passion for life waned as he sought acceptance on personal and collective levels. Along with many others, he has struggled to access what should be a natural sense of belonging rather than the need to pretend and feeling safe only when acting 'as-if'. Mike felt, on the outside, unaccepted and diminished. Without inclusion, the self registers an aching in the soul, a longing to be correctly seen and respected. If sensitive and aware, a person can relate to this sense of estrangement as they face their own unconscious exclusion of others, both internally and externally.

Moreover, Eurocentric and Anglocentric undercurrents and biases have tended to prevail in the analytical and psychological professions. And we do not pay close enough attention to how they reflect social, economic and political conflicts and disparities. They also perpetuate the 'as-if' cover to fit and be part of the acceptable status quo, the imagined correct patient. The stranger, the immigrant, represents those unfamiliar parts of the personality we try to deny or negate; their recognition and inclusion enhance personal and cultural growth.

When there is a break in social life, the question of identity and belonging arise. At these moments, we are faced with choices between past and present, membership in one group or another, staying or leaving. Implicit becomes explicit as the psyche ruptures. The complex interrelations between place, belief system and identity force us to examine how we see ourselves and how others perceive us. The loss of or threat to a set of beliefs that form the basis for a person's ideals and behaviour can provoke helplessness, depression and alienation. Out of the need to escape these feelings, the person resorts to becoming 'as-if'. This rupture indicates the intricate dialectical tension between inner states and social realities.

For example, Mike struggled against the imposition and dehumanisation of the sociocultural impress of being othered. As a defence he learned to hide his hurt and act 'as-if' he was a part of and could fit with the mannerisms, dress and language of the dominant culture. He learned to imitate well because he imagined being seen for who he was would be met with a crushing loss of respect and value. He had no safety, however, and being excluded destroys hope. Exclusion also stirs longing as without sufficient inclusion the self is disturbed in its development, as expressed in the gaps, complexes and projections put onto him. Loneliness sets in from the resultant emptiness and isolation.

Although Mike stopped showing his reactions long ago, traumatic childhood memories remained; maintaining the façade 'as-if' required energy while simultaneously perpetuating self-deception. Mike's underlying grief, mourning and emptiness appeared as his interest, curiosity and passion waned and hope was almost abolished. In a dream he related, *I am lost in a strange city. I find myself on a street with many openings. No one helps. Do I belong? I wander around disorganised, afraid and lonely. Will I be picked up? Panicking, I remind myself things will work out.* The dream illustrates loss of direction, confusion, being without help, facing the threat of being marked as 'one of those'. Yet, all these troubling emotions were answered by self-assurance at the end.

His dreams offered a literal accounting of reality and a figurative representation of emotional truths. They were a glimpse into the tensions integral to his experiences of an undemocratic and hierarchical society, but this remained unsayable. Mike's identity and pride were a road littered with terror and trauma.

Dream language is symbolic and unfolds beyond the literal. Dreams reveal other personality parts unleashed to enlarge the world and how we move through it. Access to the psyche feels blocked when we are lost and emotionally stymied. This dream portrays the feeling of being without assistance and at threat of exclusion and possible denigration. Jung commented about the transformative process occurring through the world of dreams: 'When my conscious mind no longer sees any possible road ahead and consequently gets stuck, my unconscious psyche will react to the unbearable standstill' (1966b, CW 16, para. 123). As in the dream Mike reported a daily oppressive weight of depression and fear and sometimes being without motivation to live. He felt the insecurity and unease of one who knows he is different from the mainstream and as such feels subjected to the manipulations of others. To be invisible, he acted 'as-if' he was like them.

Mike was a related spouse and father who did not enact his culture of machismo and the required stereotypical, patriarchal authority figure. A self-educated man, he did not fit the typical Hispanic male image. This did not make it easy for him. The Mexican machismo is a set of behaviours and rules of conduct inculcated to boys to be strong, tough, independent and stoic. It denotes a strong sense of masculine pride, an exaggerated masculinity, associated with a man's responsibility to provide for, protect and defend his family. It refers to the condescension of the swaggering male and the trappings of manliness used to dominate women and keep them in their place. Although the construct of machismo holds both positive and negative aspects, emerging research suggests it has associations with negative cognitive-emotional factors (that is, depression symptoms, trait anxiety and anger, cynical hostility) among Hispanic populations. Men are expected to maintain the integrity of the family unit and uphold the honour of family members. The term *fatalismo* is used by Latinos to express their belief the individual can do little to alter their fate.

Mexican philosopher Emilio Uranga (2018) proposed an ontological account applicable to my example here. Uranga describes Mexican sentimentality, melancholy and inferiority, concluding these are symptoms of the fact that to be Mexican is to be groundless and conscious of a lack of permanent foundation. He characterises the Mexican as feeling weak or fragile inside, a quality of being threatened by nothingness, by the threat of falling into non-being. The Mexican's emotive life psychologically expresses or symbolises this condition as felt insufficiency transforming into pervasive inferiority.

Jungian psychology regards the self as formed by the personal and collective experience of the individual. The normative aspects of the personality are created out of unconscious internalisations of the social and cultural order, meaning the inside replicates the outside and vice versa. The person from a group ascribed as 'the enemy', the interloper, the one accused of taking jobs from those who really belong, is too often rejected and considered undeserving. This sets up longing, doubt about acceptance, identity, legitimacy and, in its most painful aspects, can escalate to crushing despair. The psychological injury of not belonging, separation from family, home and loved ones appears in dreams and through the transference and countertransference in psychological treatment.

Mike's depression expressed the violation of his natural self and opened a descent into the psychological ashes, like at the beginning of the first alchemical stage called the *nigredo*. This stage, like his previous dream, indicated the psychological process starting with a painful loss of bearings in the alchemy of dissolution, a *massa confusa* prior to the reforming. Jung paradoxically said, 'The secret is that only that which can destroy itself is truly alive' (1968b, CW 12, para. 93). Mike embarked on a process of taking apart and putting together, looking at the pieces of himself and accessing openly the reality of who he was without the façade. Much can evolve but, of course, had not yet occurred.

Trauma

The traumas Mike suffered as an adult replicated those in childhood. Nothing really goes away but there comes a time when the old defences become unbearable, unchanging and no longer controllable (Kimbles & Singer, 2004, p. 85). The psyche communicates these unconscious experiences to be intercepted by individual and collective acts of consciousness. The famous Spanish poet Frederic Garcia Lorca wrote eloquently (1919) about hopes lost, frozen and deserted. French psychoanalyst Julia Kristeva, herself from another country than the one where she lives, said, 'Within depression, if my existence is on the verge of collapsing, its lack of meaning is not tragic – it appears obvious to me, glaring and inescapable' (Kristeva, 1992, p. 3).

Jungian psychology attends to the cross-cultural aspects of the personality through the collective unconscious, the symbolic, imagistic, archetypal and psychological layers. 'The multicultural nature of the psyche includes a matter of opening our hearts and minds to that which is foreign' (Kimbles & Singer, 2004, p. 140). The psychological issues of unity and diversity, monism and pluralism have historical and archetypal roots passing from generation to generation in an unending spiral. Life can become desiccated from past cultural traumas as the memories and their severity are stored in the psyche and body, often emerging years later. A person can be haunted by these past ghosts dragging their luggage of transgenerational trauma. They provide guidance when addressed, however, as these experiences and their residue exist within to be acknowledged and dealt with.

For Mike, current internal and external situations presented material he formerly could not decode. In trauma situations, the psyche shatters. The defence, as traumatic as the original trauma, focuses on mere survival while attempts to find oneself are fraught and despairing. The adoption of the 'as-if' façade is a protective mechanism reflecting the annihilation anxiety in a response of folding in on oneself.

Personal complex

Identity opens us to the realisation of psychological and cultural complexes and how they become powerful enough to autocratically rule the personality. The complex, as referred to in Jungian psychology, is a situation, both inner and outer, of emotional intensity, loaded with conflicting feelings. The complex references the parts that we might be unaware of, but they can powerfully rule the personality. They exert different influences and arise from how we were affected by various events in our lives. Complexes associated with the emotion of longing are laden with feelings of shame, anger, terror and aloneness.

> The complex is not under the control of the will and for this reason it possesses the quality of psychic autonomy ... Abreaction then is an attempt to ... incorporate it gradually into the conscious mind as an accepted content, by living the traumatic situation over again, once or repeatedly.
>
> (Jung, 1966b, CW 16, paras. 267–8)

During times of transition and change the loss of self combines with blocked access to familiar cultural signifiers of identity and belonging. When identity becomes negated, it introduces the question of where and how one belongs. Amid the diversity of changing populations and beliefs, people become disconnected and estranged from what they knew previously. The world becomes disorganised with social and psychological immersion in the unknown and unfamiliar. A person can be left adrift in a sea of insecurity and ambiguity, with no way of navigating the storms. This creates a type of loneliness in which emotions escalate, like with Mike, into a creeping psychic terror. When excluded from society and without its holding and containing qualities, a person becomes vulnerable, fearful and insecure. The psyche seeks equilibrium and will do much to avoid discomfort. But the rejected, uncomfortable material retains its pressure and, if not integrated consciously, manifests in various symptoms. 'The emotion arousing the yearning for belonging and identity occurs in the interaction between people and similarly in therapy, as it is what moves us to a greater wholeness' (Kimbles & Singer, 2004, p. 273).

An axiom of Jungian psychology is that each phenomenon contains the means for interpretation and resolution of the issues. Within the psyche a principle of synthesis supports self-discovery and repair as the symbols guide the process for belonging between self and others. 'The work of the therapist consists of holding to elicit from the unconscious product a meaning that relates to the subject's future attitude' (Jung, 1971, CW 6, para. 702).

Mike faced grief, mourning and emptiness as the repressed returned. Mike commented about his childhood school experience.

> In grade school I suffered repeated physical torment, harassment and humiliation by ruthless bullies. I did not fit the machismo culture of gangs and guns. I began to believe that in some cosmic way, I deserved the abuse. I developed my first suicidal thoughts in the third grade; I was nine years old. I knew I could not ever belong with people like them.

Mike had a difficult time in school, living at the edge of constant fear, goading and bullying from peers. He lived in an area known for drugs, gang violence and a general lack of attention to learning.

> The shadow is a moral problem that challenges the whole ego-personality, for no one can become conscious of the shadow without considerable moral effort. To become conscious of it involves recognizing the dark aspects of the personality as present and real. This act is the essential condition for any kind of self-knowledge.
>
> (Jung, 1968a, CW 9ii, para. 14)

There he learned to live 'as-if' – a façade to protect him from danger. This was a different façade than the one he presented when outside his neighbourhood. There, Mike used many flexible presentations to feign 'as-if' he belonged.

The following describes his childhood of emotional neglect.

> As a child I would cry myself to sleep while hugging a ragdoll my mother made for me. I would repeatedly pray with hopes to be magically transported out of my window and through the sky back to my mother at night so I wouldn't have to stay with my father and my stepmother. But come morning, no magic change.

Mike vividly recalled the exclusion and fear, the aloneness and despair. To this day, he is wary of the macho culture of his neighbourhood. This feeling transferred to the larger world, and he preferred to be unnoticed, under the radar, using aliases on social media so he would not be traceable.

Over time, sometimes after a long time, we become more conscious of what we carry psychologically from our sociohistorical experiences. Mike's father was a brutal and harsh military man who dealt with ethnic prejudice by fighting, carrying a gun, teaching his son to be aggressive and in support of the dominant white culture of the United States. However, this son could comply with none of it. The current emotional and physical losses and subsequent grief Mike reported were present from childhood. Mike retained an apprehension of authority, of being misunderstood, a pervasive fear of being stopped by the police. He knew how to act but worried he would be accused and unable to convince 'the man'. However, he did not fit in the system, be it the American culture, his heritage as interpreted by his father, the neighbourhood gangs or with other Hispanic family members. Low self-esteem was the result, creating anxiety and depression. His right to exist teetered precariously.

From an intrapsychic perspective, trauma can be conceptualised as inner displacement (Luci, 2020, p. 275). Mike relied on his wife for emotional support, but often did not tell her how bad the negative, self-deprecating and fearful thoughts were. One event after another put him into suicidal ideation. The rift in the constitution of his identity reflected the perils of societal and self-criticism, the voices that enslave and disallow self-acceptance or love.

Dreams emerged, arousing curiosity, emotions and memories. In one dream *Mike is up high and eating a zebra with knife and fork. Others are around and watching.* He was upset at the dream because zebras are showy, and they cannot hide. They are black and white, and Mike wants to be grey. That is why he needs to eat the zebra. He has lost his self-definition in the inertia from depression with its general lack of sustained interest or focus. Mike felt unsafe being seen and had disguised himself to blend in 'as-if'. This dream situation replicated Mike's conscious experiences featuring a persecutor and innocent victim.

> With this loss of psychic skin in trauma, there is an inner displacement in the self due to a dramatic change in the interplay between inner and outer worlds that profoundly alters the previous organization between the ego-complex and other autonomous complexes.
>
> (Luci, 2020, p. 269)

Mike could hardly manage the fears as he anticipated the loss of his wife to threatened deportation. He dreamt about *being in a Grand-Canyon-like place but there is no one else there. Then the scene shifts to the mountains and there is snow and cold but again no one there and in both parts of this dream there is no way out.* Mike did not expect help, as his previous experiences validated no one would understand, much less care. In this dream image there is a sense of what is both absent and present, the psyche yearning, cold, distant and alone in these vast spaces. The Grand Canyon itself represents a huge abyss where many do get lost and die. Mike is an example of what happens when the ordinary defences fail in the face of such unbearable psychic pain and anxiety, stemming in part from the feelings of not belonging and his identity being demeaned. His life was and is defined by peril.

Liminality and impasse

Liminality is an in-between state, a position neither here nor there, encompassing the psychological themes of rebirth and death. Dante (2000), the famous writer of the Middle Ages, referred to this in the *Inferno*, Canto I:1–60 The Dark Wood and the Hill:

> In the middle of the journey of our life, I came to myself, in a dark wood, where the direct way was lost. It is a hard thing to speak of, how wild, harsh, and impenetrable that wood was, so that thinking of it recreates the fear.

This literary excerpt refers to the sociological concept and psychological space of *liminality*, a word derived from the Latin *limen* meaning 'threshold'. Life crises bring up questions of identity and belonging, periods when we are in between, neither who we used to be, nor who we will become. At such times we resemble the snake, an ancient symbol of transformation, shedding its skin in the moulting process and during that time of change from old to new is raw and vulnerable.

Liminal spaces contain fear of the unknown. They represent times when we are naked, stripped because the former persona does not work and there is no replacement yet. Liminality depicts a period when life is full of confusion and bewilderment, disorientation, sickness of spirit and confrontation with the shadow. During liminal times our sense of direction is beclouded. We cannot move; the way is uncharted, unmarked, and there is a breakdown of identity. Consciously held values and former ways are outmoded. Old habits no longer guide at the crossroads; we are confused and torn. Essentially, ego consciousness has yet to work out a new relationship with the unconscious.

In-depth psychological treatment recognises the formerly denied, the losses and feelings of anger, guilt, sorrow and yearning. 'As far as we can discern, the sole purpose of human existence is to kindle a light of meaning in the darkness of mere being' (Jung, 1963, p. 326). According to André Green, the fundaments of analysis are that it strives to complete the mourning process. Green (1986, p. 142) contended that experiences of self are achieved against a background of loss and absence. This influences how we do or do not cope with the inevitable lacks, disappointments and directional changes in life.

Julia Kristeva speaks about the notion of the stranger as the foreigner, outsider or person who feels alien in a society not their own – as well as the notion of strangeness within the self, a deep sense of being, or its absence. She suggests we touch the otherness, escape its hatred and burden though accepting the differences it implies (Kristeva, 1994, p. 3). If we can recognise the foreign within us, we will neither have a problem with whoever and whatever seems foreign, nor will we need to create distance. Kristeva noted analysis is a journey into the strangeness of the other – and into the self (Kristeva, 1994, p. 182).

The shadow

Jung's concept of the shadow, the parts cast off as unwanted or unused, are representative of the unknown others. 'In many cases in psychiatry, the patient who comes to us has a story that is not told … In most cases exploration of the conscious material is insufficient … the problem is always the whole person, never the symptom alone' (Jung, 1963, p. 117). In the classical interpretation of Jungian psychology, from an individual and a collective point of view, there is a universal tendency to project the shadow outwards, so a patient separates from the unknown, despised, shame filled and different. The shadow is difficult, as its recognition can feel destabilising, disruptive and challenging. An examination of themselves and their relationships includes these unfamiliar and unsettling aspects.

There is need for acceptance or else a person feels lonely, depersonalised. They may withdraw intra-psychically, yet remain raw, prickly and sensitive. This can escalate to a void of futility, meaninglessness, feeling deadened and numb while at the core resides the dependency needs propelling the search for connection

(Ashton, 2007, p. 21). At this core is the hidden dependence because without the search for meaningful relationships a person feels lifeless. For Mike, a cultural shadow was cast, forming a crucible for depression but not for safe connection.

Mike felt acutely the cultural shadow projections and hostility, heightened by the threat of his wife's deportation. He questioned in therapy if he would be met with denigration or understanding due to his ethnic identity. The anticipation of estrangement, even in therapy, mirrored his frequent intrapersonal and societal experiences.

Mike dreamt that *someone takes his chest of jewels, and he calls out to stop the thief but there are people obstructing the way and he cannot get to the thief.* He said he was lonely, without self-direction or a place to express his creativity. He felt weak and helpless like in the dream; his jewels, perhaps slang for his genitals, meaning his maleness and sense of self, respect and regard, needed to be reclaimed. The therapy situation ideally provides enough security for the self to unfold in its authenticity (Solomon, 2007, p. 240). This might be where he can recover the jewels as intersubjective experiences can affect self-development and foster his capability for transformation. Concerning early

> relational trauma it is the containing relationship in psychotherapy making it possible to dream what was previously the undreamable. It is a prelude to becoming able to think the unthinkable, and as a foretaste of creating experience, not in terms of the historical past, but in terms of the relational present.
>
> (Wilkinson, 2006, p. 54)

The recognition of belonging and not belonging occurs in psychotherapy and is exposed in the transference and countertransference for the self to merge. Jung said, 'In this world created by the Self we meet all those many to whom we belong, whose hearts we touch; here there is no distance, but immediate presence' (Jung, 1973, p. 298). It takes psychological work to repair the suffering experienced in interpersonal relationships lacking recognition and belonging. Green (1986, p. 42) explained this as a person needing the container of the therapist for the content to be presented. It is a self-to-self interweaving, a mutual steeping in the issues. Jung commented, 'Individuation involves the transformation of the analyst as well as the patient, stirring up in his or her personality the layers that correspond to the patient's conflicts and insights' (Jung, 1966b, CW 16, p. 172).

Therapy confronts a person with the need to express so the self becomes consciously present. The narrative demands the presence of another to witness, hear and understand the story as it unfolds. Jung commented, 'Analysis is a mutual and dialogical process. There is no understanding without the one who understands. This understanding is negotiated between the author and listener, patient and analyst' (1966b, CW 16, para. 314). New insights involve analysing personal and collective structures and images, as both patient and analyst reflect on their meanings.

In the search for understanding the disruptive inner and outer emotions aroused from the lack of belonging, several factors are involved in the psychological treatment. Within the dynamism of the therapeutic interplay are the tasks of linking the known and unknown, conscious and unconscious, and balancing the tension between. 'The repressed content must be made conscious so as to produce a tension of opposites without which no forward movement is possible ... Life is born only of the spark of opposites' (Jung, 1966a, CW 7, para. 78). If the tension can be sustained without succumbing to the urge to identify with one side or the other, the third and completely unexpected image unites the two in a creative new way. The psyche is fluid, multidimensional, alive and capable of creative development. The challenge is to emerge from the crises and find authenticity and intimacy with self and others. The task delves into discovering what is called in Jungian psychology the 'treasure hard to attain' or the knowledge residing in the unconscious, the body and the discovery of self.

Analysis dwells in exposing the innermost ravages and co-constructing the patterns of self and others. The analytical relationship can offer a corrective experience, a kind of repair that involves remembering the wrenching and broken connections of self to self and self to others. After all, the self naturally becomes conscious of itself in relation to another (Mattoon, 1985, p. 131). Yet, therapists can lack awareness of what diverse systemic social traumas mean due to their own preconceived concepts and projections. Theory can be used as a defence when the therapist assumes recognition or attempts to slot the client into something familiar. Both therapist and client are involved in the shadows to open the subjective material and find the expressive symbols. Both witness the emotions around the neglected feelings becoming unwrapped from the injuries of not belonging.

Cultural complex

Complexes are personal, cultural and historical processes reflected in therapy. 'Cultural complexes structure emotional experience and operate in the personal and collective psyche like individual complexes but with different content' (Kimbles & Singer, 2004, p. 6). Cultural differences pose a question of how to be reconciled with the universals of human nature on the one hand and cultural variations on the other. The issues of class, wealth distribution and skin colour are closely intertwined. 'And when we flee from or struggle against the foreigner, we are fighting our unconscious' (Kristeva, 1994, p. 191). To become conscious of prejudice can display a powerful cultural complex with its capacity to contaminate the personal and collective psyche.

Personal and social identity denotes the fact that a person or a group has certain particular and characteristic qualities marking them as separate and distinguishable from others. 'The Mexican ... is familiar with death. [He] jokes about it, caresses it, sleeps with it, celebrates it. It is one of his favorite toys and his most steadfast love' (Octavio Paz, quoted in Uranga, 2018). The post-Jungian concept of the cultural complex refers to active unconscious elements in the psyche, problematic for both patient and analyst and possibly presenting therapeutic challenges. The cultural complexes are delineated in the following way:

- Complexes operate at the group level of the cultural unconscious
- Function autonomously within each individual or group
- Organise the attitudes, emotions and behaviours making up the group life
- Facilitate the individual's affective relationships to the group's cultural patterns
- Provide both the individual and the group with a sense of belonging and identity

(Kimbles & Singer, 2004, pp. 229–230)

Cultural complexes repeat the psyche disfigured by the imprisoning contours of traumatic and wounding private experience. From early in life, Mike was deprived of individual and collective significance or meaning. He described something within was killed or lost and the good experiences gone. To hide all this, Mike learned to fit into the predominant culture, familiar with its mannerisms, slang and dress, acting 'as-if'. However, there is both danger and attraction to this persona adaptation. Tending to fit in can serve as pretence, devoid of real connection or integration, and either deflect or lead into the deeper issues of self-development.

Transcendent function

Mike came to therapy afraid, with the world divided into oppressor and oppressed. The social structure he knew all his life seemed worse than it was previously. He felt even those like him did not understand. What was the use of his voice as so many were for assimilation and getting rid of people like him? He lived as if a child – hidden yet present in a group who did not support or care about him. What he read and how he thought and perceived the world was antithetical to his cultural neighbourhood.

Jung described coming to a standstill, energy dammed up, as setting up the situation for the possible emergence of the transcendent function. The transcendent function moves the psyche, yet it depends on the ego's ability to hold the opposing forces and sustain their dynamic interaction. In the process of the old breaking down, there is pain and resistance even as the steps are taken towards movement. 'From the activity of the unconscious there now emerges a new content, constellated by thesis and antithesis in equal measure and standing in complementary relation to both' (Jung, 1971, CW 6, para. 825). The paradoxes and processes of going back and forth from the varied positions in the unconscious bring the psyche out of the polarisation and oppositional states. The transcendent function brings out the synthesis for repair, rebalancing and regulation of the psyche.

The personality expands as the conscious and unconscious form a dynamic relationship – rather than being stuck in old emotions, discontent and stress – creating new visions and opportunities. The transcendent function as the third area or position may be described as 'a space for the creation of the meaning-making function of the psyche' (Colman, 2007, p. 565). This emerges through dreams, life situations and the therapeutic process. The 'often perilously obtained clinical experience and information along the hazardous journey is difficult and requires much patience on the parts of both participants' (Solomon, 2004, p. 635). The process takes perseverance and time, although the ego worries and wants the suffering to stop immediately. As Jung said, 'It is a new content that governs the whole attitude, putting an end to the division and forcing the energy of the opposites into a common channel ... and life can flow on with renewed power towards new goals' (1971, CW 6, para. 827).

The unknown information is a feature for emergence of the therapeutic third, a jointly created unconscious life from the flow between the therapeutic pair (Colman, 2010). This psychological work brings us back to the suffering experienced in interpersonal relationships. Wounds and blows to the heart signify the past unmourned grief and loneliness and the deconstruction and reconstruction of the self for finding meaning and value. In reference to this Green stated, 'The mind has the capacity to bring something back again which has been related to an object, without the object being there' (1979, p. 30). This refers to the psychological origins for renewal, transcending the limits of time and space.

Transference

People make sense of themselves through the webs of meaning supplied by their personal and collective social, historical and symbolic systems.

> To the extent that the transference is projection and nothing more, it divides quite as much as it connects ... because relationship to the self is at once relationship to our fellow man, and no one can be related to the latter until he is related to himself.
>
> (Jung, 1966b, CW 16, para. 445)

The capacity for growth, development, creative agency and love is dependent upon existing in the mind, eyes and gaze of an-other in a dance of attuned, rhythmic and imperfect resonance.

> Analytic work encompasses relational as well as interpretive agents to bring about the integration and increased connectivity between and within both hemispheres of the mind-brain leading to a change in the nature of attachment which will then permit the self to emerge more fully through the process of individuation.
>
> (Wilkinson, 2006, p. 113)

From staying with this process, symbols arise to move the personality from formerly constricting situations. The self is supported in its development through the symbolic nature of the transcendent function and the creative resources residing in the unconscious that become accessible (Solomon, 2007, p. 244). Symbols and metaphors are central to the interpretation of the unconscious. 'The psyche accomplishes its transformation through the creation of symbols which are capable of bringing together opposing aspects of the self' (Solomon, 1998, p. 227). Symbols are also impersonal metaphors, sharing meaning from past and current conventions, myths and cultural artefacts, a medium of communication revealing our inherent intersubjectivity.

In therapy symbols began to appear, familiar to Mike's ethnic culture and representing the desire for acceptance. The therapeutic relationship bridged culture and time, creating the linkages and security for the psyche to express its multicultural aspects. 'Culture is a deeply imbedded structure that underlies the perception of our self, our reality, and the ways we become individuals' (Mattoon, 1992, p. 124). The differences in culture between analyst and analysand are recognised in the transference and countertransference. It is important to define rather than assume the cultural themes and social trends the person identifies with and that symbolise what they are moving towards. 'The political and social isms of our day preach every conceivable ideal, but, under this mask, they lower the level of our culture by restricting or altogether inhibiting the possibilities of individual development' (Jung, 1959/1968, CW 9i, para. 617).

Awareness of the contents of the personal unconscious, including our own cultural background, entails also accessing the layers of images and motifs comprising the collective unconscious, a vast cultural array including the hauntings of tragedies. A much greater part of our personality than we generally believe is collectively determined (Alho, 2006, p. 662). Jungian theory about the collective unconscious reflects many of our deepest human instincts like love, fear, social projections, sex, wisdom and good and evil. We tap into this layer for connection, sustenance and meaning. 'This widened consciousness ... brings the individual into absolute, binding, and indissoluble communion with the world at large' (Jung, 1966a, CW 7, para. 275). Embodying a psychological attitude includes acknowledging the universal longing to belong. The understanding of this also means awareness of our tendencies for polarisation, the shadow of blame, shaming, bullying, rejecting and accepting differences. All this requires thoughtful reflection and response. This psychological attitude to the personal and cultural taps into the past, changes the present and leads to a more fulfilling future.

Our existence is fundamentally interpersonal. Human beings are not isolated, free-floating objects, but subjects existing in perpetual, multiple, shifting relationships. Life is defined by these myriad interactions – by the push and pull of intersubjectivity as well as the overt and covert social contracts. Many people experience helplessness, powerlessness and the resultant loneliness as one of the most painful experiences of human existence. It can radically cut people off from human connection, a kind of wilderness where a person feels deserted and abandoned. When experiencing too much loneliness, a person loses the ability to experience anything else and cannot make new beginnings. As soon as they begin to talk about loneliness, they transform one of the most deeply felt human experiences into an object of contemplation, reflection and ownership. Everybody experiences loneliness, but they experience it differently. 'There are positive forces that seek to move the psyche into the future, there are powerful retrograde forces that seek to prevent such movement' (Solomon, 1998, p. 142).

How do we make space to open encounters with others, both inner and outer, so a transformative spirit may emerge? The inclusion or exclusion divide can create psychological distress, leading to the collapse of the inter-relationship between culture and the individual personality. Mike talked of sitting outside my office and looking at a mountain called Camelback with rocks shaped as a monk sitting on the edge of the mountain. The scene reminded him of the hallucinations he had from fevers as a child when he imaged the monk in a mountain. He took this as a reassuring and restorative image. The past and the present became contiguous through such images. He said he must break the inner lock and wondered if this meant writing a novel. Doing so might express the heart and emotions put away years ago and now wanting to be heard.

He noticed a tree in the yard outside my office and described one branch reaching out and leaning on the other. He said it was not burdened as the connection gave support. In relation to this, British Jungian analyst Jean Knox said being an analyst requires constant focus on the subjective, to fine-tune to the intuitive, poetic, symbolic narrative that emerges in an analytic session (Knox, 2004, p. 13). This requires the therapist's capacity to resonate with the multiple and sometimes contradictory threads of the patient's narrative in the co-construction of symbolic space. The analyst's search for unconscious meaning in the patient's communications becomes an agent of change. Taking the other perspective is necessary to resolve conflict, whether inner or outer, as conflicts are perpetuated from adopting a single perspective. 'All that other people are and the world is, from rivers and elephants to ashtrays and toasters is essentially what I call me' (Hillman, 1993, p. 252).

'Opening for flight'

In an address to the US Congress on 21 February 1990, Václav Havel, president of the Czech Republic, said, 'The salvation of this human world lies nowhere else than in the human heart, in the human power to reflect, in human meekness and human responsibility'. From the perspective of Jungian analytical psychology, the self seeks union of its disparate aspects of unconscious to conscious, personal to cultural. This acknowledges the longing for connection, a sense of belonging and identity. 'The limits of your ambition were expected to be set forever. You were born into a society which spelled out with brutal clarity that you were a worthless human being. You were not expected to aspire' (Baldwin, 1992, p. 7). Engagement with others gives voice to these many selves and an increased consciousness and inclusion rather than foreclosure on the different and pretending 'as-if'. Mike had an image of himself as a bald eagle, strong, his wings slowly opening for flight. He was amazed about the image and reluctantly admitted he was like a bald eagle now, able to see the bigger picture and navigate through with confidence and power.

The capacity to gather the personal and collective threads for the co-construction of belonging occurs through the transcendent function in Jungian psychological treatment. The Jungian process of individuation is a coming to oneself as personality transformation occurs through fulfilling the basic longing for inclusive acceptance. Engagement with the other brings about recognition of the self, reconciliation and mutual understanding that evolves from a sense of personal and collective belonging and pride in identity. The integration results in communication between self and others, the shadow and the stranger.

References

Alho, P.M. (2006). Collective complexes – Total perspectives. *Journal of Analytical Psychology*, *51*(5), 661–80. doi: 10.1111/j.1468-5922.2006.00626.x.

Ashton, P. (2007). *From the brink: Experiences of the void from a depth psychology perspective*. Routledge.

Baldwin, J. (1992). *The fire next time*. Vintage.

Colman, W. (2007). Symbolic conceptions: The idea of the third. *Journal of Analytical Psychology*, *52*(5), 565–83. doi: 10.1111/j.1468-5922.2007.00686.x.

Colman, W. (2010). Mourning and the symbolic process. *Journal of Analytical Psychology*, *55*(2), 275–97. doi: 10.1111/j.1468-5922.2010.01840.x.

Dante, A. (2000). The inferno, cantos, I–VII. In *The Divine Comedy* (A.S. Kline, trans.). www.poetryintranslation.com/PITBR/Italian/DantInf1to7.php.

Green, A. (1979). *The tragic effect*. Cambridge University Press.

Green, A. (1986). *On private madness*. International Universities Press.

Hillman, J. (1993). Concerning the stone: Alchemical ideas of the goal. *Sphinx: Journal of Archetypal Psychology and the Arts*, *5*, 234–65.

Jung, C.G. (1959/1968). *The collected works of C.G. Jung: Vol. 9i. The archetypes and the collective unconscious*. Princeton University Press.

Jung, C.G. (1960/1969). *The collected works of C.G. Jung: Vol. 8. The structure and dynamics of the psyche*. Princeton University Press.

Jung, C.G. (1963). *Memories, dreams, reflections*. Random House.

Jung, C.G. (1966a). *The collected works of C.G. Jung: Vol. 7. Two essays on analytical psychology*. Princeton University Press.

Jung, C.G. (1966b). *The collected works of C.G. Jung: Vol. 16. The practice of psychotherapy*. Princeton University Press.

Jung, C.G. (1968a). *The collected works of C.G. Jung: Vol. 9ii. AION*. Pantheon Books.

Jung, C.G. (1968b). *The collected works of C.G. Jung: Vol. 12. Psychology and alchemy*. Princeton University Press.

Jung, C.G. (1971). *The collected works of C.G. Jung: Vol. 6. Psychological types*. Princeton University Press.

Jung, C.G. (1973). Letter to Mary Mellon. In (C.G.J. Letters, çev.): Vol. I, 1906–50. Routledge & Kegan Paul.

Kimbles, S. & Singer, T. (eds.) (2004). *The cultural complex: Contemporary Jungian perspectives on psyche and society*. Brunner-Routledge.

Knox, J. (2004). From archetypes to reflective function. *Journal of Analytical Psychology*, *49*(1), 1–19. doi: 10.1111/j.0021-8774.2004.0437.x.

Kristeva, J. (1992). *The black sun*. Columbia University Press.

Kristeva, J. (1994). *Strangers to ourselves*. Columbia University Press.

Lorca, F.G. (1919). Another song. https://federicogarcialorca.net/obras_lorca/libro_de _poemas.htm#68.

Luci, M. (2020). Disintegration of the self and the regeneration of 'psychic skin' in the treatment of traumatized refugees. *Journal of Analytical Psychology*, *65*(2), 260–80. doi: 10.1111/1468-5922.12304.

Mattoon, M. (1985). *Jungian psychology in perspective*. Free Press.

Mattoon, M. (1992). *The transcendent function: Individual and collective aspects*. Daimon Verlag.

Solomon, H.F. (1998). The self in transformation: The passage from a two- to a three-dimensional internal world. *Journal of Analytical Psychology*, *43*(2), 225–38.

Solomon, H. (2004). Self-creation and the limitless void of dissociation: The as if personality. *Journal of Analytical Psychology*, *49*(5), 635–56. doi: 10.1111/j.0021-8774.2004.00493.x.

Solomon, H. (2007). The self in transformation. *Karnac*.

Uranga, E. (2018, 25 June). Essay on the ontology of the Mexican. In *The Philosophy of Mexicanness* (C.S. Sánchez & R.E. Sanchez, trans.). *Aeon*. https://aeon.co/classics/to-be -accidental-is-to-be-human-on-the-philosophy-of-mexicanness.

Wilkinson, M. (2006). *Coming into mind*. Routledge.

Chapter 12

Living on

A woman dreamt *of two women swimmers crisscrossing into water around a cylinder that was empty. She was on shore watching as they wove in and out with bubbles covering them. As they swam, the empty cylinder they were swimming through was coming together.* This dream illustrates the analytical process of coming together from the unconscious, the hole in the self being repaired and the natural process as the women easily swam back and forth in the waters of life and the unconscious. Likewise, the dreamer was gradually gaining confidence, the centre filling because she was less afraid and more able to trust and find the love she wanted. She was beginning to recognise that she could be visible and no longer hide herself.

> There is a pain – so utter –
> It swallows substance up –
> Then covers the Abyss with Trance –
> So Memory can step
> Around – across – upon it
>
> Emily Dickinson (1926, p. 294)

External solutions do not address the internal emptiness and distress expressed by the 'as-if' person. Who am I? What do I want? What will fix me? What will allow me to have pleasure and enjoy life? These questions are more than personal issues but point to a widespread crisis of sterility and lack in contemporary consciousness. The focus on the superficial and immediate fosters emptiness, anxiety, despair, loss of meaning, addictions and the sacrifice of the real. At the same time, distress plunges the 'as-if' person into a longing for Eros or relatedness.

Jungian analytical thought involves searching for what is called the 'treasure hard to attain'. This refers to aspects of the personality hidden and unused, ignored, maybe even despised, but ones that connect us to our personal self with its collective nature. This book covers a variety of Jungian concepts and how they can be applied in psychotherapy as well as in everyday life. This exposé illustrates elements of the 'as-if' personality through symbols, dream images and composite clinical examples. The cross-cultural and cross-disciplinary range of theories and perspectives widens understanding and stretches beyond familiar borders. The

DOI: 10.4324/9781003315254-13

interweaving of these brings psychological awareness with its intricacy, challenges and rewards.

Behind the façade of the 'as-if' person, the blank spaces, the vulnerability and confusion hold the promise for development. Absence seeks to be filled. The inner search involves mixing metaphors, shifting narratives, embracing multiplicity and making space for differences between self and others. These aspects reside in the conscious and unconscious and are expressed psychologically, culturally and physically, releasing the 'as-if' person from defensive and regressive singularity and isolation into a richer, thoughtful life.

The point is to make clear what has been clouded by the façade of the 'as-if' person. Exploring what lies under the surface of this personality requires thoughtful reflection as promoted in these pages. The psyche of the person living 'as-if' is complex but when peeled off layer by layer becomes an interesting mix of meanings leading to self and other relationships. Holding onto images based on false preconceptions and indifference to what is other than oneself is limiting. Engagement with others gives voice to our many selves. The transformation process is hopeful when consciousness connects with the unconscious. The personality opens from acknowledging what has been dissociated, deadened and numbed. In addition, the dreams and life experiences of people reveal the difficult but rewarding journey from 'as-if' to the real.

This book provides openings to the process of psychological awareness, uniting reality and fantasy, the shadow and the body. Psychotherapy is a way to bring consciousness to bear on the images the psyche presents. The forces for unmasking compel inward and outward movement through examining self-deceptive fictions. With an aptitude for mimicry, the 'as-if' person watches the world but remains aloof, alone and above it all. A solitary sadness takes over and deprives the person of joy and the permission to be real. The necessary acknowledgement of vulnerability and incompleteness provides an end to the flight from reality. The various psychoanalytical and philosophical approaches in each chapter plus the myths and stories add a broad platform for recognising the fragility of the ego moving into the more complete self.

This personality type gets stuck in the tendency to cover up, in superficiality and the persona as it searches for easy fixes, especially as found on the internet. Over time the 'as-if' system falls apart as it is too rigid to maintain. Being real rather than 'as-if' and shedding the guise of the imposter is a process of release and personal emergence, from void and loss to desire, excitement and aliveness. Psychologically, the hope is for the re-emergence of the 'as-if' person's true nature. The Jungian individuation process theoretically and therapeutically reveals the possibility for the 'as-if' person to reconnect with the self, to discover and accept who they really are.

Revisioning is the act of looking back, seeing with fresh eyes and acknowledging the assumptions blocking the 'as-if' person from themselves. Perceiving the past with a wider lens allows the patient to reassemble the material rather than passing on the traditional or unconscious way of being. The unconscious is not linear but loops back to re-incorporate the sentient and the imaginative in newly emergent ways. By attending to the inner world, the self can be healed, bringing unity between body and mind and becoming active with a sense of purpose and meaning.

'Relationship to the self is at once relationship to others, and no one can be related to the latter until he is related to himself' (Jung, 1966, CW 16, para. 445). This is a gathering of the multiple personal and collective threads, the social and historical forces conditioning existence. To see one's life as a kind of palimpsest reinforces taking the risks to take off the cloak of 'as-if'.

During the writing of this book, I had a dream that *Julia Kristeva called me on the phone. There was background noise as there were people working in my area. I apologised but she said she had time and not to worry. She wanted to say my book was about healing and related to the Greek god Asclepius, the god of healing.* I was amazed upon awakening and felt encouraged and supported. I refer to her in this book and in previous writings. I appreciate her mind and way of being. She lives in a different culture than her birth and puts forward her ideas, representing an analytical slant on the psyche different from mine. The dream evokes the archetype of healing in the sense that healing is to be oneself, unafraid, taking chances and going forward into individuation. I also ponder who the healing refers to in the dream and note it is the Greek male god of healing. Is it also the masculine healing as healer? Is it personal and collective? These questions are an excellent way to answer the questions of living fully and with purpose although we never finish.

The 'as-if' personality, able to unmask the issues both personal and cultural, also represents hope. This is needed to untie the constraints and create new ways of being throughout life. What is made along the way is an individual and unique self.

> I have to learn how to dance
> In time for the next party
> My room is too small for me
> Suppose I die before graduation

Audre Lorde (1978)

References

Dickinson, E. (1926). *The complete poems of Emily Dickinson*. (T.H. Johnson, ed.). https://en.wikipedia.org/wiki/There_is_a_pain_—_so_utter_.Wikipedia—

Jung, C.G. (1966). *The collected works of C.G. Jung: Vol. 16. Practice of psychotherapy.* Princeton University Press.

Lorde, A. (1978). *Hanging fire. The collected poems of Audre Lorde.* W.W. Norton & Co.

Index

131, 205; processes 74, 146, 149; projective identifications 122; psyche 195; reactions 16; realms 5, 134; recognition of 2; river of life 15; situation 114, 123; thoughts 139; turbulence 25; tyranny 183; wounds 7
Uranga, E. 195

violence 11, 95, 119, 157, 185; childhood of 95; feelings of 72; gang 198; inner 48; internal 55, 62, 108; internalised 49; lifeless 108; physical 17; psychic 48;

void 64, 67, 69–70, 86, 88, 100, 102, 107–8, 115–16, 122, 180, 200, 210
vulnerability 21, 28, 30, 53, 56, 71–3, 91, 122–3, 125, 129, 139, 157, 162–3, 168, 181, 210; avoiding 20; expression of 134; of narcissism 84; tender 1, 146; terrifying 10

Wilde, O. 23
Winnicott, D. 9–10, 86, 109, 112, 175
withdrawal 39, 86, 89, 177; destructive 55
Wordsworth, W. 144

For Product Safety Concerns and Information please contact our EU
representative GPSR@taylorandfrancis.com
Taylor & Francis Verlag GmbH, Kaufingerstraße 24, 80331 München, Germany

www.ingramcontent.com/pod-product-compliance
Lightning Source LLC
Chambersburg PA
CBHW050645280326
41932CB00015B/2791

9 781032 324807